D0469251

How Christian Is Christian Counseling?

HOW CHRISTIAN IS
CHRISTIAN
COUNSELING?

The Dangerous Secular
Influences That Keep Us from
Caring for Souls

GARY L. ALMY, M.D.

CROSSWAY BOOKS • WHEATON, ILLINOIS
A DIVISION OF GOOD NEWS PUBLISHERS

How Christian Is Christian Counseling?

Copyright © 2000 by Gary L. Almy

Published by Crossway Books
        A division of Good News Publishers
        1300 Crescent Street
        Wheaton, Illinois 60187

All rights reserved. No part of this publication may be reproduced, stored in a retrieval system, or transmitted in any form by any means, electronic, mechanical, photocopy, recording, or otherwise, without the prior permission of the publisher, except as provided by USA copyright law.

Cover design: David La Placa

Cover photo: © Tony Stone Images

First printing 2000

Printed in the United States of America

Unless otherwise noted, Scripture is from the *Holy Bible: New International Version®*. Copyright © 1973, 1978, 1984 by International Bible Society. Used by permission of Zondervan Publishing House. All rights reserved.

The "NIV" and "New International Version" trademarks are registered in the United States Patent and Trademark Office by International Bible Society. Use of either trademark requires the permission of International Bible Society.

Scripture references marked NKJV are from the *New King James Version*. Copyright © 1982, Thomas Nelson, Inc. Used by permission.

Scripture references marked RSV are from the *Revised Standard Version*. Copyright © 1946, 1953, 1971, 1973 by the Division of Christian Education of the National Council of the Churches of Christ in the U.S.A.

Library of Congress Cataloging-in-Publication Data

Almy, Gary, 1943-
    How Christian is Christian counseling? : the dangerous secular
influences that keep us from caring for souls / Gary L. Almy.
        p.   cm.
    Includes bibliographical references and index.
    ISBN 1-58134-135-0 (trade pbk. : alk. paper)
    1. Pastoral counseling. 2. Pastoral psychology. 3. Psychotherapy—
Religious aspects—Christianity. I. Title.
BV4012.2.A46 2000
253.5'2—dc21   99-054975
                                                          CIP

15	14	13	12	11	10	09	08	07	06	05	04	03	02	01	00
15	14	13	12	11	10	9	8	7	6	5	4	3	2		

CONTENTS

From Psychoanalysis to Caring for Souls

Paul wrote to Timothy that, in the last days, "People will be lovers of themselves, lovers of money, boastful, proud, abusive, disobedient to their parents, ungrateful, unholy, without love, unforgiving, slanderous, without self-control, brutal, not lovers of the good, treacherous, rash, conceited, lovers of pleasure rather than lovers of God—having a form of godliness but denying its power" (2 Tim. 3:1-5).

Few would deny that these characteristics are increasingly a part of our society and, regrettably, even of the church. There was a time when I was an active promoter of ideas that helped develop the kind of people Paul warns about. This book is a product of the changes God has wrought in my heart, and of His opening my eyes to His truth. He has brought me to a place I would never have predicted, and this writing reflects some of what I have learned along the way.

I chose psychiatry as a career during my years in medical school at the University of Nebraska. I immersed myself in the "scriptures" of Freud and his followers and was convinced that psychoanalysis was the epitome of medical and intellectual achievement. I went to California for my specialty training and in my first year of residency was faced with the scientific flaws in psychotherapy. Everyone's favorite teacher in that training program was a research-oriented, atheistic psychiatrist who consistently pointed the residents-in-training toward what he believed was a medical-scientific approach to the human mind. My Freudian foundations began to crumble as I was unable to refute scientifically my teacher's thesis that psychoanalysis and psychotherapy were religious superstition rather than science.

I finished the specialty training and passed the board certification exams, trying to ignore the scientific approach to psychiatry so that I could begin earning a good income as an insight-oriented psychotherapist. The talking-therapy aspect of my practice produced enough income to purchase a Ferrari. The patients and their families were largely convinced that I was leading them toward "insight" into the "why" of their lives. They were awed by my powers as a therapist and were supposedly discovering how the traumatic experiences in their past explained their present difficulties. They paid their costly therapy bills and wanted to keep coming for the hour of "talk."

I gave lectures on anorexia and other psychological disorders, spreading the word as to what psychiatry had to offer. In retrospect, I was giving just enough of the secret language and secret knowledge of psychotherapy to let the listeners believe I really had answers. This was not a conscious deception at the time, but now I realize that I was truly the blind leading the blind.

In spite of all my worldly success, I could not get away from the increasing conviction that the talking-therapy aspect of my psychiatry practice was an abysmal failure. It was obvious that nothing really changed with these patients, and that they either moved from one therapist to the next or became too old or impoverished to continue the hopeless quest for a "cure." I can now look back and thank God for this inexplicable conviction by the Holy Spirit that made me increasingly uncomfortable with psychotherapy.

Part of this awareness of failure was my own obvious need for a therapist. While supposedly giving great insight to others, I was increasingly a failure in my personal life. I was determined to ignore any concept of sin; however, the consequences of my own sin made that increasingly difficult. As my sinful actions made a marriage relationship impossible, my Christian wife called a pastor who came to our home and counseled me from God's Word. I had to face the reality that neither the knowledge of psychoanalysis nor my successful career in psychiatry was going to bring the contentment and glory of which I had dreamed. Holes in the fabric of the system were increasingly apparent; less and less was I able to patch the holes and pretend that it would eventually be intact. Finally, I had no choice but to acknowledge my sin and admit that I was lost.

I was in desperate need of a Redeemer. God used that pastor to point me to the Messiah and to the fact that He had made full atonement for my sins in His death on the cross. When I realized this, there came to me "grace, mercy and peace from God the Father and Christ Jesus our Lord" (2 Tim. 1:2).

Slowly but surely I began to see the dissonance between what I had been taught about the human mind and what Scripture has to say on the subject. It took time, but I could not ignore the gross incompatibility of insight-oriented psychotherapy with the *care of souls* as shown in Scripture. Increasingly, the difference seemed not only significant but of fundamental importance to the transmission of the Gospel, described by Paul as "the power of God for the salvation of everyone who believes" (Rom. 1:16).

Peter wrote that "His divine power has given us everything we need for life and godliness through our knowledge of him" (2 Pet. 1:3). I concluded that my study of psychiatry had led me away from life and godliness, but that a loving and merciful God had used that experience to cause me to despair of mankind's efforts to achieve "life." Aware of the tremendous increase in the number of Christian counselors in recent years,[1] and aware of the nature of the training most of them receive, I began to wonder how Christians could claim a need to add Freud to Scripture. Why are evangelical seminaries, colleges, and even churches increasingly populated by psychologists? I began to wonder just how "Christian" so-called Christian counseling really is.

The church needs to examine the theories underlying counseling psychology; it needs to examine counseling psychology's claim to be an effective and scientific method of solving human problems. The belief that psychology is simply a part of "God's truth" outside of Scripture needs serious evaluation. Does psychology really fill in gaps not covered in Scripture? Is counseling psychology really even a science?

It does not require great intellect to see that counseling psychology has no base at all in rigorous empirical science. It is a house built on subjective notions that cannot be measured; it is applied speculation, and its claim to have discovered scientific truth is a lie. (Other authors who make this clear are listed in "Recommended Reading.") Sadly, this false claim that counseling is a science continues to be actively promoted in the church. Worse yet, many within the church seem not to care that its scientific claims are false; it has become too useful in numbers and finances. The church shows no inclination to separate itself from the destructive body of doctrine underlying counseling psychology; instead, it seems to actively suppress any attempt to expose the truth in this crucial area.

I have written this book for those who care about learning the truth concerning counseling psychology as it is practiced today. The book is divided into four sections, each addressing a different aspect of the subject.

Section 1 addresses what I define as the "pillars" of insight-oriented psychotherapy—so called because it claims to solve human problems by helping its clients achieve insight or self-understanding. Chapter 1, "The Freudian Foundation," analyzes insight-oriented psychotherapy, pointing out what I believe to be the basic doctrines, the "pillars," of psychotherapy. Many psychotherapists claim to have gone far beyond Freud or even to have rejected his teachings today. However, you will see by observing the practice of psychotherapy, whether in or out of the church, that its use of Freud's fundamental pillars has not changed. The presuppositions by which the counselor sees the client and his life and by which he moves toward "treatment" have not changed at all. When we examine these foundations, we will clearly see that they are incompatible with the Bible. Integration of Scripture and Freud is impossible.

Chapter 2, "The Biblical Foundation," shows what Scripture teaches about mankind, our problems, and the proper "cure" for those problems. Scripture leaves no gaps needing to be filled in with Freud or Carl Jung or Abraham Maslow or Erich Fromm. The Bible contains a complete "psychology" of mankind, truly giving "all we need for life and godliness" (2 Pet. 1:3).

Chapter 3, "Ideas Have Consequences," describes the consequences for a culture and for the church when it follows the doctrines underlying insight-oriented psychotherapy. The pleasure forever promised by counseling psychology is never attained, and in its pursuit people are led away from any conviction of sin and toward blaming others for their problems. People are led away from the cross of Christ as increasingly they view the therapist as the only mediator they need. But the fulfillment clients anticipate as they write their checks to the counselor proves ever more elusive.

Yet the idea of sin being merely a dysfunction is so attractive to every one of us heirs of Adam that we continue to follow the therapist to self-destruction. Only by the direct intervention of the Holy Spirit, bringing genuine repentance for sin, can any of us say with Bunyan's Faithful, "It came burning hot into my mind that whatever he said, and however he flattered, when he got me to his house, he would sell me for a slave" (*The Pilgrim's Progress*).[2]

Section 2 examines "The Origins of the Psychotherapeutic Ethos," tracing the development of psychotherapy's underlying ideas. Chapter 4, "Darwin, Haeckel, Fliess, and Freud," traces the founding of Freud's psychoanalysis to an especially opportune time late in the nineteenth century. Freudian doctrine originated in the philosophy of fallen, rebellious humans unable or unwilling to place their theories under the light of Scripture. Freud did not claim the light of Christ for his thinking; what is the excuse for Christian leaders failing to use that light?

Chapter 5, "Descartes' Dualism vs. Materialistic Monism," seeks to show that the doctrines of psychotherapy are an outgrowth of atheistic naturalism, or materialism, which looks only to "matter-in-motion" as it considers the origin, development, function, and purpose of human life. Charles Darwin's theory of evolution by natural selection opened the floodgates of atheistic naturalism, and the church continues in its determination to integrate Darwin's theories as science. We will examine the implications of these theories.

Chapters 6, 7, 8 and 9—on Augustine, Pelagianism, gnosticism, and Platonism—trace the origins of psychotherapy back to antiquity. In these chapters we will see that the legacies of Pelagius and the gnostics, and some aspects of Plato's legacy, are at the very deepest foundations of insight-oriented psychotherapy. We will also discover the fascinating role of Augustine and the "anti-psychoanalytic" effect of his influence. We will see that, regrettably, the church eventually forgot much of Augustine's unfolding of Scripture and thereby contributed to the existence of psychotherapy today.

Section 3 addresses "The Effects of the Psychotherapeutic Ethos" on all of us today. In chapter 10, "Caring for Souls: Then and Now," we will take a closer look at what often passes for Christian counseling today, compared with how earlier believers understood their duties in this area. Among Christian psychologists, long-term therapy relationships are more and more common, along with specialized training, graduate degrees of uncertain quality, obscure jargon, and journals filled with techniques for so-called diagnosis and treatment. In general, what has been called Christian counseling is taking on the trappings of psychotherapy. Special training in methods is becoming the norm. The temptations to blend "Christian counseling" with its secular counterpart are more powerful than most would guess, and this marriage has created a lucrative industry. I hope to encourage even the new believer in the truth of 2 Corinthians 3:5-6 that, "Our competence comes from God. He has made us competent as ministers of a new covenant." The believer is not only, in the words of psychologist Jay Adams, competent to counsel;[3] he or she is expected to do so—but always to do so from Scripture.

Chapter 11, "Jane's Story: Modern Psychotherapy vs. Truth," addresses one of the most serious problems of insight-oriented psychotherapy: its total disregard for truthfulness. After looking at a tragic example of psychotherapeutic malpractice involving "false memory," we will consider the Freudian concept of "psychic reality" and the modern concept of the "personal narrative." The development of this unique kind of personal life story—whether that story is true or not—is considered essential to gaining insight into personal problems.

Chapter 12, "Recovered Memory Therapy: Have We Recovered from It?" focuses more fully on the false-memory epidemic that has been one of the awful consequences of insight-oriented psychotherapy. Even the powerful therapy industry has found it difficult to suppress media attention to the horror produced by so-called "recovered memories." This bizarre epidemic, likened by many to the Salem witch trials, could only have developed in a culture where one's own personal psychic reality is considered to be entirely relative. The *truth* of the patient's narrative simply doesn't matter; truth is utterly unimportant to the therapist. We might expect such methods to develop outside the Christian community, but they have run rampant within the church as well. Sadly, this reflects a church where witnesses and truth are treated as unimportant, a church functioning outside of scriptural guidelines. Lawsuits brought on by these fictions are reducing the frequency of such diagnoses in secular society, and it appears that only lawsuits will stop them within the church.

In section 4 we will look at some "Alternatives to Psychotherapy." Chapter 13, "Psychiatry's Twin Failure: No Cause, No Cure," reviews the history and futility of psychiatry's search for the cause and cure of mental illness. Chapter 14, "One Person, Two Paradigms," reviews a typical counseling case, giving two different ways to view the problem, one psychological and the other biblical. Chapter 15, "A Biblical Approach to Depression," applies Scripture to the most prevalent complaint of people seeking the help of counselors today. Then, in the Epilogue, I shall recount a true-life example of how Christians can care for one another's souls—how "Christian counseling" can be truly Christian.

As believers in Jesus Christ, we are surely called to be like the Bereans and search the Scriptures, "to find out whether these things are so" (see Acts 17:11, NKJV). I trust that this book will be a help to all true Bereans.

THE PILLARS OF THE PSYCHOTHERAPY INDUSTRY

ONE

❧

THE FREUDIAN
FOUNDATION

In this first chapter we will examine the "pillars" of insight-oriented psychoanalysis, as established by Sigmund Freud. Until the end of his life in 1939, Freud generated a vast literature developing and expanding these psychoanalytic theories. Freud's pillars are the foundational beliefs of the psychoanalytic movement, and they continue today as fundamental doctrines of the psychotherapy industry. If one closely examines the beliefs and practices of modern insight-oriented psychotherapy, whether conducted by a classical psychoanalyst or by a bartender consoling a depressed drinker, these fundamental pillars will be evident.

Paul C. Vitz, professor of psychology at New York University and a widely-known critic of psychology, agrees that certain very basic presuppositions underlie all varieties of insight-oriented psychotherapy. These presuppositions are: *atheism* (rather than theism), *reductionism* (rather than constructionism), *determinism* (rather than freedom of the will), *individualism* (rather than interdependence), *self-centered morality* (rather than God-centered morality), and *subjectivism* (rather than realism). Vitz shows that each of these presuppositions is completely at odds with Christianity.[1]

Throughout this century, numerous schools of psychology and psychotherapy have come and gone, usually the product of charismatic leaders who rise in popularity for a time, then fall. A listing of such leaders and schools would include: Freud's Psychoanalysis,

Alfred Adler's "Individual" Psychotherapy, Erik Erikson's Object Relations, Carl Rogers's Client-Centered Therapy, Abraham Maslow's "peak experience," Albert Ellis's or Aaron Beck's Cognitive Therapies, Viktor Frankl's "search for meaning," and Joseph de Rivera's mutualist self-therapy. The list would include the work of Erich Fromm, Gordon Allport, Carl Jung, and Karen Horney; it would include such varied approaches as Family Therapy, Feminist Therapy, Gestalt Therapy, Group Therapy, Impasse-Priority Therapy, Implosive Therapy, Marathon Therapy, Naikan Therapy, Orgone Therapy, Play Therapy, Poetry Therapy, Reality Therapy, and Reevaluation Therapy.

A standard textbook of psychiatry describes more than 250 different kinds of psychotherapy.[2] Others assert that "there are as many psychotherapies as there are psychotherapists."[3] This assertion becomes obvious with a bit of investigation; however, it does not discount the reality that at the foundation of all the insight-oriented "psychotherapies" are the pillars that Freud elaborated nearly a hundred years ago.

Paul Gray, in a 1993 article in *Time* titled "The Assault on Freud," quoted Seattle-based psychoanalyst George H. Allison: "I think Freud's influence in mental health as well as in the humanities is much greater than it was 40 years ago."[4] He also quoted Allison in reference to the profusion of "talking cures competing in the U.S. mental health market place." Allison says that these methods "are really based on Freudian principles, even though a lot of people who head these movements are anti-Freudian officially."

As beings who bear the image of God and are thus able to reason, we should investigate Freud's foundational ideas to determine whether they are consistent with God's Word, and whether they even live up to their own claims to be scientific. Such an investigation will show these ideas to be neither consistent with God's Word nor the products of rigorous scientific inquiry. We should therefore be more than a little concerned that these pillars have been so thoroughly woven into the fabric of what is loosely called Christian psychology or Christian counseling.

Seminaries proudly offer degrees in psychology, and many

Christian counselors boast of having "integrated" Freud's pillars into their counseling practice. They exult in their modernity, their "balance," and their resultant professional credibility. In a recent Seminary and Grad School Directory in *Christianity Today* (October 5, 1998) Wheaton College "is pleased to announce that the doctoral program in Clinical Psychology is now accredited by the American Psychological Association." They claim to offer a "holistic Christian approach."

Like the equally popular field of evolutionary biology, psychoanalysis simply does not play by the rules of empirical science. The attribution by Freud and his predecessors of truthfulness to data collected by the historical method set the course for both of these areas of inquiry. Such methods diverge from rigorous, objective, provable/falsifiable science—whether we are considering fossilized remains or the memories of a counseling client.

The observed data supposedly supporting both evolution and psychology are not measurable phenomena, but are entirely descriptive and subjective. The hypotheses are biased toward an expected or desired outcome. There are no experiments capable of proving or disproving such hypotheses. There can be neither independent confirmation nor replication of such theories. In recent years, a significant literature has emerged (both secular and Christian) showing that Freud's fundamental theories of counseling psychology are not "truth."[5] Neither evolutionary biology nor psychoanalysis/counseling psychology are truly scientific, nor are they capable of generating truth. This should be obvious to anyone who attempts a dispassionate examination of the issues.[6] For instance, "repression," the very centerpiece of Freud's theory of the mind, is an idea for which there is no scientific evidence. This is increasingly obvious after sixty years of research on the subject.[7]

Why are such pseudo-scientific theories as evolution and psychoanalysis so widely accepted as science? How do they elude exposure as false religions? Basic to both of these theories is the denial of God's existence and the conclusion that man can be his own god.[8] As his own god, man claims the ability to perfect his future. The Word of God becomes untrustworthy and irrelevant. It is no longer regarded as ultimate truth and therefore is no longer seen as a benchmark for measuring ideas.

The desire to be God opened the minds of late-nineteenth-century Europeans to both Darwinism and Freudianism in the same way that it "opened the eyes" of Adam and Eve to setting their own standard of good and evil. Darwinism and Freudianism appealed in a special way because they offered a socially and "scientifically" acceptable expression of this desire to be God. They offered ways to overcome the concept of original sin and the "onus of hereditary degeneration."[9] Such concepts as original sin and the Fall do little to raise the self-esteem of the godman, while the theories of Darwin and Freud seem to do so—by offering solutions to problems, cultural revitalization, and a brighter future controlled by mankind himself.

It is the quest for an answer, outside of Scripture, to the "why's" of life that drives many to therapy. Most therapists agree that therapy can provide a "rationale" for the client's life and troubles.[10] It is the industry's claim of this secret knowledge that keeps the consumers coming. Commenting on the staying power of psychoanalysis and its Freudian pillars, Paul Gray said:

> For all of [Freud's] . . . sins of omission and commission that critics past and present correctly lay on his couch, he still managed to create an intellectual edifice that *feels* closer to the experience of living, and therefore hurting, than any other system currently in play. What he bequeathed was not (despite his arguments to the contrary), nor has yet proved itself to be, a science. Psychoanalysis and all its offshoots may in the final analysis turn out to be no more reliable than phrenology or mesmerism or any of the countless other pseudo-sciences that once offered unsubstantiated answers or false solace. Still, the reassurances provided by Freud that our inner selves are rich with drama and hidden meanings would be missed if it disappeared, leaving nothing in its place.[11]

Freud's vision of psychoanalysis (and the insight-oriented psychotherapy industry that grew out of that vision) has failed as science and as a treatment. That objective reality is increasingly being admitted even by those prominent within the world of psychotherapy. Alan A. Stone, Touroff-Gloueck Professor of Psychiatry and Law at Harvard University, recently commented on the survival of psychoanalysis and insight-oriented psychotherapy in our culture:

> Psychoanalysis, both as theory and as practice, is an art form that belongs to the humanities and not the natural sciences. It is closer to literature than to science and therefore. . . . that is the domain in which Freud and psychoanalysis will survive. . . . in popular culture, where it has become a kind of psychological common sense, and in every other domain where human beings construct narratives to understand and reflect on the moral adventure of life.

He goes on to say:

> I still believe that a traditional psychoanalytic experience on the couch is the best way to explore the mysterious otherness of one's self, but I do not think psychoanalysis is an adequate form of treatment. . . . When a patient's symptoms are treated, he may need a psychoanalyst to help him deal with his ordinary human suffering. That is the therapeutic domain in which the art of psychoanalysis will survive.[12]

Many in the church apparently agree that the rationale of insight-oriented psychotherapy is better than "any other system currently in play" and "would be missed if it disappeared." They behave as though the truth of Scripture were not currently "in play," as though it could not possibly replace Freud's edifice "to deal with ordinary human suffering." The foundational ideas of Freud and his followers have been accepted in the modern church for the same reasons that they were accepted by late-nineteenth-century Europeans. Freud offered a conception of mankind, his problems, and their resolution that appeared far more attractive than what Scripture offered. He offered a purely man-centered redemption. His psychoanalysis required no burdensome concept of sin, and it certainly released mankind from the requirement of atonement for his sin and from any need for submission before a holy God. The modern church has accepted Darwin's and Freud's ideas as truth. With that acceptance, the simple message of the Gospel and the offense of the Cross have been supplanted by systems of thought that seem so much better and so much deeper.

THE FIRST PILLAR: ENVIRONMENTAL DETERMINISM

The first and most foundational pillar of Freudian theory and psychotherapy is the assertion that human mental and emotional difficulties are the result of improper external environmental influences. Darwin excited late-nineteenth-century Europe with his assertion that natural selection, the effects of the environment upon the development of the species, explained the form and substance of humankind. The outworking of this Darwinian notion in the theories of Freud and his followers sees mankind as having been born with a clean slate, naturally poised for success. With the acceptance of Darwin and Freud, mankind is no longer seen as inherently predisposed toward evil.

Environmental determinism denies the doctrines of the Fall and original sin. Belief in mankind's inherent goodness was popularized by Ernst Haeckel (1834–1919) in his many quasi-religious writings. Haeckel asserted that the human soul was rational and pure, but was defiled by environmental influences that caused the eruption of the archaic residues of man's primitive animal past.[13] According to Haeckel's "biogenetic psychology," during the development of the human personality, ontogeny recapitulates phylogeny. Simply stated, that means that the evolutionary stages of the development of human consciousness (phylogeny) can be observed in the post-natal personality development of each human individual (ontogeny). Freud believed that these stages were "layered over" or "repressed" along the road to maturity. The genetic theory (now proven wrong) of Chevalier de Lamarck (1744–1829), that external events could influence genetic endowment and lead to the inheritance of acquired traits, was also a key ingredient in Freud's thinking.

From these basic premises, Freud asserted throughout his career that "man is basically a socialized animal; he is not responsible for his actions."[14] By this Freud meant that, if we were reared properly, by enlightened and sensitive parents, and if all external stimuli were of the right sort and came at the right time, we would emerge successfully through those stages to be perfect human beings.

Freud correctly observed, however, that "children are completely egotistic; they feel their needs intensely and strive ruthlessly to satisfy them."[15] In his own version of Haeckel's biogenetic psychology, Freud asserted that "this frightful evil is simply the initial, primitive, infantile part of mental life which we can find in actual operation in children, but which, in part, we overlook in them on account of their small size, and which, in part, we do not take seriously since we do not expect any higher ethical standard from children."[16]

As one Freud scholar explains, "The crucial point about Freud's view of this frightful evil is that he does not see it as a permanent, inescapable condition of human beings, but only as a developmental stage, which all healthy individuals are biologically destined to leave behind them as they grow to maturity."[17] Freud said, "We do not on that account call a child 'bad'; we call him 'naughty': he is no more answerable for his evil deeds in our judgment than in the eyes of the law."[18]

Freud regarded repression as a normal biologic process that, in conjunction with proper environmental influences and the inherited influences of civilization, would result in the leaving behind of primitive or "infantile" instincts and behaviors, and would eventually lead to healthy maturity. "And it is right that this should be so; for we may expect that before the end of the period which we count as childhood, altruistic impulses and morality will awaken in the little egoist and . . . a secondary ego will overlay and inhibit the primary one."[19] This "secondary ego" is what Freud eventually termed the "superego."

In accordance with his theories of infantile sexuality, repression, and fixation, and with his acceptance of Lamarck's theory of the inheritance of acquired traits, Freud believed that, "If this morality fails to develop, we like to talk of 'degeneracy,' though what in fact faces us is an inhibition of development."[20] For Freud, the "frightful evil" seen in children is not the permanent or inherent nature of man; it is a developmental phase. If it remains, something in the environment has not been manipulated in a correct manner. Degeneracy should naturally and biologically be replaced by "maturity." If that natural and biologic process fails, then the environment is to blame.

For Freud, evil was not a spiritual problem but simply a technical one. Thus Freud believed that people could learn to control evil both in themselves and in society. He offered psychoanalysis as a cure for those who refused to accept what they called "the despair of degeneracy." For those not eager to rest in such foolishness as a Redeemer paying for their degeneracy on a Roman cross, Freud offered a "better" way.

Freud's belief that the thoughts, feelings, and behaviors of infants are biopsychologic and developmental, rather than inherent in the human heart, laid the supposedly scientific foundations for a doctrine of original innocence, replacing the Christian doctrine of original sin. The attractive fantasy of childhood innocence swept the Western world. Freud appeared to provide not only an external cause for the travails of modern humanity, but at the same time a positive, humanistic hope for regeneration through the techniques of psychoanalysis. He thus laid the foundation, the pillar, of the now universal belief that if we are not "emotionally healthy," it is, by definition, due to the wrong actions of someone else.

THE SECOND PILLAR: PSYCHIC DETERMINISM

The second pillar of Freudianism is the belief that there exists in each person a "dynamic unconscious" that determines and controls our every thought and action. Freud asserted that the mind, outside of our awareness, is a powerful repository of instincts, experiences, sensations, perceptions, emotions, and thoughts. This repository is always active, and it controls our thoughts, feelings, behaviors, and relationships.[21] The content of this so-called unconscious is kept out of awareness by repression.[22]

Freud's unconscious can be likened to having a videotape recorder inside our mind that operates from birth, recording everything we experience with total accuracy and with total credibility. Freud viewed this repository as powerful, as if under pressure, and as having a need to express itself, to be released. This repository controls us without our realizing it. We have no control over its effect on our life.

Freud claimed that the unconscious can express itself in cryptic or symbolic ways through dreams, slips of the tongue, odd emotions, and unsatisfying relationships.[23] These cryptic expressions can be deciphered only by an analyst or therapist with special experience and training. For Freud, the most important aspect of the human mind was not that of the conscious mind but rather that of the unconscious. He viewed the content of the unconscious as the decisive influence over our daily lives.

This is why a typical psychotherapist will for the most part disregard the overtly conscious experiences of a patient's day-to-day life and concentrate instead on the supposed content of the patient's unconscious. Psychotherapy goes after the "why" beneath the "what." The "deeper" meaning of the behavior was for Freud vastly more important than the behavior itself. Freud was convinced that, without understanding the content and influence of the unconscious, people would always be in hopeless bondage to the traumatic experiences of their past. These experiences, he believed, were recorded in the unconscious mind, from whence they determined everyday life. Like any other practitioner of the occult, Freud convinced himself that he could know the content of the unconscious and that, moreover, he could control it.

THE THIRD PILLAR: INSIGHT

The third pillar, Freud's chief contribution to the methodology of psychotherapy, is his belief that access to the out-of-awareness mind is not only essential but fully possible: In order to reach "maturity," we can and must discover the content of what he called our unconscious. Only by understanding the content of the unconscious can we understand and control its influence over our lives. Freud claimed to offer a way of doing this with his special techniques of recollection, free-association, dream interpretation, symbol interpretation, hypnosis, facilitated recall, and revivification. He also advocated "catharsis"—the dramatic, emotional release of repressed, problem-causing unconscious mental content. He claimed that we must vent or express such repressed content, and relive repressed traumatic experiences, in order to be truly released from bondage to our unconscious.

THE FOURTH PILLAR: THE THERAPIST

The fourth pillar of Freud's system is the importance and necessity of a specially trained and experienced psychotherapist to assist the patient in the quest for insight. This fundamental pillar is the basis of what is reputed to be in this country a $200 billion industry,[24] and by one estimate nearly 80 percent of the American public has at some time in their lives sought its help![25] One cannot, says Freud, simply accomplish the quest for insight and mastery on one's own. A professional, skilled, credentialed, and paid expert is required. The expert therapist possesses a special knowledge that enables him or her to interpret the overt as well as symbolic and cryptic expressions of the unconscious, to explain the client's difficulties, and to provide a solution.

The therapist's special knowledge provides a framework through which the client can understand the "why" of his problems and, in so doing, can have hope of a self-cure. This hope of self-cure is enhanced when the therapist through his special knowledge is able to prescribe specific treatment activities. These activities will differ depending on which therapeutic fad the therapist is basing his practice on at the time.

The therapist-expert will have been trained by other experts and will be a member of an elite group claiming to possess secret psychological knowledge and skill. This knowledge supposedly allows the therapist to predict what he or she will find at the root of a client's problems. Numerous theories of human psychology have come and gone over the years; common to all of them remains the fundamental pillar of the therapist as the facilitator of self-cure.

It is essential that the therapist provide "an intense, confiding relationship."[26] He must inspire confidence and trust in the client. He must seem concerned about the client's welfare. This will engender in the client the all-important hope for success. The therapist must also provide a setting for the treatment that is conducive to the healing process.

One hallmark of psychotherapy is that no specific kind of treatment has proven to be consistently superior to any other,[27] leading to the conclusion that, "If a multitude of different systems can legitimately claim success, then their diversity may be illusory and they share core features that in fact are the curative elements responsible for therapeutic success."[28] The "core feature" identified most often is simply the presence of the therapist, the "therapeutic alliance," the "beneficial therapist qualities," the "opportunity for catharsis," the "provision of a rationale for the client's problems," and "the creation of positive expectations" he provides.[29] The psychotherapy industry rests upon the pillar of the therapist. Who he is, what he believes, and what he does is not nearly so important as the fact that he is there, and that clients see him as able to provide answers—if they are willing and able to spend enough time and money!

THE FIFTH PILLAR: SELF-SUFFICIENCY

The fifth pillar of Freudian practice is the notion of self-sufficiency and self-cure. By this Freud meant that people could solve their own problems without the help of God or any other supernatural source. This desire for self-cure was not an invention of Freud. The notion became prominent during the Enlightenment in eighteenth-century Europe, with its faith in the power of human reason. This belief in man's ability of self-empowerment was fundamental to the thinking of Freud and is foundational to psychotherapy today.

There is scant understanding or agreement among psychotherapists as to what constitutes a "cure" for their clients. The essential importance of the therapist is unquestioned, but little else is clear. There are, however, two additional, generally accepted notions of what defines success. One is the acquisition of "mastery" on the part of the client. This means the practice of new behavior under the guidance of the therapist, which then leads to success, self-satisfaction, and feelings of accomplishment (mastery) over problems. The second factor is the belief that "change will last only if the patient attributes improvement to himself (as opposed to the therapist or the treatment)."[30]

Self-mastery over one's problems and the attribution of success to oneself are considered essential to a successful psychotherapeutic outcome.

THE SIXTH PILLAR: THE PLEASURE PRINCIPLE

The sixth and final pillar is the ultimate psychotherapeutic objective of pleasure. Freedom from guilt, shame, fear, anxiety, and suffering is the unabashed, openly-stated goal of psychotherapy. This was true for Freud and remains true today. Discomfort is the anathema of insight-oriented psychotherapy. The desire to avoid suffering is a major reason for the existence of the therapeutic community. Suffering is to be avoided at all costs, and pleasure is to be pursued at all costs. Freud did not invent this motivation; people have always tried to avoid suffering. Freud did, however, offer his method as an effective means to that desired end. All forms of insight-oriented psychotherapy today are offered as a means to ease discomfort.

The particular promises offered to clients vary somewhat, depending on the theories upon which the therapist bases his practice. Some therapists see it as their purpose to train the client to have more self-control over "unhealthy" impulses. These impulses are seen to emanate from the unconscious, which has been damaged or derailed in its development by unhealthy environmental influences.

Other therapists may try to help the client uncover his own innate goodness or discover his own self-actualizing nature, which has been deformed by maladaptive external influences or lack of proper opportunities. The goal is "to move away from facades, oughts, pleasing others, and to move toward self-direction—being more autonomous, increasingly trusting and valuing the process which is in himself."[31]

Other therapists try to help clients carve out their own existence in a relativistic, valueless world, learning those skills necessary for "optimal" or self-satisfying functioning within the culture.

Then there are the "transpersonal" New Age therapists, who guide their clients toward accepting their own role as part of "the larger self," with the goal of experiencing its "illimitibles or measureless states—compassion, sympathetic joy, all-embracing kindness and equanimity."[32]

Jung spoke of the "individuated" self. Otto Rank espoused creativity as the ultimate goal. One author, surveying the vast and confusing literature attempting to define psychological "health," has pointed toward the achievement of self-satisfaction, self-actualization, personal integration, autonomy, and mastery of the environment as the central goals of all psychotherapy, the essence of the ephemeral goal of psychological "health."

Personal pleasure; an absence of ill feelings; avoidance of guilt, shame, sadness, anxiety, depression; a filled-up love tank; being "together"—all these and more are the "self-ish" goals and promises of therapy. Self-satisfaction is for sale. Self-satisfaction is the commodity of an industry that claims to be able to provide that satisfaction.

If you add to all of this some key evangelical terminology and twisted interpretations of a few Bible verses, you end up with what today is often called Christian counseling.

CONCLUSION

The foundational ideas, the "pillars" of insight-oriented psychotherapy outlined in this chapter are common to all forms and practices of psychotherapy that seek to solve human problems by achieving "insight." These fundamental ideas run through the entire movement regardless of what school of therapy and regardless of what charismatic leader may be popular at the moment. In a community characterized by fad and fancy, my assertion of the commonality of these pillars may seem overly simplistic. Close inspection, however, of the actual practices of psychotherapists, their claims, and their published articles will reveal these fundamental ideas in operation—sometimes overtly, sometimes covertly, but always in play. Wherever troubled clients are seeking insight—outside of biblical truth—into the causes and cures of their mental and emotional problems, you will see these six pillars in operation.

The six fundamental ideas of psychotherapy may be restated and summarized as follows:

1. Our current mental and emotional well-being has been determined by our past experiences. We are determined by our environment.
2. Our past experiences are recorded deeply in our unconscious, where they powerfully control our daily thoughts, feelings, and behaviors. We are controlled by our unconscious.
3. We can and must access our unconscious and correct its maladaptive control over our life. Such "insight" is possible and essential.
4. We need a skilled and experienced therapist to help us gain this insight.
5. We can and must make ourselves better or more mature (more perfect).
6. The goal of life is obviously pleasure. Feelings of discomfort mean failure.

Chapter 2 will explore the contrast between these six fundamental ideas of Freudian psychology and the six foundations of counseling revealed in the Bible.

TWO

℘

THE BIBLICAL

FOUNDATION

The foundational ideas, the "pillars" outlined in chapter 1, represent the core beliefs Freud held throughout his long and influential career. They also represent the foundational beliefs of insight-oriented psychotherapy today. It is currently popular among psychotherapists to dismiss the importance of Freud and his beliefs. And of course, Christian psychologists will claim to have left Freud behind. However, a close inspection of what actually occurs in the therapist's assessment of a client's problems, along with observation of the actual interventions the therapist makes against those problems, will reveal that Freud's six pillars continue to be foundational for Christian and non-Christian therapists alike.

The extent to which Freud's beliefs have been incorporated into the beliefs and practices of Christian counselors should be of grave concern to Christian leaders, for Freud's pillars are thoroughly incompatible with Scripture. Like Bereans, Christians should constantly compare these ideas—this "human wisdom"—with the teachings of Scripture. The Bible warns the church to expect false teachers to arise, and it directs us to be constantly on guard:

> Even from your own number men will arise and distort the truth in order to draw away disciples after them. So be on your guard! (Acts 20:30-31)

See to it that no one takes you captive through hollow and deceptive philosophy, which depends on human tradition and the basic principles of this world rather than on Christ. (Col. 2:8)

This chapter will show the Bible's perspective on the six pillars of psychotherapy outlined in chapter 1. We will see that Scripture does offer basic principles for counseling. There is a biblical way to care for souls, but it differs sharply from Freud's doctrine, and there can be no integration of the two methods.

As a quick review, Freud's six pillars could be stated in terms of six questions a person might ask, along with the six answers a typical psychotherapist will give:

1. *Why am I unhappy?* I am unhappy because I was improperly reared and thus have been wounded.
2. *What is wrong inside my mind?* My life is controlled by my past experiences, which are recorded deeply in my mind, out of my awareness.
3. *How can I make sense of my problems?* I can and must explore and understand the depths of my mind in order to be able to change.
4. *Who can help me solve my problems?* A skilled and experienced therapist is able to lead me toward this change and is essential to my improvement.
5. *How can I be happier?* I can and must make myself happier.
6. *What is the purpose of my life?* The purpose of my life is to achieve a general feeling of pleasure.

How does the Bible answer these six questions?

TRUTH NUMBER ONE: ORIGINAL SIN

"Why am I unhappy?" Psychotherapy tells us that we are unhappy because of bad experiences early in life. Those early traumas have prevented us from reaching our "full potential." Our culture today accepts as axiomatic that we are the product of the environmental influences of our developing years. Few of those who accept this view are aware that it is the result of the thinking of Darwin, Haeckel, Fliess, and Freud. Fewer still know how valiantly the early church fought against this heresy.

The ignorance of this history of ideas comes at a time when people either actively reject the Bible or regard it as little more than an object of sentimental devotion. As a result, the vast majority of both non-Christians and professing Christians believe that we humans are essentially born innocent and basically good, and that we would all be leading lives of health and happiness, at our full potential, if only a bad environment had not intervened. If I am not healthy, happy, and functioning at an optimal level, then the responsibility lies outside of me. My misery and general lack of success must be due to my parents, my family, the neighborhood, the culture, the environment. The only exception to this paradigm is the emerging claim that genetics can play a determining role in complex patterns of human behavior. But even this, of course, is not my responsibility; my misery and my troublesome behavior are out of my control—it is all outside of me, in my environment or in my genes.

Scripture gives a very different understanding of the human situation. It wastes no time in pointing us to our own sin as the root of our problems. Most importantly, it teaches what has been called the doctrine of original sin. We are not sinners simply because we have sinned; rather, we sin because we are sinners by nature. My sin comes from inside me. This is in direct opposition to psychotherapeutic doctrine. As J. C. Ryle explains, man is born in sin and with an inclination to keep on sinning as he rebels against his Creator.[1] This is surely among the most fundamental truths about mankind revealed by God in His Word; if our eyes were not veiled by our own sin we would see it as one of the most obvious characteristics of humankind. The idea that people are born innocent, or have a natural inclination toward purity, is inconsistent with Scripture and with personal experience. It is inconsistent with the observations of any objective historian and of any mother caring for her own children.

The Bible records God's warning to Adam and Eve not to rebel against Him, and Satan's effort to negate that warning:

And the LORD God commanded the man, "You are free to eat from any tree in the garden; but you must not eat from the tree of the knowledge of good and evil, for when you eat of it you will surely die." (Gen. 2:16-17)

"You will not surely die," the serpent said to the woman. "For God knows that when you eat of it your eyes will be opened, and you will be like God, knowing good and evil." (Gen. 3:4-5)

Our rebellious nature as humans has three basic attributes: our refusal to believe God, our determination to set our own moral standard, and our refusal to submit to authority. The serpent told the first couple that what had been forbidden to them by their Creator was actually "desirable for gaining wisdom" (Gen. 3:6). Man wants to be like the Creator God; he does not easily accept his position as a created being. However ideal the environment, it is not in the nature of any human to submit to authority. Unregenerate man joins Satan in refusing to allow any authority over him; he refuses to acknowledge the Creator for who He is. Throughout its pages, Scripture emphasizes mankind's basic, inborn sinful nature:

. . . every inclination of his heart is evil from childhood. (Gen. 8:21)

Surely I was sinful at birth, sinful from the time my mother conceived me. (Ps. 51:5)

Even from birth the wicked go astray; from the womb they are wayward and speak lies. (Ps. 58:3)

Jews and Gentiles alike are all under sin. As it is written: "There is no one righteous, not even one." (Rom. 3:9-10)

God sees me as a sinner and abhors my blaming others for my sin (Ezek. 18:2-4). The Creator as authority holds me responsible for my sinful omissions as well as my sinful commissions (James

2:10). He holds me responsible even for my unintentional sins (Num. 15:22-24). Scripture says nothing about environmental causation for sin. It gives no hint of diagnoses such as sexual addiction, kleptomania, alcoholism, or oppositional defiance disorder. Never does Scripture suggest the need to, in the words of Freud, "remember, repeat, and work through"[2] our past environmental influences in order to be made righteous before God.

Blaming a bad environment is nothing new. It was one of the sins for which God sent the Jews into Babylonian exile. Ezekiel spoke to this issue:

> The soul who sins is the one who will die. The son will not share the guilt of the father, nor will the father share the guilt of the son. The righteousness of the righteous man will be credited to him, and the wickedness of the wicked will be charged against him. (Ezek. 18:20)

The Bible consistently stands against environmental determinism. My father will answer to God for sins committed against me as well as for his other sins; however, Scripture assigns to my father neither blame nor credit regarding my own justification and sanctification (Deut. 24:16). At the final judgment, I will stand alone before a sovereign and holy God without excuse, without anyone to blame, to await perfect justice. My parents cannot take the punishment for me. No oppressor, no bad parent, no unfriendly environment, no genetic disability, no psychiatric diagnosis will stand there to mitigate my guilt. My only covering, my only advocate, will be the shed blood and righteousness of the Messiah.

God accomplished redemption for my sin on a hill called Golgotha. This redemption comes to me from the outside. It does not arise from within me. Within me is my sinful nature—not the wounded inner child so promoted in some Christian circles today. We constantly try to reverse this reality of sin within and redemption without. This reversal (sin from without, redemption from within) is surely a large part of the attraction of the false gospel of insight-oriented psychotherapy. It allows us to pretend that our sin is outside ourselves and has been rudely forced upon our innocent "inner child." Psychotherapy tells us that we can find redemption within ourselves if only we will avail ourselves of the correct methodology.

Regardless of feelings or sociological studies, Scripture's certain word is that we are lost and under the wrath of a holy God due to our own sin. Salvation is all of God, and though God uses the environment for His purposes, it neither aids nor stays His hand. The church in our day seems either ignorant of this or unwilling to believe it. Augustus M. Toplady lived about one hundred years before Sigmund Freud, but he would surely have seen the deception of psychotherapeutic doctrine. As recorded in his beloved hymn "Rock of Ages," Toplady's redemption was fully outside of himself, and he knew it:

> *Not the labors of my hands can fulfill Thy law's demands;*
> *Could my zeal no respite know, could my tears forever flow,*
> *All for sin could not atone; Thou must save, and Thou alone.*

> *Nothing in my hand I bring, simply to Thy cross I cling;*
> *Naked, come to Thee for dress; helpless, look to Thee for grace;*
> *Foul, I to the fountain fly, wash me, Savior, or I die!*

TRUTH NUMBER TWO: THE HEART

It is natural to ask, "What goes on inside my mind?" We think there is more to us than meets the eye. We observe an "out-of-awareness" aspect to our mind and conclude that this is where memories are stored, where other thoughts are stored while we are paying attention to one particular object or perception. We conclude that learned facts must be stored there for future retrieval and use, and we think that dreams offer some kind of access to that out-of-awareness mind.

Man has devoted much time and energy to such speculation about the human mind—about the conscious as well as the out-of-awareness part of the mind; about the material as well as the immaterial. As we as a society moved away from the authority and sufficiency of Scripture and began to rely on introspection and human reason, we began to build a concept of the mind based on our own experience and derived from philosophy. However, it was not until the late nineteenth century that the "unconscious" became a fully developed working concept.

Freud defined our out-of-awareness mental aspect as the *Freud's* "unconscious." The unconscious is supposedly a lifelong archival *unconscious* repository of inherited instincts and external influences. The contents of that unconscious determine conscious thoughts, feelings, and behaviors. The unconscious may control the conscious in obvious ways, but more often it does so in cryptic (symbolic) ways. Most importantly, the content of the unconscious can be reliably examined by a trained therapist, who can read the secret symbols; the content of the unconscious can then be changed by special techniques, as devised by Freud.

Freud synthesized ideas from a variety of sources to formulate this notion of the unconscious, but he deserves full credit for the concept as it is understood today. His view of the unconscious mind as an archival repository of life experiences powerfully influencing our daily thoughts, feelings, and behaviors is accepted without serious questioning in most circles. His concept of the deterministic unconscious remains the foundation of psychotherapy today. Most of us at the close of the twentieth century answer the question, "What is wrong inside my mind?" with Freud's answer: "It is all the effect of my unconscious."

Scripture does not deny our out-of-awareness mind. Moreover, it offers an authoritative and utterly sufficient explanation of that mind. The Bible describes it using the words commonly translated "heart," "soul," and "spirit." Additional truths about the functioning of the human mental apparatus are delineated through the words commonly translated as "mind." Following this terminology, we can see the answer Scripture gives to the question, "What is wrong inside my mind?"

We humans have two aspects: material and immaterial. Philosphers have observed and discussed this truth from the dawn of recorded history. Of all creatures, only we humans were created in the image of God, with both an immaterial heart/soul/spirit and a material aspect, a physical body. Our two aspects are in many ways distinct from each other, but there is an incomprehensible unity of the two, making us truly unique beings:

> The LORD God formed the man from the dust of the ground and breathed into his nostrils the breath of life, and the man became a living being. (Gen. 2:7)

> The dead will be raised imperishable, and we will all be changed. For the perishable must clothe itself with the imperishable, and the mortal with immortality. (1 Cor. 15:52-53)

> If Christ is in you, your body is dead because of sin, yet your spirit is alive because of righteousness. (Rom. 8:10; see also 1 Cor. 7:34; 2 Cor. 7:1)

> "Do not be afraid of those who kill the body but cannot kill the soul. Rather, be afraid of the One who can destroy both soul and body in hell." (Matt. 10:28)

> . . . and the dust returns to the ground it came from, and the spirit returns to God who gave it. (Eccles. 12:7)

> I know a man in Christ who fourteen years ago was caught up to the third heaven. Whether it was in the body or out of the body I do not know—God knows. And I know that this man . . . heard inexpressible things, things that man is not permitted to tell. (2 Cor. 12:2-4)

Throughout Scripture, the words commonly translated as "soul," "spirit," and "heart" are used interchangeably. Scripture calls the heart "the wellspring of life" (Prov. 4:23). It is the center of our character, where things are stored. This immaterial aspect of humanity is naturally wicked and given to every form of sin:

> "But the things that come out of the mouth come from the heart, and these make a man 'unclean.' For out of the heart

come evil thoughts, murder, adultery, sexual immorality, theft, false testimony, slander." (Matt. 15:18-19)

The hearts of men, moreover, are full of evil and there is madness in their hearts while they live, and afterward they join the dead. (Eccles. 9:3)

"Are you so dull? . . . Don't you see that nothing that enters a man from the outside can make him 'unclean'? . . . All these evils come from inside and make a man 'unclean.'" (Mark 7:18, 23)

"Woe to you, teachers of the law and Pharisees, you hypocrites! You clean the outside of the cup and dish, but inside they are full of greed and self-indulgence. Blind Pharisee! First clean the inside of the cup and dish, and then the outside also will be clean." (Matt. 23:25-26)

We humans ultimately cannot understand the heart; this knowledge is reserved for the God who created it:

"The heart is deceitful above all things and beyond cure. Who can understand it? I the LORD search the heart and examine the mind." (Jer. 17:9-10; see also Rom. 7:15; 1 Cor. 2:10-12; 1 John 3:20)

Many verses describe the heart as the seat of emotions. It can be stilled and quieted by the Holy Spirit:

But I have stilled and quieted my soul. (Ps. 131:2)

The Spirit himself testifies with our spirit that we are God's children. (Rom. 8:16)

The heart represents our innermost being, and God searches it:

The lamp of the LORD searches the spirit of a man; it searches out his inmost being. (Prov. 20:27)

This human heart/soul/spirit is closely involved with the conscious mind:

> For if I pray in a tongue, my spirit prays, but my mind is unfruitful. . . . I will pray with my spirit, but I will also pray with my mind; I will sing with my spirit, but I will also sing with my mind. (1 Cor. 14:14-16)

Scripture promises that the Christian's heart/soul/spirit, indwelt with the Holy Spirit of God, will produce a kind of fruit different from that produced by the unbelieving heart:

> Your beauty . . . should be that of your inner self, the unfading beauty of a gentle and quiet spirit. (1 Pet. 3:3-4)

Scripture clearly teaches that only God can reliably know the human heart. Our efforts to do so are not only fruitless but ultimately rebellious; the attempt to know another person's heart is an attempt to be as God. Any therapist's notion that he can access the content of the "heart" is not only a delusion but is disobedient to Scripture. The truth about our immaterial aspect cannot be known from experience, nor can it be discovered by anyone's questioning or methodical analysis. We are called to accept what Scripture says about the content and influence of our immaterial aspect; it is idle foolishness to attempt otherwise:

> He who trusts in himself is a fool, but he who walks in wisdom is kept safe. (Prov. 28:26)

> All a man's ways seem innocent to him, but motives are weighed by the LORD. (Prov. 16:2)

> O LORD, you have searched me and you know me. . . . Search me, O God, and know my heart; test me and know my anxious thoughts. See if there is any offensive way in me, and lead me in the way everlasting. (Ps. 139:1, 23-24)

Though body and soul/spirit/heart are united in life, the immaterial departs the material at death, only to be reunited at the time of our bodily resurrection and judgment:

... hand this man over to Satan, so that his sinful nature may be destroyed and his spirit saved on the day of the Lord. (1 Cor. 5:5)

The body without the spirit is dead. (James 2:26)

While they were stoning him, Stephen prayed, "Lord Jesus, receive my spirit." (Acts 7:59)

I desire to depart and be with Christ, which is better by far; but it is more necessary for you that I remain in the body. (Phil. 1:23-24)

We are confident, I say, and would prefer to be away from the body and at home with the Lord. (2 Cor. 5:8)

Scripture teaches that "in this life, there is a continual interaction between our body and our soul and they affect one another. But it is not at all clear *how* they interact; this remains a mystery to us."[3] We know from the Bible that our immaterial aspect is designed to be beyond our comprehension; it is known only by God our Creator. Scripture does, however, tell us that the heart (the immaterial aspect) of the unregenerate person is in hopeless bondage to sin. God Himself is the only source of redemption and constructive change. Unless atonement is made for our sin and the Holy Spirit comes to indwell our immaterial aspect, we are in bondage to that sin forever. Without atonement, we are lost in sin and await only what Scripture calls the "second death"; no amount of psychotherapy can change that fact.

TRUTH NUMBER THREE: CONVICTION OF SIN

Psychotherapy's third pillar is "insight." The customers of psychotherapy pay for supposed insight into their unconscious, into the why of their troubled lives. Psychotherapy promises help for the client who asks, "How can I make sense of my problems?" It claims that such insight is not only possible and reliable but also efficacious. It promises that clients will have better feelings and will function more successfully when they understand their own personal why.

The insight-oriented therapist focuses on *why* people think, feel, and do. Counseling psychology may acknowledge the *what,* the day-to-day events of the client's life, but beginning with Freud the emphasis has been on insight, on understanding the *why* behind the *what:*

> What all schools of psychotherapy have in common is a developmental, historical account of the individual . . . a believable self-description . . . that help[s] them make sense of their personal histories.[4]

Attempts to remember past experiences are of utmost importance to the therapeutic process since, of course, Freudian doctrine says that the stored memories of these experiences control and explain the client's life. Maximum effort must therefore be expended toward recall of supposedly traumatic and maladaptive experiences. ,

However, the therapist's attempt to discover the content of the client's heart becomes a process in which the client believes only what he wants to believe and/or what the therapist wants him to believe. Human self-analysis leads not only to increasing bondage but to personal delusion. In telling his "own personal narrative," the client comes to believe what serves the purpose of the therapist at the time. Thinking they could play God and know the heart, both client and therapist end up believing a lie. A recent and tragic example of this, as we shall see in chapter 12, is the False Memory Syndrome pandemic that has flourished over the last several years. Therapists and their clients together create and believe false memories of past abuse.

Scripture closes the door on inquiry into the *why's* of life, except for what is clearly stated in Holy Writ. God asks, "Where were you when I laid the earth's foundation? Tell me, if you understand" (Job 38:4). Psychotherapists continue to claim just such understanding. Counselees continue their quest for the why, rather than relying on the sufficiency of the information God reveals in His Word. Counselors are glad to assist their clients in this futile quest, for it brings great status and monetary gain—within the church as well as in secular society.

Scripture and popular psychology differ sharply in the area of insight. As opposed to a quest for insight, Scripture speaks of conviction of sin. As opposed to man-centered introspection, Scripture calls the believer to objectively examine both the Bible's teachings and his own deeds, as well as the deeds of others. We are to examine ourselves from God's perspective as revealed in Scripture. Our assessment of our past will always be blinded by our self-centered nature, unless we make our assessment in the light of God's perspective as revealed in Scripture. We are to examine ourselves, but never in the morally relative manner of psychotherapy. Self-examination should always be carried out using Scripture as the sole standard of comparison. Scripture is to be authoritative in our life; it is the benchmark for our thoughts, feelings, and behaviors:

> . . . the sacred writings which are able to instruct you for salvation through faith in Christ Jesus. All scripture is inspired by God and profitable for teaching, for reproof, for correction, and for training in righteousness, that the man of God may be complete, equipped for every good work. (2 Tim. 3:15-17, RSV)

Rather than primarily examining the heart, we are to look at *what comes out of* the heart—the *fruit* of the heart/soul/spirit—in ourselves and in others. This task should not be taken lightly, for this fruit shows whether or not the Holy Spirit is truly at work in the heart of a professing believer:

> Let us examine our ways and test them, and let us return to the LORD. (Lam. 3:40)

A man ought to examine himself before he eats of the bread and drinks of the cup. . . . If we judged ourselves, we would not come under judgment. (1 Cor. 11:28, 31)

Examine yourselves to see whether you are in the faith; test yourselves. (2 Cor. 13:5)

But the fruit of the Spirit is love, joy, peace, patience, kindness, goodness, faithfulness, gentleness and self-control. (Gal. 5:22-23)

"By their fruit, you will recognize them." (Matt. 7:20)

Dear children, do not let anyone lead you astray. He who does what is right is righteous, just as he is righteous. He who does what is sinful is of the devil, because the devil has been sinning from the beginning. . . . This is how we know who the children of God are and who the children of the devil are: Anyone who does not do what is right is not a child of God. (1 John 3:7-8, 10)

We can and should examine the fruits, the outward deeds of ourselves and others. But we must leave to God the task of examining the contents of the heart, for He alone knows what is within the unconscious:

The crucible for silver and the furnace for gold, but the LORD tests the heart. (Prov. 17:3)

We are not trying to please men but God, who tests our hearts. (1 Thess. 2:4)

Test me, O LORD, and try me, examine my heart and my mind. (Ps. 26:2)

O LORD Almighty, you who examine the righteous and probe the heart and mind . . . (Jer. 20:12)

He who trusts in himself is a fool, but he who walks in wisdom is kept safe. (Prov. 28:26)

The typical psychotherapist views present deeds as simply a result of past experiences; therefore he will focus intensely on the client's ability to remember his or her past. Freud's formula, "remember, repeat, and work through," could be the slogan for a psychotherapist's ad, for it concisely summarizes the process of insight-oriented psychotherapy.

The idea of remembering and recalling is hardly foreign to Scripture. Those terms appear frequently throughout the Bible. But a simple word study will show that what is to be remembered are the commandments, the warnings, the blessings, the mercies, the actions, the covenants, the love, and the wonders of God throughout the history of Israel and in the life of the individual believer. Our memory of the past as well as our hope for the future is to be focused on our Creator-Redeemer—who He is and what He has done. Psychotherapy would have us remember all our good and evil past actions and all the good and evil influences in our lives. Scripture, quite to the contrary, teaches that God has removed our past sins "as far as the east is from the west." We are to remember what God has done in the past, rather than what we have done:

> For He established a testimony in Jacob, and appointed a law in Israel, which He commanded our fathers, that they should make them known to their children; that the generation to come might know them, the children who would be born, that they may arise and declare them to their children, that they may set their hope in God, and not forget the works of God, but keep His commandments. (Ps. 78:5-7, NKJV)

> Remember the wonders he has done, his miracles, and the judgments he pronounced. (Ps. 105:5)

> Surely God is good to Israel, to those who are pure in heart. But as for me, my feet had almost slipped; I had nearly lost

my foothold. . . . If I had said, "I will speak thus," I would have betrayed your children. When I tried to understand all this, it was oppressive to me till I entered the sanctuary of God. (Ps. 73:1-2, 15-17)

Our faith in God's goodness may waver at times, but it is sin to "speak thus" (v. 15), that is, to complain against God and others . . . as a therapist urges us to remember an environmental cause for our current discomfort. Psychotherapy "remembers" in order to find a perpetrator; therapeutic remembering makes our sins appear "understandable" (v. 16) due to a bad environment. Freud's manner of remembering tends to induce desire for revenge; the fruit of therapeutic remembering is bitter.

God doesn't remember our sins, and neither should we:

"I will forgive their wickedness and will remember their sins no more." (Heb. 8:12)

"I, even I, am he who blots out your transgressions, for my own sake, and remembers your sins no more." (Isa. 43:25)

If we remember our sins at all, it should lead only to rejoicing for our salvation from those sins:

Do you not know that the wicked will not inherit the king-dom of God? . . . And that is what some of you were [remember?]. (1 Cor. 6:9, 11)

Remember those earlier days after you had received the light, when you stood your ground. . . . So do not throw away your confidence; it will be richly rewarded. (Heb. 10:32, 35)

Therefore, prepare your minds for action. . . . As obedient children, do not conform to the evil desires you had when you lived in ignorance [remember?]. (1 Pet. 1:13-14)

... and may not be like their fathers, a stubborn and rebellious generation, a generation that did not set its heart aright and whose spirit was not faithful to God. (Ps. 78:8, NKJV)

But one thing I do: Forgetting what is behind and straining toward what is ahead, I press on toward the goal to win the prize for which God has called me heavenward in Christ Jesus. (Phil. 3:13)

"A woman giving birth to a child has pain because her time has come; but when her baby is born she forgets the anguish because of her joy that a child is born into the world." (John 16:21)

Our focus should be on the good things of our present life with Christ, not on the sins of our past:

Whatever is true, whatever is noble, whatever is right, whatever is pure, whatever is lovely, whatever is admirable—if anything is praiseworthy or excellent—think about such things. (Phil. 4:8)

God gives each person a conscience. Therapists view the conscience as producing guilt and shame, both of which (they say) we should avoid. Scripture speaks of our conscience as a reflection of God's image in us. Therefore, the conscience is to be used for God's glory and our good. It is an immaterial, supernatural register of our conformity to God's higher standards. Our conscience is also a register of our conformity to the standards of our parents and society. It registers its data through our body in terms of feelings that we describe as contentment, guilt, or shame. As we conduct our lives, our conscience assesses dissonance between what we are thinking, feeling, and doing, and what we *ought* to be thinking, feeling, and doing. God, through what theologians call His "common grace," weaves His "oughts" into each human heart. Even nonbelievers receive this common grace, and thus God's oughts, His moral standards, are woven into the very structures of society as all humans have a conscience to guide them toward "decent" behavior and away from being as evil as they might otherwise be:

> When Gentiles, who do not have the law, do by nature things required by the law, they are a law for themselves, even though they do not have the law, since they show that the requirements of the law are written on their hearts, their consciences also bearing witness, and their thoughts now accusing, now even defending them. (Rom. 2:14-15)

This common grace is, however, not saving grace. Even though it does contribute to a more decent society, it does not bring individuals to salvation. Unregenerate people become hardened against their own conscience and reject God's free gift of salvation:

> Furthermore, since they did not think it worthwhile to retain the knowledge of God, he gave them over to a depraved mind, to do what ought not to be done. . . . Although they know God's righteous decree that those who do such things deserve death, they not only continue to do these very things but also approve of those who practice them. (Rom. 1:28, 32)

Salvation comes only when the individual becomes convinced, through the convicting truth of the Law and through the Holy Spirit's work on the conscience, that he is hopelessly lost in sin and in need of salvation from outside of himself.

The God-given conscience promotes decent behavior. In a Christian, the desire to keep a clear conscience in obedience to God is a strong motivation toward righteous behavior. This conscience acts in conjunction with the indwelling Holy Spirit to bring a convicting knowledge of God's Word:

> It is necessary to submit to the authorities, not only because of punishment but also because of conscience. (Rom. 13:5)

The goal of this command is love, which comes from a pure heart and a good conscience and a sincere faith. (1 Tim. 1:5)

I thank God, whom I serve, as my forefathers did, with a clear conscience, as night and day I constantly remember you in my prayers. (2 Tim. 1:3)

But do this with gentleness and respect, keeping a clear conscience. (1 Pet. 3:15-16)

Therapists view the conscience as the result of past experiences, and no reasonable person would dispute that we are *shaped* by our past experiences. We have all been influenced, trained, acclimatized, acculturated, and stamped by families, neighborhoods, schooling, and the larger culture. Our individual differences are to some degree explained by this shaping. However, Scripture regards such shaping influences as utterly unimportant as it warns us of our duties before our Creator and Judge.

Shaping is far different from *determining*. The fundamental idea of insight-oriented psychotherapy is that we are *determined* by our environment and that we are the created products of the influences that played upon us during key moments and periods of our life. Thus counseling psychology sees those external determinants as being responsible for what we are. Scripture, quite to the contrary, describes us as having been the *willing slaves* of sin before our redemption. We have chosen sin over and over because we are born sinners and have given ourselves over to that slavery. We are thus dead in trespasses and sins. Our freedom cannot come from remembering and repeating a supposedly self-affirming personal narrative; supernatural intervention is required. The release comes from outside of us and has been accomplished once for all in history when "the LORD [made] his life a guilt offering" (Isa. 53:10).

TRUTH NUMBER FOUR: OUR COUNSELORS

The operation of the multi-billion-dollar psychotherapy industry depends on the existence of a multitude of therapists. When the average person asks, "Who can help me solve my problems?" the automatic answer is, "You need to find a good therapist." From all walks of life, students enroll in a vast and highly variable sea of training curricula designed to supply the ever-enlarging demand for therapists and counselors. Most of these students do not realize that there is no standardized, agreed-upon, or proven curriculum for their chosen profession. By the time they do realize it, it often is of little concern to them or their customers. The lack of scientific support for insight-oriented psychotherapy has little impact on the throngs of individuals who pursue the revered mantle of "therapist." Nor does it seem to dissuade the troubled millions who seek their help.

While the therapist is the central figure in psychotherapy, the Bible's teaching on the "care of souls" describes no such central figure. It speaks only of exhorting and encouraging one another, of discipling the new believer, and of discipline within the church. In so speaking, Scripture presents a complete, authoritative, and sufficient theology of soul care. It is a theology both distinctive from and clearly opposed to that which has evolved in the practice of psychotherapy.

Scripture speaks of what we might call counseling, but it speaks against those who pretend to read minds and communicate with spirits, even for the supposedly noble purpose of helping another in distress. It urges those of us who follow Christ to know and use God's Word, to care for fellow believers, and to confront sin in those for whom we show that care. The church is to rebuke, train, encourage, and generally disciple those who are troubled or are going astray. To do this is one of the ways we "love one another" (1 John 4:7). To fail to do this, or to substitute human wisdom for God's revealed wisdom, is to fail to love.

This stands in contrast to most "Christian therapists," who have taken on not only the fundamental doctrines of the secular insight-oriented psychotherapy industry but also its practices and trappings. Among these counselors who characterize themselves as "Christian," all too often we find:

- the claim to possess the secret knowledge of an elite corps, along with the use of a vocabulary so elusive and complex that an aura of sheer magic surrounds it
- credentials framed on the wall
- fifty-minute therapy sessions, after which they charge fees for what should be considered discipling

These counselors move within the church more as people possessing secret knowledge than as loving church leaders fighting the good fight.

Quite apart from these professional counselors, Christians have the following four sources available for counsel: the Holy Spirit, the Word of God, other Christians, and the organized church.

I. The Holy Spirit

God exists eternally in three persons. Each of these three persons possesses all the attributes of the triune God. While Scripture does not explain how or why this is true, it does portray the three persons as being associated with certain activities. The Holy Spirit has attributes that are personal. He has intelligence and possesses a mind; He has a will and feelings (Rom. 8:27; 1 Cor. 2:10; Eph. 4:30). As God, the Holy Spirit is to be obeyed, although we humans often lie to, resist, insult, and even blaspheme Him (Acts 5:3; 7:51). The Holy Spirit convicts the world of sin, guides believers toward truth, and does not abandon the believer in whom He has come to dwell:

> "I will ask the Father , and he will give you another Counselor to be with you forever—the Spirit of truth. . . . He lives with you and will be in you. I will not leave you as orphans." (John 14:16-18)

> "Unless I go away, the Counselor will not come to you; but if I go, I will send him to you. When he comes, he will convict the world of guilt in regard to sin and righteousness and judg-

ment. . . . But when he, the Spirit of truth, comes, he will guide you into all truth." (John 16:8-9, 13)

For as many as are led by the Spirit of God, these are sons of God. For you did not receive a spirit of bondage again to fear, but you received the Spirit of adoption by whom we cry out, "Abba, Father." The Spirit Himself bears witness with our spirit that we are children of God. (Rom. 8:14-16, NKJV)

The indwelling Holy Spirit acts as a counselor as He convicts of sin and guides toward truth. This conviction operates through the believer's conscience. The conscience makes itself known to us by generating feelings in response to thoughts and behaviors. When we do wrong, our conscience, unless it is hardened, will bring a sense of guilt and shame, a feeling of dissatisfaction. If it is controlled by the Holy Spirit, our conscience will generally stimulate us toward change. The Holy Spirit guides us toward truth and opens our understanding in the study of Scripture, pointing always to Christ and His Word. He shows us what would be pleasing to God as we think and act upon the events and circumstances of our daily life.

II. The Word of God

The second source of counsel for the Christian is God's written revelation, the Bible. The Bible contains God's words of personal address; it is His Word spoken through humans and written down by humans.[5] The Bible has established itself as being clear, authoritative, necessary, and sufficient for the Christian life.[6] The Bible is the most readily available, most effective, and most authoritative source of written counsel. It is truly the Creator's handbook and thus is the most enduring book of moral principles ever written. However, the person without the Holy Spirit is not able to discern God's Word or use it as counsel. "Unless the Spirit of Wisdom is present, there is little or no profit in having God's Word in our hands."[7] The unbeliever is unable to accept God's truth for his life. He is unable to comprehend what he reads in the Bible:

The man without the Spirit does not accept the things that come from the Spirit of God, for they are foolishness to him, and he cannot understand them, because they are spiritually discerned. (1 Cor. 2:14)

Those who are indwelt by the Holy Spirit, on the other hand, recognize that God is speaking to them through His written Word.[8] When the believer reads the Bible, asks for the aid of the Holy Spirit in understanding, and is willing to obey what the Bible says, he will always grow in righteousness:

"My sheep listen to my voice; I know them, and they follow me." (John 10:27)

Like newborn babies, crave pure spiritual milk, so that by it you may grow up in your salvation. (1 Pet. 2:2)

III. Other Christians

The third source of counsel for the Christian is other believers. Scripture calls all believers to exhort and encourage one another. The mature and experienced are to impart godly wisdom to those less mature and experienced. And if the "mature and experienced" are "humble and contrite in spirit" and are the kind of people in whom God delights (Isa. 66:2), they will in turn receive counsel from even the newer believers. They will recognize the Spirit's Word to them even if it comes from those less mature in the faith. We are instructed to "bear one another's burdens" (Gal. 6:2, NKJV). Relying on God's Word and seeking the counsel of the Holy Spirit, all believers are, as previously stated, not only "competent to counsel" but clearly expected to do so:

I am convinced, my brothers, that you yourselves are full of goodness, complete in knowledge and competent to instruct one another. (Rom. 15:14)

> Let the Word of God dwell in you richly as you teach and admonish one another with all wisdom, and as you sing psalms, hymns and spiritual songs with gratitude in your hearts toward God. (Col. 3:16)

> We proclaim him, admonishing and teaching everyone with all wisdom, so that we may present everyone perfect in Christ. (Col. 1:28)

> Likewise, teach the older women to be reverent in the way they live, not to be slanderers or addicted to much wine, but to teach what is good. Then they can train the younger women. (Titus 2:3-4)

Believers are to come alongside other Christians in difficult times; they should not always wait to be invited, and they certainly are not to request compensation for doing so. Believers are to "invade" each other's lives as an act of true Christian love. The right to privacy has been used as an excuse not only to abort our offspring but also to avoid godly counsel and discipline. In Scripture, the concept of "counseling" includes what we would think of as counseling today, but it also includes teaching, training, discipling, exhorting, encouraging, and rebuking. We are not to do these things in sessions for which we charge a fee; rather, these things should be a part of the normal interaction between believers:

> We dealt with each of you as a father deals with his own children, encouraging, comforting and urging you to live lives worthy of God. (1 Thess. 2:11)

> Warn those who are idle, encourage the timid, help the weak, be patient with everyone. (1 Thess. 5:14)

> I long to see you so that I may impart to you some spiritual gift to make you strong—that is, that you and I may be mutually encouraged by each other's faith. (Rom. 1:11-12)

All scripture is inspired by God and profitable for teaching, for reproof, for correction, and for training in righteousness, that the man of God may be complete, equipped for every good work. (2 Tim. 3:16-17, RSV)

But if we walk in the light, as he is in the light, we have fellowship with one another, and the blood of Jesus, his son, purifies us from all sin. (1 John 1:7)

IV. The Organized Church

The fourth source of counsel for believers is the church itself. The organized church should provide for believers several avenues that help them along their Christian walk, over hills and valleys, through times of trial and persecution, through doubt and despair. The organized church is to be a help to the individual believer in persevering in a life that will more and more "prove what is that good and acceptable and perfect will of God" (Rom. 12:2, NKJV). These avenues include the preaching of the Word, baptism, the Lord's Supper, and church discipline.

The church exercises church discipline to remove from its midst the "leaven"—the contamination or defilement of sin that openly detracts from the glory of Christ's name. Discipline is also for the purpose of protecting believers and challenging them to godliness. It is a means of producing soundness of faith and restoring disobedient believers. Scripture instructs the church to discipline those who are sinning (Matt. 18:15-20; Gal. 6:1), the lazy (2 Thess. 3:6), false teachers (Titus 1:10-16), those who are divisive (Titus 3:8-11), and those who are immoral (1 Cor 5:11); sometimes, even church leaders need such discipline (1 Tim. 5:19-20). As an instrument of God on earth, the church is instructed to discipline with certain attitudes and principles:

Rebuke them sharply, so that they will be sound in the faith. (Titus 1:13)

Brothers, if someone is caught in a sin, you who are spiritual should restore him gently. (Gal. 6:1)

Those who sin are to be rebuked publicly, so that the others may take warning. (1 Tim. 5:20)

Don't you know that a little yeast works through the whole batch of dough? Get rid of the old yeast that you may be a new batch without yeast—as you really are. (1 Cor. 5:6-7)

Now instead, you ought to forgive and comfort him, so that he will not be overwhelmed by excessive sorrow. (2 Cor. 2:7)

We should praise God that the church has one solid truth, one authoritative method, one sufficient promise for "the care of souls." The world of psychotherapy is a place where, as we have noted, "there are as many psychotherapies as there are psychotherapists," where there is no authoritative manual or guidebook, where each therapist brings to the client his own home-grown wisdom and advice. We should genuinely pity those trying to build their lives on such a foundation of sand.

TRUTH NUMBER FIVE: SANCTIFICATION

Psychotherapists attract their customers with the promise of insight into the why of their unsatisfactory and degenerated lives. They lead their clients to believe that, with the help of the therapist, they will be able to "work through" maladaptive or unhealthy responses and will thereby achieve happiness. The costly process requires the guidance of a therapist, but the promise is that by using the power of self, a life of increased personal pleasure will be achieved. For the troubled client who asks, "How can I make myself a happier person?" psychotherapists provide the answer of self-sufficiency. This promise is couched in various terms: self-actualization, self-empowerment, self-awareness, self-esteem, self-identity, discovery of the "control issue"—to name only a few. But no matter what the terminology, the promise remains at its most fundamental level that of self-mastery over one's own problems; success is attributed to self.

The Bible is completely different in method, different in purpose, and different in source. The scriptural process of change is termed sanctification. For the regenerated person, it is assumed to be an inevitable process.

Sanctification has been defined as "a progressive work of God in man that makes us more and more free from sin and like Christ in our actual lives."[9] Ryle describes it as "the invariable result of that vital union with Christ which true faith gives to a Christian."[10] Sanctification is a progressive work that follows upon the conversion of a repentant sinner, as that person becomes a trusting child of God. It is "the outcome and inseparable consequence of regeneration . . . the only certain evidence of that indwelling of the Holy Spirit which is essential to salvation . . . the only sure mark of God's election."[11]

While justification is an instantaneous act on the part of God, sanctification is the progressive work of God with the new believer. It involves continual growth and change, which comes by grace through faith as a believer trusts and obeys:

> Therefore, since we have been justified through faith, we have peace with God through our Lord Jesus Christ. . . . And we rejoice in the hope of the glory of God. Not only so, but we also rejoice in our sufferings, because we know that suffering produces perseverance; perseverance, character; and character, hope. And hope does not disappoint us, because God has poured out his love into our hearts by the Holy Spirit, whom he has given us. (Rom. 5:1-5)

> You, however, are controlled not by the sinful nature but by the Spirit, if the Spirit of God lives in you. . . . For those God foreknew he also predestined to be conformed to the likeness of his Son. (Rom. 8:9, 29)

> And we, who with unveiled faces all reflect the Lord's glory, are being transformed into his likeness with ever-

increasing glory, which comes from the Lord, who is the Spirit. (2 Cor. 3:18)

And he died for all, that those who live should no longer live for themselves but for him who died for them and was raised again. (2 Cor. 5:15)

He has given us his very great and precious promises, so that through them you may participate in the divine nature and escape the corruption in the world caused by evil desires. (2 Pet. 1:4)

From the moment of salvation, as a new believer, you will be "dead to sin and alive to God in Christ Jesus. . . . Sin will have no dominion over you" (Rom. 6:11, 14, RSV). This means that the new believer, for the first time in his or her life, has received from God the power to put off sinful thoughts, feelings, and behaviors, and to put on righteousness. All true believers are being "changed into His likeness from one degree of glory to another" (2 Cor. 3:18, RSV).

We must remember, however, that sanctification is a process, continuing until our ultimate glorification, when the "perishable" puts on the "imperishable" (1 Cor. 15:53). We will never achieve total sanctification in this life: "Sinners we were when we began, sinners we shall find ourselves as we go on; renewed, pardoned, justified, yet sinners to the very last."[12] Yet, even though we will not achieve perfection in this life, we should eagerly pursue it as God's will for us:

In the same way, count yourselves dead to sin but alive to God in Christ Jesus. Therefore do not let sin reign in your mortal body so that you obey its evil desires. . . . For sin shall not be your master, because you are not under law, but under grace. (Rom. 6:11-12, 14)

Not that I have already obtained all this, or have already been made perfect, but I press on to take hold of that for which

Christ Jesus took hold of me. Brothers, I do not consider myself yet to have taken hold of it. But one thing I do: forgetting what is behind and straining toward what is ahead, I press on toward the goal to win the prize for which God has called me heavenward in Christ Jesus. (Phil. 3:12-14)

The Christian is not alone or on his own in the process of progressive sanctification. His progress or "success" does not depend on self-empowerment, self-actualization, or self-cure. God is at work in the process:

It is God who works in you to will and to act according to his good purpose. (Phil. 2:13)

God causes the believer to desire His will, just as He gives him the power to obey it:

May the God of peace . . . equip you with everything good for doing his will, and may he work in us what is pleasing to him. (Heb. 13:20-21)

This is love for God: to obey His commands. And His commands are not burdensome, for everyone born of God has overcome the world. This is the victory that has overcome the world, even our faith. Who is it that overcomes the world? Only he who believes that Jesus is the Son of God. (1 John 5:3-5)

Christ is our provider and our example. His death provides our sanctification and His life is our guide:

. . . Christ Jesus, who has become for us wisdom from God— that is our righteousness, holiness and redemption. (1 Cor. 1:30)

. . . Jesus, the author and perfecter of our faith . . . (Heb. 12:2)

. . . because Christ suffered for you, leaving you an example, that you should follow in his steps. (1 Pet. 2:21)

Whoever claims to live in him must walk as Jesus did. (1 John 2:6)

. . . being confident of this, that he who began a good work in you will carry it on to completion until the day of Christ Jesus. (Phil. 1:6)

This work is carried out by the Holy Spirit who indwells the heart/soul/spirit of the believer. He leads us to truth as a counselor and produces in us the "fruit of the Spirit" (Gal. 5:22) as He changes the very conduct of our lives. The converted person desires to yield himself to God, to strive for holiness, to abstain from immorality, and to obey God's commands. He desires to purify himself and grow in righteousness:

Those who belong to Christ Jesus have crucified the sinful nature with its passions and desires. Since we live by the Spirit, let us keep in step with the Spirit. (Gal. 5:24-25)

Those who are led by the Spirit of God are sons of God. (Rom. 8:14)

Offer yourselves to God, as those who have been brought from death to life; and offer the parts of your body to him as instruments of righteousness. (Rom. 6:13)

Everyone who has this hope in him purifies himself, just as he is pure. (1 John 3:3; see also 2 Pet. 1:5-7)

In sanctification, God provides us His power "both to will and to do for His good pleasure" (Phil. 2:13, NKJV). God is there to equip us with everything we need in order to do His will and be pleasing in His sight.

As the believer is sanctified, his thinking is renewed after the image of his Creator. He gains discernment, and knows more and more of God. He has more and more ability to control his thoughts, emotions, and "sinful desires":

Since, then, you have been raised with Christ, set your hearts on things above, . . . not on earthly things. . . . since you have taken off your old self with its practices and have put on a new self, which is being renewed in knowledge in the image of its Creator. (Col. 3:1-2, 9-10)

And this is my prayer: that your love may abound more and more in knowledge and depth of insight. (Phil. 1:9; see also Col. 1:9-10)

We take captive every thought to make it obedient to Christ. (2 Cor. 10:5)

The Christian, as he experiences this process of sanctification, will "see more and know more and feel more and do more and repent more and believe more as [he gets] on in spiritual life and in proportion to the closeness of [his] walk with God."[13]

Gratitude for redemption and the resultant love for God is the principal motivation for a believer's striving for holiness. If the satisfaction of his own "felt needs" remains the primary goal, he needs to follow Paul's instruction to test himself to see if he is in the faith. If felt needs are the only focus, the person has probably never faced his real need—his need for salvation—and thus sanctification will not occur.

Believers are motivated to strive and press on toward sanctification by remembering their rescue from God's wrath. True believers have gone to God "as sinners with no plea but that of utter need and cast our souls on Him by faith for peace and reconciliation with God."[14] As such, "we must press on and be ever making fresh applications to Christ, . . . to live the life of daily faith in the son of God, and to be daily drawing out of His fulness the promised grace and strength which he has laid up for His people—this is the grand secret of progressive sanctification."[15]

Without holiness no one will see the Lord. (Heb. 12:14)

"If you love me, you will obey what I command." (John 14:15)

I desire to do your will, O my God; your law is within my heart. (Ps. 40:8)

There are several means by which we may receive the grace we need for sanctification. Prayer, study of and meditation on the Word, and objective self-examination, using the truth of Scripture as our benchmark, are forms of what Ryle calls "diligence in the use of private means of grace."[16] Participation in worship, with its corporate prayer, praise, preaching of the Word, and sacraments, constitutes "careful use of the public means of grace."[17] These activities should produce in us a watchfulness over our conduct in everyday life. We will thus better control our tempers, our tongues, and our use of time.

Sanctification is not just a private undertaking but also a corporate process. No believer is autonomous in the process. We are part of a body of believers striving together, encouraging, rebuking, and coming alongside each other, teaching and building each other up, and together striving to glorify God. We glorify our Creator and Redeemer in a church body as well as in our individual lives:

> Let us consider how we may spur one another on toward love and good deeds. Let us not give up meeting together, . . . let us encourage one another—and all the more as you see the Day approaching. (Heb. 10:24-25; see also 1 Thess. 5:11)

> The body is a unit, though it is made up of many parts . . . baptized by one Spirit . . . there should be no division . . . its parts should have equal concern for each other. If one part suffers, every part suffers with it; if one part is honored, every part rejoices with it. (1 Cor. 12:12-13, 25-26)

> If we walk in the light, as he is in the light, we have fellowship with one another, and the blood of Jesus, his Son, purifies us from all sin. (1 John 1:7)

The believer's sanctification is God's business; the Holy Spirit uses the Word, the church, and other believers in the process and has provided for all the needs of His redeemed. How we should pity those who don't know this all-sufficient Lord, and therefore turn instead to psychotherapy with its secular "cures" and its counselors claiming special insight.

TRUTH NUMBER SIX: SACRIFICE

We are living in what has been aptly described as a "sensate culture,"[18] where people live for pleasure and make decisions based on personal feelings. What is pleasing to the senses they choose to pursue. What is unpleasant to the senses, they choose to avoid. Surely one of the reasons for the tremendous growth of psychotherapy is the sensual appeal of its answer to the question, "What is the purpose of my life?" Insight-oriented psychotherapy answers, "Continuous and pervasive personal pleasure is available for you through our methodology; this is as far as we expect you to go in defining the true meaning and purpose of life." This promised result seduces many into therapy.

Troubled people seek out insight-oriented psychotherapy because they are experiencing a lack of pleasure, because they are dissatisfied. Feelings of guilt, shame, fear, depression, and anxiety are the "presenting complaints" of most psychotherapy customers. Our post-Christian, sensate culture defines such feelings as unacceptable, having no value, something to be eliminated at all cost.

The Puritan writer Jonathan Mitchell declared, "A Christian may and ought to desire many things as means, but God alone as his end."[19] The Westminster Shorter Catechism declares that "The chief end of man is to glorify God and enjoy him forever."[20] For the Christian, our relationship with the eternal Creator God is to be a primary source of pleasure. As for this present life, while our sensate culture tells us to pursue pleasure, Scripture tells us that suffering has meaning and purpose in the believer's life. Suffering and trials are the expected lot of mankind—especially of Christians—for we live on a fallen planet. Unredeemed people respond to life's normal and expected troubles with recoil, avoidance, and resentment. And since they lack any perspective apart from the desire for peace and prosperity, we can hardly expect them to react in any other way. The fundamental pillars of insight-oriented psychotherapy are not only the products of this view of life, they also function to perpetuate it. The only escape from this vicious cycle of pleasure-seeking is the radically different worldview and the radically different purpose in life that we find in Christ the Messiah:

> Dear friends, do not be surprised at the painful trial you are suffering, as though something strange were happening to you. But rejoice that you participate in the sufferings of Christ, so that you may be overjoyed when his glory is revealed. If you are insulted because of the name of Christ, you are blessed, for the Spirit of glory and of God rests on you. . . . If you suffer as a Christian, do not be ashamed, but praise God that you bear that name. (1 Pet. 4:12-14, 16; see also 3:14)

As we learn the positive value of suffering, Christ is our great example:

> Although he was a son, he learned obedience from what he suffered. (Heb. 5:8)

As we live out the life of obedience through faith and the grace of God, we will encounter insults and persecution and will experience suffering often greater than that of our nonbelieving neighbors. We should expect such suffering and, rather than fleeing from it, we should welcome it:

> Consider it pure joy, my brothers, whenever you face trials of many kinds, because you know that the testing of your faith develops perseverance. Perseverance must finish its work so that you may be mature and complete, not lacking anything. (James 1:2-4; see also 1:12)

> Endure hardship with us like a good soldier of Christ Jesus. . . . If we died with him, we will also live with him; if we endure, we will also reign with him. (2 Tim. 2:3, 11-12)

But he said to me, "My grace is sufficient for you, for my power is made perfect in weakness." Therefore I will boast all the more gladly about my weaknesses, so that Christ's power may rest on me. That is why, for Christ's sake, I delight in weaknesses, in insults, in hardships, in persecutions, in difficulties. For when I am weak then I am strong. (2 Cor. 12:9-10)

The fundamental goal of psychotherapy is to achieve a life of pleasure and to avoid suffering at all costs. The contrasting fundamental goal of the Christian life is to glorify God through all aspects of our lives, trusting that our suffering will be used in just the way Scripture promises. These two goals are diametrically opposed. A goal of personal peace and prosperity can never produce a life that glorifies God. One goal eliminates the other; these purposes cannot be integrated. For the believer, trials on the road of life are the milestones in sanctification. Our perseverance in the face of these trials, our relying on the strength that God provides, is the means by which we grow and begin to experience the reality of His promises.

Are we to pursue self-esteem or Christ-esteem? Are we to strive for assertiveness or for humility? Are we to clothe ourselves with pride or with gratitude? Are we to strive for autonomy or for serving one another in love? Are we to search our past or are we to "press on toward the goal"? (Phil. 3:14). The answer is not, "some of each; a bit of both." The answer must be one or the other. One is right, the other is wrong. Only by perverting the meaning of Scripture, ignoring its context, overlaying it with non-Christian theories, or ignoring it altogether can the apologists of psychotherapy claim that we are to love and serve self.

Christians must look to Scripture for the right answer. There, the purpose and meaning of life is not defined by the pursuit of personal pleasure. Paul's great desire was, "that I may know Him and the power of His resurrection, and the fellowship of His sufferings" (Phil. 3:10, NKJV). May our desire be the same!

CONCLUSION

There are six fundamentals of authentic biblical counseling that contrast with Freud's six pillars of psychotherapy:

1. the doctrine of original sin
2. a biblical understanding of the human heart/soul/spirit
3. the necessity of a conviction of sin
4. the sources of counsel provided by God for believers
5. the process of sanctification following true salvation
6. the sacrificial life of a Christian in gratitude to his Redeemer

These six biblical fundamentals stand in sharp contrast to the six worldly fundamentals common to all insight-oriented psychotherapy. The contrast is so sharp, so clear, and so distinct that a Christian can only conclude that psychotherapy offers its customers a false gospel. Moreover, the acceptance of that false gospel will harden the clients of psychotherapy against the true Gospel. What person, eagerly pursuing self-sufficiency and assured by his therapist that he is making progress toward it, will recognize his hopeless state and cry out for a Savior? In believing the claims of psychotherapy, the customer is buying ideas in direct opposition to Scripture. The addition of evangelical language, the insertion of a few Bible verses taken out of context, the labeling as Christian psychology or as biblical counseling—with "Christian music" playing in the waiting room—will not change that fact.

The contrast between the doctrinal base of psychotherapy and biblical fundamentals is so stark that anyone claiming to "integrate" psychotherapy with Scripture is surely either ignorant of Scripture or knowingly going against it. Those who would integrate the claims of counseling psychology with the truths of Scripture are thus open to the accusation of being false teachers. They are wolves among the flock, leading the sheep away from the saving Gospel to one that can only destroy. Replacing the rich, authoritative, effective, and sufficient Word of God with flashy, facile, and foolish human ideas offers the troubled in spirit nothing of value and, worse yet, leads them toward destruction.

> Take heed to yourselves and all the flock, among which the Holy Spirit has made you overseers, to shepherd the church of God which He purchased with His own blood. For . . . savage wolves will come in among you, not sparing the flock. Also from among yourselves men will rise up, speaking perverse things, to draw away the disciples after themselves. Therefore watch. (Acts 20:28-31, NKJV)

> Guard what has been entrusted to your care. Turn away from godless chatter and the opposing ideas of what is falsely called knowledge, which some have professed and in so doing have wandered from the faith. (1 Tim. 6:20-21)

THREE

IDEAS HAVE CONSEQUENCES

When we bring the "pillars of the psychotherapy industry" into bold relief, we can clearly see that they are in complete disagreement with Holy Scripture. These ideas, first formulated by Freud, remain at the core of insight-oriented psychotherapy today. This belief system permeates our society and is accepted as axiomatic by most people, Christian and non-Christian alike. It is so firmly established that it no longer needs to be presented as scientific to find acceptance. Freud's principles, his pillars, are used throughout our society, not only in counseling but in all walks of life. Any challenge to this doctrine has come largely from libertarians scattered here and there; sadly, the church's challenge to these devilish ideas has been little more than a whimper.

But in the words of University of Chicago philosopher Richard Weaver, "Ideas have consequences."[1] The ideas people choose to believe have definite consequences in their own lives and in the lives of their children. The stark dissonance between the six fundamentals of insight-oriented psychotherapy and the six fundamentals of scriptural counseling is not merely an interesting intellectual or theological issue (though it certainly is that). Choosing to believe and follow the fundamentals of psychotherapy brings destruction to the lives of men, women, and children. Absolute truth exists. If one idea is true, then its opposite cannot be true and must therefore be a lie, and those who choose the wrong answers to the basic questions of life eventually suffer the consequences of believing those lies.

This chapter examines the consequences, in individual lives and in our culture, of choosing the human wisdom and philosophy related to psychotherapy over the truth of Scripture.

VICTIMIZATION

If the doctrine of original sin is wrong and we are all born with a clean slate, then the ultimate cause of mental and emotional distress must be harmful external stimuli, perhaps assisted by flawed genetics. Ultimately, therefore, life's problems are due to what someone or something else has done to us. People with problems are actually victims of outside malevolence beyond their control; the troubled individual is not responsible. Wrong influences of certain types, occurring at certain critical times in our development, have had a decisive and permanent effect on our ability to function in life.

This notion of victimization is so widely accepted today that it is the language of explanation for the most diverse of human malfunctions and misbehavior. The troubled individual is not encouraged to look to Scripture and to his own sinful state as regards his mental and emotional distress; he is instead encouraged to look for perpetrators, oppressors, and abusers in his past. A costly search is made for a dysfunctional family, a hurting inner child, verbal abuse, satanic ritual abuse, lack of affirmation, lack of self-esteem. These terms and concepts are the language of our day.

The "Unabomber," according to this line of thinking, murdered because he was not held by his mother during a hospitalization in his first year of life.[2] The Menendez brothers murdered because they were supposedly abused by their parents from the earliest days of their lives. Adopted children are rebels because of empty love tanks produced by a lack of "bonding." Men commit adultery because of dysfunctional parenting, resulting in a midlife crisis. "A two-year-old boy who loses his father or a five-year-old boy who is molested will carry his unmet need for masculine love and affirmation into his adult years. The adult homosexual has choices to remain celibate, to engage in sexual activity, or to seek therapy to resolve the unfinished business of childhood."[3] An imperfect father-figure may drive a woman to have an abortion or to reject faith in God: "Does the word 'father' bring feelings of hurt and bitterness? Accepting God Almighty as your heavenly Father may be difficult if you have broken relationships with your authority figures here on earth."[4]

Even within Christian counseling, as we shall see in chapter 10, visualized forgiveness rituals are often a part of therapy. Books and seminars on forgiveness flood the Christian marketplace. Most of these books and seminars, however, promote a muddled, emotional, and utterly self-centered view of forgiveness, leading people even farther from Scripture. After all, some would say, I can hardly become a Christian until someone helps me work through my damaged "father-image." Many seminaries are frantically trying to produce enough professionals with counseling degrees to offer this "hope," but strangely enough, as more "doctors" appear in the church to help people in this way, there seem to be ever greater numbers who need such help! Yet the church fails to look at the statistics and ask why this is so. They move on with the blindness of the world, and conclude that they were simply missing the hordes of people in the past with a skewed father-image, and that the answer can only be to produce more counselors to meet this long-neglected need. Salvation and sanctification are no longer sufficient; everyone must either see a therapist or become one! Surely that viewpoint springs from the psychotherapeutic pillar of original innocence. Misbehavior is always someone else's fault.

This concept of environmental determinism works its influence not only upon psychology and social engineering, but upon economics and politics in general. It is the fundamental belief of the liberal politician. Ellen Willis, writing in *The New Yorker,* laments our government's retreat from massive federal welfare programs and acknowledges her conviction that we humans are indeed perfectible, with the key to human happiness being proper manipulation of the environment:

The purpose of politics in a democratic society should not be moral improvement, which is properly the business of individuals, but a cooperative effort to promote the general welfare—that is, to create social conditions conducive to the pursuit of happiness. Give people the power to shape their lives to their liking, and their souls will take care of themselves.[5]

With the increasing rejection of Scripture as anything other than a personal devotional tool, the church has accepted this same conviction. This view not only feeds the vast Christian counseling industry, it also undergirds most of Christian missionary and social action in underdeveloped countries and in American inner cities. Once we have accepted Freud's view of humanity, no amount of talk of biblical principles or of making the counseling church-sponsored will change the destructive results of such counseling. Whether our politics be right-wing or left-wing, the result will be the same, because the view of man and his problem is essentially the same. We have adopted the view that man's environment is the problem, and that the proper manipulation of that environment will bring in God's kingdom.

BONDAGE TO OUR "UNCONSCIOUS"

If, as Freud says, our "unconscious" is in tyrannical control of our thoughts and behaviors; if it is a genuine repository of all our past experiences and influences; if it expresses itself sometimes clearly but more often cryptically; then we are in hopeless bondage to a malevolent inner force created by outsiders and over which we have no control. And if we find ourselves in this situation with no belief in God, then our only recourse (other than suicide) is to seek self-actualization through our own efforts, with the guidance of those who claim to understand the unconscious. No wonder the psychotherapy trade is replete with techniques for escaping this bondage. Psychotherapists tell us we can plumb the depths of our unconscious mind and there find the insights needed to climb the ladder to a better life. Bookstore shelves everywhere are filled with volumes telling us how to curb the maladaptive effects of our powerful unconscious.

But God Himself, in His wisdom, prevents a satisfactory end to this quest for self-understanding. Not only is the supposed insight unavailable, but what insight we think we have found is unreliable. As a result, multitudes aimlessly move from one therapist to the next. Increasingly hopeless, they try to find the *why* of life—with their only discovery being the lie of blaming someone else for the unsatisfactory *what,* the reality of life.

With so many on such a quest, why would not the church take people to Scripture, as it so clearly speaks about the real bondage we suffer, and about the answer to that bondage:

> I myself in my mind am a slave to God's law, but in the sinful nature a slave to the law of sin. Therefore, there is now no condemnation for those who are in Christ Jesus, because through Christ Jesus the law of the Spirit of life set me free. (Rom. 7:25; 8:1-2)

How tragic for those who claim Christ's name to look on a world in bondage to sin and, in the name of Christ, offer them the lie of "insight into the unconscious" . . . while God's Word is there all along, offering a true and lasting "peace with God through our Lord Jesus Christ" (Rom. 5:1).

"RECOVERED" MEMORIES

If our out-of-awareness mind is truly knowable, "replayable" and "re-experience-able"; if insight into its content is essential to our changing its influence upon our life; if the data of this historical search for the influences of our past is reliable and credible; then this quest for insight should be the single most important pursuit in all of life.

Since the quest for insight is directed entirely toward self, it stands to reason that the methodologies of this quest are entirely subjective, introspective, and almost exclusively historical rather than scientific. Given the subjective nature of the data collected, it is not surprising that expediency and plausibility are the sole standards of data validation. "What works for me" becomes the standard for truth. The meaning of one's life is devised from one's own perspective, based upon one's own subjective data. This inward-directed personal perspective replaces any need for reference to God's perspective. When Christian counselors add Scripture, all too often they add it only as an afterthought.

Out of this has emerged the common belief that one's own "personal narrative," whether true or entirely fictitious, is the credible data base for personal growth—even when the narrative includes such things as horrific accusations of incestuous abuse. Such accusations are sometimes derived from therapist-coached efforts at "remembering and repeating" past trauma, with no real concern about whether the trauma actually occurred. The subjective narrative apparently is of more importance than objective, verifiable truth. Rarely will the counselor or counselee try to verify the accounts; truth is considered to have no real place in the process. The importance of the narrative to self is the crucial concern, and any damage such "revelations" cause to others is of a far secondary importance. Each counselee is called to follow his own autonomous course toward personal enlightenment. Except for occasionally adding some "Jesus-words," the process is no different in Christian counseling.

Practitioners of insight-oriented psychotherapy are under increasing pressure to cease their efforts to "recover" such personal histories. This pressure has come from unjustly accused parents, from former patients who come to their senses and "recant" their concocted narratives, from media exposure of the disastrous results, and most effectually from the courts. Sadly, this pressure has not come from the Christian church evaluating these methods from a biblical vantage point.

It is the secular society that has become concerned about recovered memories, and there are two principal reasons for this. The first is that the belief that we are victims of deterministic past experiences and therefore not personally responsible for our misdeeds has become so troublesome and is bringing such chaos as to finally incite some negative public reaction. This is especially noticeable in the legal arena, but it is also becoming more apparent in the news media and commentary. The second reason is that the false memory accusations brought on by these therapists (many of them Christian counselors) have reached prominent civil and church leaders. The proliferation of such memory-induced accusations has promoted new research into human memory. This research has found psychotherapeutic recall to be far from reliable. The outrageous consequences of the theories of insight-oriented psychotherapy are becoming apparent even within the hallowed confines of the psychoanalytic academy. Quoting internationally prominent Harvard professor Alan A. Stone, psychoanalyst and past president of the American Psychiatric Association:

> The important challenges for psychoanalytic therapy, as posed by our critics, are first that these developmental events have no causative relationship to the phenomena of psychopathology. . . . Developmental experience may have little to do with most forms of psychopathology. . . . Child development explains very little about Axis 1 [major] disorders. . . . Psychoanalysts can no longer assert that what they learn about their patient's childhood will help them explain the etiology [the assumed cause] of the patient's psychopathology, or even of the patient's sexual orientation. . . . If there is no important connection between childhood events and adult psychopathology, the Freudian theories lose much of their explanatory power. . . .
>
> The self-descriptions generated by our explanatory theories are both irrelevant and unverifiable. . . . We have no reason to assume that a careful historical reconstruction of those developmental events will have therapeutic effect. . . . Everything we have learned in recent years about memory has emphasized its plasticity, the ease with which it can be distorted, and the difficulties of reaching hypothetical veridical [truthful] memory. . . . Much of what psychoanalysis considered infantile amnesia may be a function of the (normal) reorganizing brain rather than of a repressing mind. . . . If

memory cannot be trusted to construct a self-description, what does one do in therapy?[6]

"What does one do in therapy?" That is the question. Even Freud himself knew that personal narratives were unreliable. Yet that did not change his practice of psychoanalysis. It is lawsuits rather than medical research or the church that are challenging the practice at the moment. But, because of the implicit answer to Stone's question ("What does one do in therapy?"), it is not likely that much will actually change for long in the practice of psychotherapy. The pillars of psychotherapy have weathered many storms and most likely will do so again.

If we continue to search for deterministic past traumas recorded in our out-of-awareness mind, we should not be surprised at the outrageous consequences. We can expect such consequences not only because the theories behind the pursuit are unscientific, but more importantly, because both the theories and the pursuit are in opposition to Scripture. As we have seen, what Scripture tells us about who we are, why we have problems, what we can know about our heart, and what we are to do about our past and our problems is in complete opposition to the theories of insight-oriented psychotherapy. The two cannot be integrated. The one is incompatible with the other.

We will look at the tragic results of Recovered Memory Therapy in much greater detail in chapters 11 and 12.

PROFESSIONALISM

If the counselor does not accept absolute truth, if he sees no eternal standards, if his only perspective is personal and experiential, then all is relative. This places the therapist in a position of exalted importance and power as the counselee views him as the only available escape from directionless self-absorption. The therapist can suggest, guide, demand, and coerce because he is placed in the position of guru or possessor of secret knowledge of the unconscious mind. Not significantly different from the animistic shaman, such an exalted therapist "claims that the spirits of the deep can be understood, conjured up, appeased, and rendered harmless only by certain practitioners of mysteries, members of a restrictive guild with specialized initiation rites."[7] Out of this exaltation come the fads and fancies of modern psychotherapy with its charismatic gurus and multiple grand theories. Out of this also come the innumerable techniques and methods of achieving personal pleasure and happiness. Masquerading as science, sounding plausible, using technical jargon, claiming but never proving good results, and appealing to the ancient human desire for self-perfection, our culture is awash in an ever-changing sea of therapists and therapies, with a willing audience ready to accept them:

> The question is sometimes raised whether psychoanalysis does really make promises, extravagant or other, as inducements to prospective patients. That tempting and explicit promises have in fact been made is hardly in doubt, but the interesting and important thing is that they are not really necessary. It is said that a good con-man says relatively little, that his skill consists of letting the victim's hopes and fears work for him. The promise is issued by the patient himself, to himself.[8]

Without the Holy Spirit as our counselor, and without an authoritative and sufficient Word to provide us absolute truth, we are left to our own devices and to the guidance of others who are no less confused. This curse of professionalism pervades present-day Christian counseling, with its secret knowledge and techniques requiring special training.

Professionalism takes other forms as well, both in secular psychotherapy and in Christian counseling. Following a pattern of fifty-minute sessions, using an office lined with books, sitting behind a desk, having walls covered with framed certificates, and charging fees all evoke the image of the professional counselor. The rich trappings of the professional and his office create an expectancy of success in the mind of the client. The majority of therapists consider these trappings necessary to "successful" psychotherapy.

Perhaps Simon Magus saw himself as a "professional":

> When Simon saw that the Spirit was given at the laying on of the apostles' hands, he offered them money and said, "Give me also this ability so that everyone on whom I lay my hands may receive the Holy Spirit."
>
> Peter answered, "May your money perish with you, because you thought you could buy the gift of God with money! You have no part or share in this ministry, because your heart is not right before God. Repent of this wickedness and pray." (Acts 8:18-22)

But Paul certainly didn't see himself and his fellow apostles in this way:

> "Do not go beyond what is written." Then you will not take pride in one man over against another. . . . Already you have all you want! Already you have become rich! You have become kings—and that without us! . . . For it seems to me that God has put us apostles on display at the end of the procession, like men condemned to die in the arena. We have been made a spectacle. . . . We are fools for Christ, but you are so wise! (1 Cor. 4:6, 8-10)

ISOLATION

Autonomy is the natural and seemingly desired state of our postmodern age. It has been the desired state since the serpent beguiled Eve in the Garden. To "do it my way" is more than a phrase from a Sinatra song; it is the goal of life for most people.

"'In the pride of your heart you say "I am a God." ' . . . But you are a man and not a god, though you think you are as wise as a god'" (Ezek. 28:2). The prophet Ezekiel spoke for all time to the rebellious, defiant human heart. The biblical concept of sanctification stands always against this defiance and is possible only when the Holy Spirit makes a person not only obedient and willing, but eager for change.

The pillar of psychotherapy which I have termed "self-cure" appeals to our natural rebellious nature and our desire for autonomy. Self-assurance, self-empowerment, self-accomplishment (no matter how self-deluded) is the goal. Certainly such a goal is in stark contrast to Jesus' clear commands to lose oneself for God's glory and for the sake of others. Neither are such attempts at self-cure and self-empowerment likely to produce in an unbeliever a personal conviction of sin leading to the Redeemer. It is only at the point of hopelessness in self-effort that the grace of God brings one to salvation. The pillar of self-cure ultimately draws people away from that kind of despair, away from the truth of the Gospel, and away from salvation.

There was a time in America when this issue would not have had to be argued, since Scripture is so overwhelmingly clear on the subject. Today's church needs to be reminded (one might even say, needs to have it written in neon letters at the entrance to every church) of what was once known and thoroughly accepted by scholars and laypeople alike. President John Witherspoon of Princeton inculcated in his students the precept that the most fundamental teaching of Christianity is self-denial. For America's greatest philosopher and theologian, Jonathan Edwards (another early president of Princeton), self-denial consisted "in being emptied of himself; so that he does freely and from his heart, as it were, renounce himself, and annihilate himself." President Thomas Clap of Yale taught his students in his popular ethics class that "for a man to make the sole, supreme, or ultimate end of all being and action to be for himself alone or his own happiness, as the *summum bonum;* and to regard God and all other beings, only so far as they may serve himself or be subservient to his own happiness, or to gratify his principle of self-love, is the most absolute inversion of the order, dignity, and perfection of beings: and one of the worst principles that can be in human nature."9

To find anything remotely resembling such opinions in recent Christian writings is almost impossible; thus, we should not wonder that the Freudian pillar of self-cure has moved into the church with so little protest. This concept of autonomy continues to produce an alienation, sending ever larger numbers to the counselors for ever greater variations on self-cure. It continues to prompt the seminaries to produce ever larger numbers of counselors trained in the pillar of self-cure.

HEDONISM

The principal goal of insight-oriented psychotherapy, based on Freud's pillars, is to achieve a state of personal peace and pleasure. Absence of guilt, shame, fear, or anxiety is the goal. Mankind has always gone to great lengths to achieve this goal, but as we move into the twenty-first century, methods and emphases formerly considered outrageous are now acceptable. Many seek transcendent states of pleasure in drugs, in the occult, or in ecstatic religious experiences. Hedonism reigns in our culture where, in the words of Harold O. J. Brown,

> The so-called free market actually exalts egotism and greed under the guise of self-fulfillment . . . the mass media celebrate and extol the most degraded of celebrities, murderers, pornographers, and criminal gangs . . . the political, educational, sports, and artistic systems elevate people who exhibit little virtue in the traditional sense into prominence . . . celebrities, political leaders, even chiefs of government. Thus the general public is progressively disillusioned and led to the conclusion that high moral conduct and the sacrifice of self for the good of others are qualities that are unknown and unattainable among human beings, or if they exist, are found only among naive people worthy at best of condescending approval.[10]

In this system of thinking, abortion of burdensome babies, euthanasia of bothersome old or ill persons, and suicide when facing any loss of "dignity" all become acceptable, even desirable. Such acts are termed "advancements" and are increasingly championed as methods of assuring peace and pleasure for self and society.

Though rarely stated as such, this overarching hedonistic principle has become a goal of even Christian counseling. Seldom does the church teach glorifying God through suffering. Peace and pleasure, avoidance of offense, self-actualization, avoidance of "burnout," transcendent ecstasy—all of these hedonistic pursuits are more and more common, more and more acceptable, even within the church. Such pursuits now pervade the language, methods, and goals of so-called Christian counselors, and are increasingly elevated as somehow being a part of the Christian life. Quoting again from Harold O. J. Brown, "It is hard for those who are committed to otherworldly values to hold them consistently when the entire surrounding sociocultural system is turning away from supersensory realities and grasping for those things that appeal to the senses."[11]

John Calvin was undoubtedly scriptural when he reminded Christians that pragmatic, pleasure-seeking goals could not be a part of the Christian life:

> We are not our own; therefore, neither is our own reason or will to rule our acts and counsels. We are not our own; therefore, let us not make it our end to seek what may be agreeable to our carnal nature. We are not our own; therefore, as far as possible, let us forget ourselves and the things that are ours. On the other hand, we are God's; let us, therefore, live and die to him.[12]

CONCLUSION TO SECTION ONE

In chapter 1, "The Freudian Foundation," we examined the six fundamental beliefs ("pillars") common to all forms of insight-oriented psychotherapy. They were environmental determinism, psychic determinism, insight, the therapist, self-sufficiency, and the pleasure principle.

In chapter 2, "The Biblical Foundation," we considered the six contrasting pillars of authentic biblical counseling. These were the doctrine of original sin, the human heart/soul/spirit, conviction of sin, God's various provisions of counsel, the doctrine of sanctification, and servanthood. In this chapter we have considered again the contrasts between the psychological and the scriptural foundations.

What are the consequences of people choosing their own wisdom and philosophy to answer the great questions of life?

To the question, Why am I not happy? the nonbelieving world answers, "I am determined by my environment and if I am not happy, it is because of the maladaptive influences of that environment. I am therefore not responsible for my unhappiness; I am a victim of my environment."

To the question, What is wrong inside my mind? the world answers, "Stored inside my mind are many bad experiences, and I am controlled by them; I am in bondage to them. I am determined by my psyche."

To the question, How can I make sense of my problems? the world answers, "I can and must delve into the depths of my unconscious mind to find release from its bondage. I must recover the buried contents of my mind."

To the question, Who can help me solve my problems? the world answers, "Only a professional therapist can offer the help I need."

To the question, How can I become a happier person? the world answers, "I can and must do it for myself. I must be independent, and I must alienate myself from all who might cause me to suffer."

For the question, What is the purpose of my life? the world has a one-word answer: pleasure! The hedonistic life is the goal of modern humanity. That is all there is. Even though not openly stated as such, the goal of many Christian counselors for their clients is the same; they usually cloak it in more acceptable terminology such as a happy marriage, a more successful business, better self-esteem, less stress, less codependency. Such goals are far more consistent with those of the secular psychotherapists than with Martin Luther's description of the Christian: "A Christian is a perfectly free lord of all, subject to none. A Christian is a perfectly dutiful servant of all, subject to all."[13]

John Zubly, a Swiss Presbyterian minister who was a member

of the Continental Congress in colonial America, said, "A more unhappy situation could not easily be devised unto mankind, than that every man should have it in his power to do what is right in his own eyes."[14]

Howell Harris, the Welsh reformer, wrote in a letter dated November 1738, "I fear I have never learnt well to be quite unbottomed of self; nor am I yet able to do all clearly to the glory of Him to whom all the glory is due. O let nothing share your heart with Him; He is willing to take you as you are, a poor, blind, weak, lost, helpless worm (Rev. 3:18), if you are made willing to part with the right eye, right arm, and all for Him."[15]

B. B. Warfield taught from 1 John 3 on February 16, 1921, as follows: "The wonder of the text is that He being all that He was, the Lord of glory, laid down His life for us, being what we are, mere creatures of His hand, guilty sinners deserving His wrath."[16] Then, records biographer David Calhoun, Dr. Warfield walked home from his class at Princeton Seminary that day and died alone.

What a contrast to the gospel of psychotherapy! What a contrast to what seems to be the doctrine of the modern church. Hopefully, such men can call us back to the authority and sufficiency of Scripture.

The consequences of our selfish, pleasure-seeking rebellion against God are all around us. Huge numbers of people spend vast amounts of money on hopeless attempts to know their own souls, to find their oppressors, to recover a nonexistent myth, and to repair a poorly-parented upbringing usually more imagined than real. Others climb endless ladders of virtue in a hopeless quest for self-generated and self-sustained well-being. Bookstores and radio and television shows are filled with advice givers who pander the pillars of the Freudian edifice in one subtle variation or another.

The Bible's prescription for the care of souls will always be thoroughly opposed to the false gospel of insight-oriented counseling psychology. One message is right; the other is fatally wrong. Both cannot be true.

THE ORIGINS OF THE PSYCHOTHERAPEUTIC ETHOS

Introduction to Section Two

We have been concerned with the fundamental "pillars" of modern insight-oriented psychotherapy. We have sought to understand these ideas, in order to consider whether or not they merit the acceptance they currently enjoy. We have also examined the stark contrast between these pillars and the corresponding doctrines spelled out in Scripture. Then we looked at the consequences of these patterns of thought in society today.

In this section we will examine the origin and development of the ideas that gave rise to the pillars of insight-oriented psychotherapy. We will see that the late years of the nineteenth century were a time ripe for the flowering of these fundamental ideas; it was a time especially well suited to the amalgamation of these ideas into a seemingly rational and attractive body of psychological theory and practice. The influence of Darwinism, popular cultural issues and concerns, the weakness of the church, the philosophical trends of the day, and the state of science and medicine all created a unique opportunity for the open and effective expression of these pillars.

We will also look back further, into that period of European history known as the Enlightenment. There we find certain fundamental changes in the way people looked at their world, at their acquisition of knowledge, and at themselves. These "enlightened" ways of knowing and thinking were in themselves decisive in laying a foundation for the flowering of ideas that would not bear their full fruit until the late nineteenth century. Especially important in these earlier times was the waning influence of the church on the domains of science and philosophy, and concurrently the increasing vigor of human-centered speculation and the increasing momentum of human-centered scientific discovery. We will see how such human-centeredness has found its full flowering in the current pursuit of "mind-science."

Most importantly, we will look at the pivotal role of Sigmund Freud as the founding father of psychotherapy. Freud was the right man at the right time. He inherited the liberal influences of the Enlightenment and absorbed the new ideas and issues of his time. Freud desired to be a messiah, a redeemer, to a European culture obsessed with "degeneration." All of these factors influenced him as he compiled—in an especially attractive, rational-sounding, and seemingly scientific manner—his theory of psychoanalysis.

FOUR

❧

DARWIN, HAECKEL, FLIESS, AND FREUD

The church, if it is to be salt and light in this bland and dark world (Matt. 5:13-14), needs to recognize the false and anti-scriptural nature of the fundamental doctrines underlying psychotherapy. In this chapter we will consider the influence of Charles Darwin's theory of evolution on Freud and his successors. We will see that the church's incorporation of Darwinian evolution into its view of origins provided an open door for the integration of Freudian doctrine into its view of man.

As J. Robertson McQuilkin, former president of Columbia Bible College, warns,

> In the next two decades the greatest threat to biblical authority is the behavioral scientist, who would in all good conscience man the barricades to defend the front door against any theologian who would attack the inspiration and authority of scripture, while all the while himself smuggling the content of scripture out the back door through cultural or psychological interpretation.[1]

THE TIMES

An extensive published literature exists on the *fin de siecle* (c. 1850–1914), most of it documenting the artistic, intellectual, spiritual, scientific, psychic, theological, and philosophical tumult characteristic of those times.[2]

> It was an age of cultural ferment and generational collision in which opposing forces of rationality and irrationality, of social progress and hereditary degeneration, of positivism and occultism, scraped together like great tectonic plates and set off earthquakes and aftershocks that culminated in the Great War and its subsequent revolutions and putsches.[3]

One could trace the beginnings of the thinking that characterized the *fin de siecle* to the dawn of the Renaissance 300 years before. Over the ensuing centuries, there was a progression of new thinking born of the growing emphasis on human reason, on introspection as a valid philosophical method, on the discoveries of empirical science, and on the expectation of relentless human progress. This was accompanied by a declining reliance on the teachings of Christianity. As the nineteenth century drew to a close, this cooking pot of Enlightenment ideas began to boil with an added, almost apocalyptic, anticipation of the dawn of a new and better century. From every direction of human interest and pursuit, there was a chaotic eruption of radical ideas, theories, and proposals for a better future.

These were also times of what was then termed "degeneration." Widespread alcoholism, drug addiction, venereal disease, urban crowding, ugly industrialization, and economic hardship were viewed as the products of a degenerated European society. Along with all this, trends in art and literature came to be seen as decadent. The acknowledgment and fear of degeneration became an overwhelming obsession of late-nineteenth-century Europe.[4] It was widely believed that degenerated behavior and environmental effects could lead to "hereditary taints" that would be passed along through successive generations. These "taints," in turn, would lead to the further death and decay of European civilization. These fears fueled a turning away from the previously popular "positivism," which taught that human reason was capable of discovering all truth through observable phenomena and scientific facts.[5] Any new idea that promised a way to forestall or prevent "degeneration"—any "therapeutic" plan of better living or remediation of the "taint"—was quickly and widely disseminated.[6]

One historian characterized the late 1800s as "a recapturing of the irrational [as a] revolt against positivism."[7] If rationalism had failed as a method for human self-perfection, then the irrational, the mystical, and the occult became an option. Though man sought to change the method, however, the fundamental positivistic quest remained the same. He sought to perfect himself by taking to himself the knowledge and power of the divine. Man desired to be his own god, by whatever method he could achieve it. This was certainly nothing new, but it had unique ways of expressing itself in this period.

Examples of this turning from the rational to the irrational in search of self-perfection became obvious in the arts. Instead of what was seen as degeneration and decadence, there appeared themes harking back to a mythical, idealized past. There were, for instance, the Teutonic legends memorialized by Wagner in his operas. And there was the promise of a better future in the "reawakened people" depicted by Nietzsche in *Also Sprach Zarathustra*. Nietzsche spoke for his times when he asked, "What do we consider bad and worst of all? Is it not degeneration?"[8]

From the time of the Enlightenment, there had been an increasing emphasis on the individual and his introspective experience. People were increasingly examining life solely from the human perspective, rather than relying upon a Creator's revelation.[9] This emphasis reached a new peak in the *fin de siecle*.[10] No writer's influence was greater in this regard than that of Friedrich Nietzsche. Nietzsche powerfully condemned traditional European culture. For Nietzsche, the solution to the degeneracy of the day was the production of certain elite peoples to become *Ubermenschen*. Such "supermen" would throw off the burdens of heredity, family, society, and religion. These supermen were to be the antithesis of what Nietzsche saw as mediocrity and stagnation. He believed that such people could acquire, by personal effort and manipulation of the environment, better characteristics which would then be inherited, in Lamarckian fashion, by their descendants.

Nietzsche also advocated the selective elimination of the "inherited taints," which he saw as dooming the culture. It did not matter to Nietzsche whether the taint alone or the person carrying it was eliminated; the important thing was to prevent it from harming future generations. His goal was to transform European man into a "race of philosophers and artists who cultivate iron-clad self-control."[11] He desired to reshape humanity into a race of geniuses.

This ideal of "genius," which became very attractive in Nietzsche's day, was borrowed from the philosopher Arthur Schopenhauer. In 1844, Schopenhauer had written about his concept of the "genius as replacing God as guarantor of artistic and intellectual novelty and cultural innovation generally."[12] Where there once had been the concepts of fallen humanity and original sin, there were now the "replacement concepts" of hereditary taint and degeneration. Where there once had been the concept of redemption and sanctification, there were now the replacement concepts of "therapeutics," *Ubermensch,* and the formation of a genius race. Where there once had been a holy, sovereign Creator God, there was now superman, individuated man, and self-actualized man as god of his own private universe.

Amid the turbulence of these ideas, psychiatry arose as a medical specialty separate from neurology. Riding the crest of the apparent successes of empirical science as well as the new metaphilosophy of science—that all phenomena have a "natural" explanation—German psychiatrists such as Wilhelm Greisinger and Emil Kraepelin insisted that all mental illness was organic in nature and causation. Kraepelin's concept of *dementia praecox* (later called schizophrenia) was a product of the concept of degeneration or hereditary taint, mixed with the notion of the organic causation of mental illness.

However, this organic approach to mental illness, and its emphasis on meticulous diagnosis and empirical research, was eventually seen as failing to yield meaningful results. Psychiatry then shifted its explanatory method and therapeutic approach to the emerging "dissociationist" theory of Jean-Martin Charcot. Charcot was a French neurologist assigned to the huge institution in Paris called the Salpetriere. This was a facility for women with chronic "mental illness" who were unable to care for themselves. There were old prostitutes with degenerative conditions now known to be caused by syphilis; there were patients with epileptic seizures and destitute women found on Parisian streets. Charcot became vastly famous, with students traveling from all over Europe to attend his lectures and demonstrations. Novelists and artists crowded the lecture hall to hear the famed neurologist and to see his strange patients. Charcot demonstrated (often in a side-show type of environment) the apparently successful application of the concepts of dissociation, hypnosis, and suggestion. This, in turn, energized another Enlightenment subject of inquiry and speculation, the theory of the unconscious.[13] Among those attracted by Charcot's fame was a young Viennese neurologist named Sigmund Freud.

The quest for paranormal and psychic experiences was quite popular in the *fin de siecle*. Crystal gazing, trances, a fascination with reincarnation and spirit guides, and the analysis of "automatic writing" flowered as popular attempts at understanding the unconscious mind.[14] This unconscious came to be viewed as a repository not only of one's own past experience but of the entire past history of the human race as well.[15] The concept that the great legends and heroes of the past were embedded in the unconscious of every individual became attractive to many. It was concluded that mankind could benefit from this unconscious treasury, even to the extent of reclaiming the supposed glory of the past.[16]

Drawing upon such ideas, as well as upon the philosophy of Schopenhauer, Richard Wagner composed a vastly popular musical literature. Drawing upon his own interest in German antiquity, he wrote a voluminous life-philosophy that had a tremendous influence on the culture of his day.[17] His theater-temple at Bayreuth in Bavaria became a mecca for "Aryan peoples . . . to contemplate ancient mysteries fulfilled in a new form." His works were performed at annual festivals before adoring thousands seeking spiritual rebirth, cleansing, transcendence, and a redemption from degeneration.[18]

Not unexpected during these momentous times was the attack on orthodox Christianity. However, the attack was not expected to come as it did from within the very ranks of the church. A new form of biblical criticism arose as well as a growing emphasis on comparative religious studies. Rather than using God's Word as a bulwark against the rising tides of scientism, naturalism, and positivism, rather than functioning as salt and light amid all these erroneous philosophies, the theologians of the Tubingen School and other universities sought similarly "modern" perspectives in an apparent attempt to be relevant. In this process, belief in the supernatural events of Scripture was jettisoned while Eastern mysticism and the occult were embraced. The search for the "historical Jesus" stripped Him of His divinity just as it stripped many believers of their faith. (This same attack continues today with the Jesus Project, as reported in both *Time* and *Newsweek* magazines during Passion Week of 1996.) The comparative approach to religious studies further opened the door to pagan religions, both current and ancient. All avenues of spiritual journeying were seen as equally valid, especially if they were intellectual or gnostic. Man was eager to be a god; most repulsive was the idea of being a servant, despised and rejected. Jesus the man of sorrows was replaced as the object of veneration by the self-assured human mind.[19]

To a culture preoccupied with what it saw as the hereditary taint of degeneration, any idea appearing to offer a redemptive possibility was attractive. Schopenhauer's blueprint for the production of "genius," Nietzsche's ideal of *Ubermensch,* and Wagner's cultic transcendence through myths and legends of old all attracted wide followings.

Into this culture of desperation came yet another redemptive promise—a promise of science.

CHARLES DARWIN

Charles Darwin, the English naturalist, lived from 1809 to 1882. Since he had married into the Wedgewood china fortune, he was free from the mundane task of earning his daily bread. Between

1831 and 1836, he traveled the world aboard the *H.M.S. Beagle* observing plants, animals, and peoples in far-flung places. He observed the wonder and orderliness of God's creation, but he did so through the eyes of an agnostic naturalist. Over the years, he worked on his theory of evolution of the species by natural selection. He sought to explain his observations without reference to the supernatural—a stance still in his day considered quite radical. Fearing public and scientific reaction, he kept his work secret for twenty years.[20]

In 1859 Darwin finally published *The Origin of the Species,* which presented a highly articulated, mechanistic explanation of the origin and development of the various life forms. His work stimulated a widespread interest that continues to this day. His influence reached far beyond biology, into broad aspects of our modern culture, not the least of which is the psychology of human development and mental functioning.

Prior to Darwin, numerous theories of origins had been proposed. For the most part, they tacitly assumed the existence of a sovereign Creator God. Darwin was not the first to try to explain mankind without reference to the Bible. When theorists of the day addressed the popular concern over "degeneration," rather than accepting the biblical account of the Fall, they generally explained it in terms of a gradual decline (devolution) through the ages from original types or ideal forms of species, which they called Urtyp.[21] Darwin, however, was the first to propose that we accept evolution rather than creation as the *sole* basis of understanding the origin and development of species. He was the first to propose that all life on earth evolved from a single or a few ancestral forms, that this had taken place gradually over a great span of time, and that the general direction of the evolution was toward higher development.[22] Darwin accepted the general (Lamarckian) belief of the times that "experienced" as well as "permanent" factors could be inherited; he explained all population speciation on the overarching basis of natural selection.[23] He boldly eliminated any need for supernatural intervention in the process. Naturalism became the scientific metaphilosophy of the day. In place of the gloomy predictions associated with the wide-spread belief in degeneration and devolution from Urtyp, Darwin's mechanistic concept of natural selection seemed to produce another ray of hope. Man need only understand such a process; he could then take charge of it himself. God was not required: *Ubermensch* was at hand!

Prior to Darwin, it was generally believed that science had limits and that many of the ultimate questions of human existence were outside those limits. Descartes was the most prominent proponent of this "dualistic" approach. As we will see in chapter 5, Descartes saw the physical universe created by God as the proper realm for science, while the transcendental, the ultimate mysteries of human nature, the immaterial, were outside the realm of science and were known only to God.

Typical of this approach was Alfred Wallace (1823–1913), who formulated a theory of evolution just prior to Darwin. Wallace eventually took the view that his theory might account for man's physical existence but that it could not be invoked to explain the human mind. He saw the human mind as embodying mysteries that compel one to postulate the existence of God—or a "world spirit working above and beyond the material world." Even though some Enlightenment philosophers and scientists opposed this view, it was the widely held assumption until Darwin published his own views.[24]

With Darwin's publication of *The Origin of the Species,* the assumption of the divine origins of the human mind collapsed. Today scientists such as Roger Penrose and Antonio Damasio assert that eventually science will be able to scientifically explain every aspect of the mind, consciousness, and soul of man.[25] For the truly naturalistic scientist, nothing lies outside the domain of scientific inquiry.

Darwin's legacy touches all areas of society. The idea that God is unnecessary; an unrestrained faith in science; atheistic naturalism as the dominant metaphilosophy of science; and the mechanistic implications of natural selection (such as abortion, euthanasia, eugenics) as a "truth" we must accept—all are modern consequences of Darwin's publications.

ERNST HAECKEL

No one applied more broadly the implications of Darwin's theory than did Ernst Haeckel (1834–1919).[26] As a zoologist, artist, and prolific author, Haeckel was one of the most prominent scientists of the day. "He became Darwin's chief European apostle, proclaiming the gospel of evolution with evangelistic fervor, not only to the university intelligentsia but to the common man by popular books and . . . lectures in rented halls."[27]

It was Haeckel who in 1868 first wrote that human beings descended from apes. It was Haeckel, as we have seen, who invented the Biogenetic Law, that ontogeny recapitulates phylogeny—that evolutionary developmental stages (phylogeny) were replicated in the stages of human embryonic development (ontogeny).[28] In his popular book *The Riddle of the Universe,* Haeckel described each person as a living museum of the evolution of his race, just as Nietzsche saw each person as harboring a repository of his own personal and racial past.[29] Haeckel theorized that successful passage through these embryonic developmental stages was essential to a successful life.

In *The Riddle of the Universe* Haeckel proposed a philosophy of life that he saw as a solution to the problem of degeneration and a way to bring about regeneration. This life-governing philosophy was a direct outgrowth of Darwinism, which undergirded Haeckel's popular views on eugenics, euthanasia, utopianism, and the worship of nature. Haeckel's views on economic control, in the hands of a devoted follower named Karl Marx, led to communism. His views on the superiority of certain races, in the hands of a young Adolf Hitler, led to Nazism. These have been some of the grave consequences of the tumultuous ideas of the *fin de siecle.*

Haeckel endeavored to apply his Biogenetic Law to all of life. He assumed the manner of a messiah, speaking to large audiences with elaborate illustrations. He did not limit his theory to the physical development of the embryo within the womb. He extended his Biogenetic Law to encompass the development of human consciousness, intelligence, will, and morality. His "Biogenetic Psychology" proposed that the human soul was not something specially created by God but simply a fundamental material aspect of any biological life. This view, which remains current among many scientists today, allowed him to extend the realm of "scientific" inquiry to the spiritual nature of man, while science had previously limited its studies to the material aspects. Haeckel's correction of "Descartes' Error" (the exclusion of the immaterial from scientific scrutiny) is still today a popular proposition.[30]

According to Haeckel, the soul evolved from the simplest primordial organism to its most complex manifestation in man. He postulated that the evolution of the soul depended on the influence of external stimuli in ways more complex and profound than the evolution of the physical body. Similarly, he postulated that the development of the soul of the human child proceeded differently from the physical development of the embryo. Specifically, he theorized that the soul was in a state of "slumber" in the womb and only began its development at birth.

Haeckel proposed that the human soul or mind must pass through postnatal ontological stages of development, just as did the human embryo in prenatal development.[31] Furthermore, he believed that the stages of the postnatal development of the mind would recapitulate the phylogenetic stages of the evolution of the human soul. Accordingly, the mind would contain a "museum" of our past; this would be a repository of our own personal past as well as of the history of the human race.

Haeckel and others of his day hoped that, by using the right techniques, mankind could reclaim a supposedly more glorious past that he had lost. The contradiction of this "glorious past" with Darwin's primordial ooze seemed to concern no one. Haeckel's theories began to influence science just as the legends and myths of the Teutons and the pagan tales of old began to characterize popular literature and music. Wagner's operas, Nietzsche's philosophy, and Haeckel's psychology derived their cult-like attractiveness from claiming to provide hope for the "degenerated" European culture.[32]

Before the turn of the century, Haeckel's view of human psychological development recapitulating evolutionary development gained wide acceptance, and many elaborate schema were published outlining the details. One author placed the psychological development of the human newborn at the level of the sea urchin, at ten weeks of age at the level of the spider, and at twelve months at the level of a monkey.[33] This line of thinking led to the notion of developmental stages through which we all must successfully pass. Equally established was the notion that external stimuli were of fundamental importance to this process. Haeckel explained this recapitulation as a fundamental biological process. Inherent in this biological conception is the notion that more primitive stages are not so much "lost" in the process of recapitulation as they are "layered over" by the more advanced or successful phylogenetic stages. Not being lost, the more primitive is "in storage."

This notion of the layering over of successive developmental stages would later provide the supposedly scientific basis for "repression," the very centerpiece of Freudian theory,[34] and for the Freudian promise of "insight into the unconscious." Freud saw the unconscious as being in storage, layered over, and recoverable by the proper techniques. He saw this gaining of insight as not only possible, but ultimately essential to normal human development.[35]

Of fundamental importance, both to the theory of evolution and to the theory-making of Freud, was Haeckel's insistence that evolutionary biology was a *historical* science involving the historical methodologies of embryology and paleontology.[36] Haeckel is credited with being "perhaps the first biologist to object vigorously to the notion that all science had to be like the physical sciences or to be based on mathematics."[37] Historical methodologies attempt to arrive at truth by understanding the past. Such methodologies can give the appearance of plausibility and explanatory power to any theory. They are a favorite tool for a researcher with "outcome bias," that is, a researcher who is determined to use science to "prove" his pet theory.

Haeckel thus expanded the scope of "science" beyond that which could be observed, measured, and tested objectively in the laboratory. While including his "historical" observations under the umbrella of science and defining all such observations as "natural phenomena," he smoothly answered any criticism with the assertion that "God reveals himself in all natural phenomena," and that all such observations, whether objective or historical, were equally "of God" and "true."[38] This oft-quoted maxim, "all truth is God's truth," is misused today in the same way to present man's fabrications and philosophies as God's truth because man considers them to be truth.

Haeckel was shown to be a fraud even in his own lifetime. He fabricated and falsely illustrated organisms and prehistoric ape-men, using them to "prove" his theories and impress his audiences. He confessed the fraud publicly in 1909, but even this did not seem to dampen his popularity or lessen the impact of his philosophy. The populace loved his teaching and saw it as a route to regeneration. Haeckel's illustrations were attractive even when known to be fabricated! Still today popular textbooks of science contain some of his fabricated illustrations of ontogeny supposedly recapitulating phylogeny; still today these texts present the illustrations as scientific truth.

As we have seen, Haeckel's influence was hardly benign and was certainly not confined to the world of ideas. "Through his obsession with the anti-God concept of evolution and his shameful fabrication of spurious data, Haeckel provided the malign influence and pernicious inspiration that were the indirect cause of two world wars and the atrocities of the holocaust."[39] Upon the fabrications of Ernst Haeckel were built not only Marxism and Nazism but the edifice of psychoanalysis and modern counseling psychology as well.

WILHELM FLIESS

The influence of Darwinism upon modern psychotherapy is clearly seen when tracing the connection between Freud and Wilhelm Fliess. Fliess (1858–1928) was a contemporary of Freud. A nose and throat specialist in Berlin, he was given to effusive flights of fancy and theoretical speculation in the areas of medical research. His interests led him to visit Charcot in Paris, where he witnessed some of "the master's" carnival-like demonstrations of hypnotism. He heard Charcot's speculative theories of the unconscious presented as fact and witnessed what appeared to be dramatic demonstrations of the truth of these theories.

Charcot claimed to enter the unconscious of his patients with the use of hypnosis. His demonstrations appeared to validate his theories that so-called hysterical symptoms were "always, always, always" caused by abnormal sexual experiences.[40] In 1887, Fliess attended lectures by Freud on neurology. The two men became fast friends, and over the next several years they carried on an extensive correspondence while working together on their theories of the functioning of the human mind. Many of these letters are pre-served, and they are studied by the psychoanalytic faithful as if they were epistles exchanged by apostles of a religion; this is, of course, exactly what they are.[41]

An example of Fliess's scientific prowess was his "discovery" of the "nasal reflex neurosis."[42] He claimed that cocaine applied to the nasal mucosa would eradicate headaches, menstrual cramps, and a variety of other bodily complaints whose physical causes were unknown at the time, and which he believed to be neurotic signs of mental unbalance. Fliess did not recognize that cocaine brought relief of symptoms by its rapid absorption through the lining of the nasal cavity into the bloodstream. Cocaine thus absorbed is instantly distributed to the rest of the body by way of the circulation and, in this way, influences neurosensory reception. With no understanding of this, Fliess postulated the existence of nerve connections or "humoral channels" between the nose and other parts of the body, especially the sexual organs. Having read Darwin and Haeckel, Fliess theorized that an archaic nasal stage of sexual evolution, which had not yet been repressed, was creating mental symptoms in his patients. Freud accepted this theory and never repudiated it, even though Fliess was later publicly ridiculed as a crackpot.[43]

More important for our purposes was Fliess's belief that newborn infants and young children pass through stages of sexual development that recapitulate evolutionary stages of development. In his theorizing with Freud, he offered fanciful propositions of nasal, oral, anal, and phallic or genital stages of sexual evolution. Fliess was thus the first to apply Haeckel's Biogenetic Law to human psychosexual development. Freud accepted these propositions and incorporated them into his developing theory of the mind.[44]

Upon these concepts imparted by Fliess, Freud eventually built his elaborate "Grand Theory" of the human mind. This theory was seemingly biologic and came from the science of the day as discussed above. It included the scientific-sounding concepts of embryonic and postnatal development, with ontogeny recapitulating phylogeny. The environment was to determine successful passage through postnatal stages. Fliess and Freud claimed this to be the inherent biological reality of living things. The appropriation of these concepts into the Freudian edifice lent his theories an undeserved aura of scientific truth.

Some of Fliess's concepts were entirely speculative even when compared with what was broadly considered "science" in the *fin de siecle*. The culture of the day provided the metaphor of a repository of experiences, instincts, and environmental influences buried in the out-of-awareness mind; it gave supposed objective and empirical validity to the collection of historical information and developed the notion that the out-of-awareness mind is not only influential but accessible. The appropriation of these cultural concepts into the Freudian edifice opened the floodgates for colorful, fanciful theorizing. By its very nature, this supposedly repressed repository lay completely outside the grasp of empirical validation, but with the use of historical methodology, any theory that seemed to resonate with life or legend and filled the intellectual vacuum, and was set forth as science, was accepted as truth.

From its very inception, Freud's theory-making was built upon false and fanciful premises. His theories were formulated in such a way as to render them incapable of clear, convincing proof of their truth or falsity.

SIGMUND FREUD

Sigmund Freud lived from 1856 to 1939. In spite of the immense impact of his ideas, most know little of his life. And while many know something of his psychoanalytic theories, few understand their origin or their connection with the general practice of psychotherapy today.

Freud had a lifelong desire to be famous as a scientist and biologist. Above all else, he desired to be a messiah who would lead people out of "degeneration." He claimed to point the way to a life free of shame, guilt, and fear. Few understand the degree to which Freud and his disciples concealed the truth and fabricated their therapeutic successes in order to accomplish this goal. By attacking and silencing his critics, Freud's disciples erected a mythical hero in the so-called science of psychoanalysis. Only in the last few years have dispassionate books and articles begun to appear that clearly assert that the praise and importance granted to this man and his ideas have been genuinely undeserved.[45]

Eager to become wealthy and famous, Freud was forever looking for ways to advance himself as a physician, neurologist, academician, and breadwinner.[46] In Wilhelm Fliess, he found an enthusiastic partner and admirer. They fed each other ideas, schemes, and praise, as evidenced in their correspondence. Both men rejected belief in God and the supernatural. Both were steeped in the writings of Darwin, Nietzsche, Marx, and other philosophers of the day. Both admired the ideas of Wagner and Haeckel. Both had a tendency to ideas some would call "crackpot," and to grandiose theories some would call "overly elastic."[47] Both were enthralled with the "unconscious," especially after coming under the influence of Charcot in Paris.

Our society's current concept of the unconscious is chiefly the product of Freud. Although it had been a subject of intellectual pursuit from the beginning of the Enlightenment, Freud conceptualized the subject in a manner never before accomplished. Like Darwin, he established an overarching theory that is still today held as axiomatic. Like Darwin's theory, Freud's theory is unprovable, unfalsifiable, grand in scope, and anti-supernatural; yet it continues to be viewed as scientific and remains generally unquestioned.

Belief in the theories of either Darwin or Freud requires great leaps of faith. Both are generally considered as having been of great value to mankind, and their critics are vilified as ignorant. This view continues in spite of a recent author's comment that "Freud has been the most overrated figure in the entire history of science and medicine—one who wrought immense harm through the propagation of false etiologies, mistaken diagnoses, and fruitless lines of inquiry."[48]

Freud's concept of the unconscious continues largely unchallenged. It has been woven into the very fabric of every form of counseling, from classical psychoanalysis to advice over the backyard fence. Upon Freud's theory of the unconscious is built the entire concept of mental and emotional problems, their causation, their assessment, and their treatment. Both the learned professional and the housewife listening to talk shows views the subject of emotions through a Freudian lens.

The story of how Freud developed his "Grand Theory" was for many years told only by his adoring disciples. In those versions, Freud was the trailblazing, relentless, ardent scientist. In more recent times (especially after the release of long-suppressed documents and personal accounts) a much different Freud is emerging.[49] In an effort to advance his lackluster academic standing as a neurologist in Vienna, Freud traveled to Paris to study under Charcot, the acknowledged grand master of neurology. Unbeknownst to Freud, the master had been experimenting with hypnosis in an effort to understand hospitalized patients with neurologic symptoms whose causes were unknown at the time. Fits, falls, catatonia, spells of blindness, and periods of paralysis all constituted the symptoms of what was called "hysteria."

Hysteria was considered a disease entity as specific as other better understood diseases such as pneumonia and cancer. Therefore, hysteria should have a definite cause, a particular slate of symptoms and signs, a specific treatment, and a predictable response to treatment. Hysteria's symptoms were highly diverse, however, and no treatment had been discovered. For this reason, hysteria drew Charcot's attention. The large asylum where Charcot worked housed literally thousands of patients with neurological symptoms fitting the diagnosis of hysteria. In examining these female patients, in obtaining their histories, and by invoking theories of other scientists and of popular folklore, Charcot came to believe that hysteria was mental in origin. He concluded that traumatic ideas could be deposited in the unconscious mind of certain predisposed (degenerated) persons, and that these traumatic ideas were then transformed into bodily symptoms.[50] Though Charcot's conclusions were based on "misdiagnosis and theoretical confabulation,"[51] Freud enthusiastically accepted them and saw them as the kind of scientific breakthrough that could bring him fame and fortune.

Returning to Vienna, Freud refined his theories and treatment of such "hysterical" patients with the help of Josef Breuer, an older neurologist of greater prominence. Thus he took Charcot's work with diseased Parisian prostitutes and applied it to the daughters of Vienna's aristocracy. Freud quickly moved beyond Charcot's hypnosis to the use of recollection in an effort to discover and release the "bottled up" idea at the source of the symptom. In this "cathartic" method, Freud usually encouraged and coached his patients' recollections. Through this coaching, he found his submissive patients to be quite productive. He used this experience to develop ever more elaborate theories as to how traumatic ideas could give rise to bodily symptoms. Modern scholarship has shown that Freud, like Charcot, misdiagnosed all of these early "hysterical" patients and fabricated all of their "success stories."[52]

Freud's first "Grand Theory" of the mind had been founded on theories from Fliess. He then added what he learned from Charcot as well as material from two other sources. From the general science of the day, he borrowed the terminology and concepts of the emerging fields of electricity, hydraulics, and physiology. He employed terminology such as "conservation of energy," "homeostasis," "excitation and repression," and "energy displacement." A prime example of this was his elaborate electrical explanation of the mind, his "Project for a Scientific Psychology."[53]

From the ancients, Freud borrowed the notion of animal spirits or humors. The flowing of these humors was supposedly the means by which the soul produced its will upon the body. In the late nineteenth century, there had been a revival of a "vitalistic" philosophical speculation about the unity of nature and spirit, a "naturphilosophie." One of its tenets was the unity of material and immaterial in a "world soul." This ultimate unity was seen as the source of both the physical universe and the human soul. This mystical philosophy, though opposed to the rationalism and materialism of Enlightenment science, had been appropriated by Haeckel as he redefined the realm of science and extended its domain of inquiry to the human body and soul.[54] For Freud, his Project for a Scientific Psychology was an ambitious proposal by which mankind could bridge the gap between material and immaterial, between the scientific and the speculative, the modern and the ancient; thus would he come to know and explain the very human soul.

Like many before him and multitudes after him, Freud thought he could reject scriptural revelation and discover his own answers to the ultimate questions about human nature. Using science and speculation, he was convinced that he could discover the "Grand Theory," the answer to these questions. Freud refused to acknowledge that the answers needed by the creature had been provided by the Creator. He refused to acknowledge the limits of science and speculation established by that Creator (Jer. 17:9-10). He was determined to reject God's Word; he did not foresee that, in his desire to grasp forbidden wisdom, he would be made a fool (see Rom. 1:21-22).

In 1895, Freud developed his explanation of hysteria and the functioning of the mind. He expanded it into a "Grand Theory" encompassing the very nature and soul of man. What he termed his Project for a Scientific Psychology became so convoluted, pseudo-mathematical, and ponderous that it finally made no sense even to Freud himself. By the end of that year, in a letter to Fliess, Freud referred to the whole Project as "a kind of madness."[55]

This first effort of Freud at a grand theory, the Scientific Psychology, came to be replaced by another grand theory, the

"Seduction Theory." Freud had begun to encourage his patients to recollect the traumatic ideas or experiences supposedly causing their hysteria. He regularly "discovered" from his patients' remembrances that those ideas were sexual in nature.[56] Such ideas were as exciting to people in those Victorian days as they seem to be to people in the church at the beginning of the twenty-first century. Freud actually *suggested* these recollections to his troubled, suggestible female patients because he had decided that sexual abuse was what *should be* discovered in accordance with his theory. Not surprisingly, patient after patient had the same revelations as they lay on his couch. Thus finding what he expected to find, Freud "confirmed" his theory that early incestuous seduction of these young women by their fathers was the cause of hysteria.[57]

From this "Grand Theory," Freud expected "eternal fame . . . certain wealth . . . complete independence, travels, and lifting [his] children above the severe worries that robbed me of my youth."[58] What he encountered, however, was horrified patients, angry fathers, and a further delay of his long-hoped-for promotion at the university. In the fall of 1897 he wrote to Fliess of his abandonment of the Seduction Theory.[59] Most of the psychotherapists creating false memories today have not shown as much common sense or fear of the consequences as did Freud in 1897, when confronted with the results of his erroneous theory.

Freud's Seduction Theory failed because it was based on false premises and on false information. It was based on outcome-biased, self-confirming, suggested sources of information. As such, it was unacceptable to the scientific community and to the public at large.

In this theoretical vacuum, Freud began to listen to Fliess, who was "proclaiming the good news" of Darwin and Haeckel. It was at this point that Darwinian principles were inserted into Freud's theories and used as foundation stones for his "Grand Theory" of the human mind. "Nowhere . . . was the impact of Darwin . . . more exemplary or fruitful outside of biology proper than within Freudian psychoanalysis."[60] In contrast to his repudiation of the Seduction Theory, Freud held to these Darwinian concepts to the end of his life.

Freud published *The Interpretation of Dreams*[61] in November 1899, as the new century was about to begin. He hoped that its release would bring him the long-coveted fame and fortune that he felt he so richly deserved. That work, plus *Three Essays on the Theory of Sexuality,*[62] published in 1905, did eventually win worldwide recognition for Sigmund Freud. In these two works, he outlined the essential pillars of his Grand Theory of the human mind and of the mind's "psychoanalysis." His many subsequent publications elaborated on the pillars of his edifice as outlined in these two works.

Freud was convinced by Fliess that human consciousness, intelligence, will, or what he often called the soul, developed postnatally in stages that recapitulated pre-human evolutionary development. He was also convinced that human sexuality developed postnatally in the same manner. He conceptualized these stages as oral, anal, and genital. Each of these stages had characteristic anatomical, instinctual, and functional aspects that set them apart from each other. The passage from one stage to the next was a biologically determined process, and the success of that process depended on external stimuli.

This process of passage involved the biologically based mechanism Freud called "repression," which involved each earlier stage of development being automatically "buried" under each more advanced stage. Any difficulty caused by improper external influences might result in "fixation" at one stage or another, or "regression" from a higher stage to a lower one.[63] Freud firmly believed all his life that human qualities such as shame, fear, disgust, and the taboo of incest were characteristics acquired by our ancestors from external experiences, which were then inherited by all following generations. In this regard, Freud agreed with Lamarck's theory that organisms change their forms to adapt to their environment, and then pass these changes on to their offspring.

Drawing directly from Charcot and indirectly from Enlightenment philosophers concerned with the conscious and unconscious mind, Freud added the notion that, out of our awareness, there functions a powerful unconscious. He saw this unconscious as a permanent repository of all our perceptions, experiences, and repressed stages of development, as well as the inherited traits, instincts, and experiences of our ancestors. Based on his observations under Charcot and his own adventures with his patients, Freud postulated that the human unconscious is a powerful determiner of our daily thinking, feelings, and behavior. Freud was convinced that by the use of free association, catharsis, hypnosis, recollection of memories, by the analysis of dreams, errors, and slips of the tongue, by the interpretation of symbols, and by evaluating the relationship between the patient and the therapist, he could analyze the unconscious. Freud believed that the unconscious could thus be corrected and that people could thereby free themselves of its tyrannical control.

Consonant with all these notions was Freud's insistence that the only real "cure" for human problems was a depth-analysis of the unconscious. To deal with the current events of a client's life rather than with this long-repressed past was to deprive the client of true redemption. The only time Freud ever doubted that the discovered content of the unconscious was anything but credible, reliable, knowable, and trustworthy was when the Vienna fathers forced him to retract his Seduction Theory.

Today, of course, the army of doubters is growing:

> The opinion is gaining ground that doctrinaire psychoanalytic theory is the most stupendous intellectual confidence trick of the twentieth century; and a terminal product as well—a vast structure of radically unsound design and with no posterity.[64]

The author of that assessment is accurate except for his conclusion that psychoanalytic theory is a "terminal product . . . with no posterity." It is true that classic psychoanalysis as a style of psychotherapy is fast waning. However its progeny, the psychotherapy industry in all its diverse forms, is far from a terminal product. It is a booming enterprise, in the church and out, and seems invulnerable to criticism, exposure, ridicule, and lack of any proof of efficacy.

Psychotherapy is riddled with flaws at its very core that seemingly should have driven it from the scene generations ago:

The movement's anti-empirical features are legion. They include its cult of the founder's personality; its casually anecdotal approach to corroboration; its cavalier dismissal of its most besetting epistemic problem, that of suggestion; its habitual confusion of speculation with fact; its penchant for generalizing from a small number of imperfectly examined instances; its proliferation of theoretical entities bearing no testable referents; its lack of vigilance against self-contradiction; its selective reporting of raw data to fit the latest theoretical fad; its ambiguities and exit clauses, allowing negative results to be counted as positive ones; its indifference to rival explanations and to mainstream science; its absence of any specified means of preferring one interpretation to another; its insistence that only the initiated are entitled to criticize; its stigmatizing of disagreement as "resistance," along with the corollary that, as Freud put it, all such resistance constitutes "actual evidence in favor of the correctness" of the theory; and its narcissistic faith that, again in Freud's words, "applications of analysis are always confirmations of it as well."[65]

In spite of all this, Freud's pillars continue to support, justify, and validate the ever-expanding world of psychotherapy. It is a growth industry purveying the empty promises of self-cure, self-actualization, autonomy, and pleasure to a population seeking redemption from its own modern "degeneration," and seeking that redemption in all the wrong places.

Most devastating is the degree to which the church has embraced Freud's pillars in an attempt to develop its own practical theology of Christian counseling. Theologians, pastors, and laypeople over the last fifty years have eagerly "integrated" the "truths" of psychoanalysis, combining counseling psychology with the teachings of Scripture. What has resulted is a *practice* of counseling among Christian counselors that is different from the secular in neither form nor content. The outcome has been a false gospel that leads counselees away from the authority and sufficiency of

Scripture, away from the curative power of the indwelling Holy Spirit, and away from the only true source of redemption from "degenerate" lives. It moves people toward the oblivion of autonomy, hedonism, and endless introspection. This provides "hell on earth," and for many, it helps to assure hell for eternity as well.

The basic fundamentals of Freudian psychoanalytic theory represent the "pillars" of his intellectual edifice. They were never repudiated by Freud and are the fundamental doctrines of psychotherapy today. Like Darwin, Freud was a product of his times. Both men became products of their times because of their determination to reject the revealed Word of an unchanging Creator. Like Darwin, Freud articulated a body of theory that was not only a consequence of the ideas of those times but which continues to exert profound influence in our own day. The sources and the consequences of those ideas need to be examined in our day.

The ideas born in the *fin de siecle* have already brought disastrous consequences. The theories of Karl Marx, Adolf Hitler, Sigmund Freud, and Carl Jung are some of the consequences of the ideas of Darwin, Nietzsche, Wagner, and Haeckel. Much suffering in this life and beyond might still be prevented if Christians would consider the sources of the ideas they are embracing.

Had we been like the Bereans, constantly comparing Darwin and Freud with Scripture, the church could not have been so confused and weakened by the theories of these men. The church should be a light to turn mankind toward the only source of truth and redemption from degeneration. Christian psychology is an oxymoron. The two religions are inherently contradictory. Believers should avoid the use of such unscientific and unbiblical concepts in their understanding of human problems. The truth of Scripture is inevitably devalued in any attempted integration. Syncretism suppresses the truth of God, and Christians should always be at work to avoid this suppression. The edifice of psychotherapy today (and this includes most Christian counseling) is the progeny of Darwin, Haeckel, Fliess, and Freud. Their ideas are what is "falsely called knowledge"; we are to "turn away" from it as "godless chatter and opposing ideas . . . which some have professed and in so doing have wandered from the faith" (1 Tim. 6:20-21).

> *In the distant future I see open fields for far more important researches. Psychology will be based on a new foundation, that of the necessary acquirement of each mental power and capacity by graduation. Light will be thrown on the origin of man and his history.*
>
> —CHARLES DARWIN
> *The Origin of Species*

FIVE

DESCARTES' DUALISM VS. MATERIALISTIC MONISM

On a stormy winter night in November 1619, Rene Descartes finally went to bed, frustrated, exhausted, but filled with what he called "enthusiasm." Throughout the preceding day and, in fact, throughout much of the preceding five years, the philosopher and mathematician had been troubled and preoccupied with thoughts about the extent to which human reason or science could explain all of human experience. He agonized over how completely we could explain all phenomena, subjective as well as objective, immaterial as well as material, mind as well as body. Descartes asked himself, "Why could not human reason and the objective, empirical methods of science fully explain everything?" The pursuit of a universal scientific explanation was not only elusive to Descartes, but the very idea of such pursuit was immensely troubling to him. With this question on his mind, he fell asleep. During the night, he was disturbed by a set of dreams. Descartes wrote of the content and his own interpretation of the dreams in a work titled "Olympia," which is now lost. That information was used, however, by Adrien Baillet in a biography of Descartes published in 1691. Quoting from Baillet:

> Then during the night when all was fever, thunderstorms, panic; phantoms rose before the dreamer. He tried to get up in order to drive them away. But he fell back, ashamed of himself, feeling troubled by a great weakness in his right side. All

at once, a window in the room opened. Terrified, he felt himself carried away by the gusts of a violent wind which made him whirl around several times on his right foot. Dragging himself staggering along, he reached the buildings of the college in which he had been educated. He tried desperately to enter the chapel to make his devotions. At that moment some people passed by. He wanted to stop in order to speak to them; he noticed that one of them was carrying a melon. But a violent wind drove him back towards the chapel.

Descartes then awoke with twinges of sharp pain in his left side. He did not know whether he was dreaming or awake. Half-awake, he told himself that an evil genius was trying to seduce him, and he murmured a prayer to exorcise it. He went to sleep again. A clap of thunder woke him again and filled the room with flashes. Once more he asked himself whether he was asleep or awake, whether it was a dream or a daydream, opening and shutting his eyes so as to reach a certainty. Then reassured, he dozed off, swept away by exhaustion.

With his brain on fire, excited by these rumours and vague sufferings, Descartes opened a dictionary and a collection of poems. The intrepid traveler dreamt of this line: "Quod vitae sectaboriter?" Another journey in the land of dreams? Then suddenly there appeared a man he did not know, intending to make him read a passage from Ausonius beginning with the words "Est et non." But the man disappeared and another took his place. The book vanished in its turn, then reappeared decorated with portraits in copperplate. Finally, the night grew quiet.[1]

The very next day Descartes was visited in his home by an Italian painter. To him, this visit of a portrait artist confirmed his own interpretation of the "triple dream" of the night before. For him, the dreams answered the question: *"Quod vitae sectaboriter?"* He was convinced that in a thunderclap he had received "the Spirit of Truth which had chosen to open up all the treasures of science to him." Thus the answer to the question, "What kind of life should one choose?" became clear to him. He believed that he was instructed to pursue a career of objective scientific inquiry. By the "est et non" (yes and no), Descartes was convinced that not all of human experience could be explained by the "dictionary" of science, that the subjective, the immaterial, the mind, the dream's "collection of poems," were properly outside the objective, material, physical realm.

Finally, the copper plates and the portrait artist's visit spoke to him of "nothing but what was very pleasant . . . indicated the future . . . and concerned only with what was to occur to him during the rest of his life." This was in contrast to the threatening warnings of the first dream, "in regard to his past life, which might not have been so innocent in God's eyes as those of men." Descartes was convinced that warning had referred to his sinful efforts to explain all of human experience with human reason or scientific methods, to know for himself the mind of God.

For Descartes, his long period of frustration and exasperation was seemingly over. Through the triple dream, he believed that he had been given a clarity of thinking and purpose where before there had been confusion and frustration. Only a few days later, he conceived a plan for a unified science based solely on mathematical laws and principles. By this unified science he believed that man could eventually explain and understand the entire material universe—but would never fully understand the immaterial. Descartes would place the immaterial outside the realm of science.

Descartes thus established the fundamental principle of *dualism*, the drawing of a philosophical line of separation between the subjective and the objective, the immaterial and the material, the mind and the body. Concerning the body, he drew a distinct separation between *res cogitans* (the thinking thing) and *res extensa* (the extended thing, i.e., the physical body). For Descartes, "the real substrate of being is thinking and the awareness of thinking."[2] *"Cogito ergo sum."* I think, therefore I am.

Out of this separation, this dualism, grew a different style of inquiry into the mind from that of inquiries concerning the body. For the philosopher, the theologian, the poet, and later the psychologist, thinking and speculating became the normal method of inquiry about the immaterial human mind. For the biologist, the physiologist, and the anatomist, mathematical measuring and weighing became the norm for studying the material human body. Today this dualism is rapidly fading. All is viewed as material, with the immaterial being viewed simply as material we have not yet come to understand scientifically, as evidenced in this description of a very sophisticated robot:

> At the Artificial Intelligence Lab at MIT, Rodney Brooks and Lynn Andrea Stein have assembled a team of roboticists and others to build a humanoid robot named Cog. Cog is made of metal, silicon, and glass like other robots; but the design is so different, so much more like the design of a human being. Cog may someday become the world's first conscious robot. . . . A conscious robot is possible in principle, and Cog is being designed with that distant goal in mind. Cog is nowhere near being conscious yet. Cog cannot yet see or hear or feel at all, but its bodily parts can already move in unnerving humanoid ways. Its eyes are tiny video cameras, which "saccade" or focus on any person who enters the room and then track that person as he or she moves about. Being tracked in this way is an oddly unsettling experience, even for those in the know. Staring into Cog's eyes while Cog stares mindlessly back can be quite heart-stopping to the uninitiated, but there is nobody there—not yet in any case.[3]

From the earliest records of human thinking, people have been asking the question, What am I? Though it is seemingly a simple question, how that question is answered has the most important of consequences. Are we more than just physical beings? Do we have spiritual as well as physical aspects, or are we actually just robots? Are we moral agents possessing free will, with responsibility for our actions, or do we simply respond like machines to deterministic input from our environment? If the latter is the case, then morality, law, and religion are only social inventions, relative at best and foolish at worst.

IS DESCARTES' DUALISM WRONG?

Antonio R. Damasio, M.D., Ph.D., is the Van Allen Professor and Chair of the Department of Neurology at the University of Iowa College of Medicine. In this position, as well as in his faculty position at the Salk Institute, Damasio has established a worldwide reputation as an expert on neurological patients affected by brain damage. Drawing upon this experience, he authored *Descartes' Error: Emotion, Reason, and the Human Brain.*[4] The testimonials on the jacket of this book reveal not only something of its content, but also the scientific and philosophical environment from which it springs and into which it is welcomed:

> An outstanding book. It links elegantly cognition and emotions through the somatic marker hypothesis.

> Damasio provides solutions to problems that have been plaguing philosophers throughout history. He . . . presents evidence strong enough to convince Descartes that "sum ergo cogito."

> This is a time of optimism and anticipation in the world of brain and cognitive science . . . a quintessential expression of that optimism.

These praises are offered by a neurobiologist, a professor of linguistics, and a mathematician/theoretical biologist.

Like every good clinical professor, Damasio uses an interesting case presentation to illustrate a point. He opens his book with the famous case of Phineas Gage. In 1848 Gage was a twenty-five-year-old construction foreman for a railroad in New England. He was athletic and likable. Known as a reliable worker, he was given responsibility for carefully placing and detonating explosive charges to clear rock from a railroad right-of-way. One day, while tamping the charge in a pre-drilled hole with an iron bar, Gage accidentally set off the dynamite. The bar was blasted like a missile through his left cheek, through the base of his skull, through the frontal lobes of his brain, and out the top of his head; it landed a hundred feet away, "covered in blood and brains." Amazingly, Gage recovered to live another thirteen years, free from the expected neurological problems of coordination and movement. He was, however, no longer his old self. "Gage's disposition, his likes and dislikes, his dreams and aspirations became fitful, irreverent, impatient, obstinate, profane, capricious, insensitive, and offensive. His personality was completely changed. He wandered from job to job and was often a well-known circus attraction, demonstrating the iron bar and the injuries it had produced."

Damasio uses the Gage case to illustrate the connection between rationality and brain anatomy and function. He reviews recent research on brain-damaged humans and animals and proposes that human reason depends on the working in concert of several brain systems across many levels of neuronal organization. To him, that is the sole composition of human reason; that is all there is.

In the same way Damasio explores feelings. Again reviewing neurobiological evidence and patients in whom brain lesions impair the experience of feelings, he concludes that feelings are no more than physical registrations of the state of the body and its supporting neural systems in its relationship with the surrounding environment. For Damasio, feelings are merely sensors of the quality of the fit between a person and his or her environment.

Finally, he confronts the mind-body problem and what he considers to be "Descartes' Error": ". . . the abyssal separation between body and mind; between the sizable, dimensioned, mechanically-operated, infinitely divisible body-stuff, on the one hand; and the unsizable, undimensioned, un-push-pullable, nondivisable mind-stuff." Damasio believes it is wrong to suggest that reasoning and moral judgment as well as the suffering that comes from emotional upheaval might exist in the mind separately from physical causation. Specifically, it is wrong to separate the most refined operations of the mind from the structure and operation of a biological organism. For Damasio, there is no duality. Mind is body; all of human reason and emotion is, or soon will be, explainable by neurobiology.

In all of his scientific and materialistic optimism, Damasio cannot completely evade the nagging problem of morality, will, and ethics. He assures the reader that these human attributes need not collapse or be threatened. He offers a "replacement hope," that man can see "how biology has contributed to the origin of certain ethical principles arising in a social context." Rather than lament that human feelings or "what humans have described for millennia as the human soul or spirit" are merely explained away biologically, Damasio says we should have an increased sense of wonder "before the intricate mechanisms that make such possible."[5]

In his postscriptum, Damasio looks forward to the further accrual of scientific understanding of human brain function as a way to "find better ways for the management of human affairs."[6] He concludes with a crescendo of scientific optimism. Social problems, bruised feelings, individual pain and suffering, lack of inner balance and happiness—all of these human aspirations and more will one day be answered by brain science.

In a similar vein, Nobel laureate Francis Crick, biochemist and co-discoverer of DNA, has recently applied his materialistic view of reality to, as the title of his recent book declares, *The Astonishing Hypothesis: The Scientific Search for the Soul*.[7] He states,

> You, and your joys and your sorrows, and your memories and your ambitions, your sense of personal identity and free will are, in fact, no more than the behavior of a vast assembly of nerve cells and their associated molecules. . . . The hypothesis is so alien to the ideas of most people alive today that it can be called truly astonishing.[8]

Crick communicates his convictions with enthusiasm and optimism. He acknowledges that scientists do not *yet* have in their hands the grand unifying materialistic theory that will completely explain, in terms of physics, every function of the human mind. Toward that end, much of his book is devoted to his ideas for scientific research into the functioning of the mind. He sees, for example, *vision* as a prototypical area to be investigated.

Crick is contemptuous of any possibility of explaining the mind outside of materialistic science. He ridicules theology as "the superstitions of our ancestors" and philosophy as having "such a poor record over the last two thousand years."[9] For the majority of scientists, quietly going about their business of working, writing, and teaching, Crick serves to express their commonly held conviction that reality is monistic. For him, there is one explanation only, and that explanation is materialistic. What am I? According to Crick, I am matter in motion, nothing more. For Crick, those who look for anything more are ignorant and sentimental.

Despite Crick's reductionistic approach and dismissive style, there are some scientists interested in the human mind for whom the answer to the dilemma is not so easily reduced to a single, simple, materialistic answer. The question that disturbed Descartes' sleep is not so easily dismissed by everyone. For these thinkers, there simply are attributes of the human mind that seem beyond current materialistic explanation. How can there really be a physical explanation of subjective experience, of consciousness, of self-awareness, of mental suffering? Is there something more? Scientists are hardly in agreement on this.

Even the definition of consciousness is a subject of debate. Some would limit consciousness to a subjective state of sentience or awareness during wakefulness—not to be confused with knowledge, attention, or self-consciousness.[10] Others view "the human mind or consciousness as not a thing or an entity, but a function— the results of processes of interaction between the brain and the whole organism, including the brain and the environment."[11] Some "eliminativists" say there is no problem with a materialist explanation of such entities as thoughts, sensations, beliefs, and hopes; they say such things don't really exist except as part of a conceptual system that might be called "folk-psychology."[12]

Those interested in comparing the human mind with computers would characterize it as a "virtual machine, the operating system of the brain, its supervisor."[13] Even the location of the human mind, or consciousness, is contested. Some insist that the brain is the sole site.[14] Others propose that the mind encompasses the entire nervous system.[15] Others propose that the human mind could not exist outside of its relation to the environment, "the culture and consciousness of others."[16] Renowned Harvard scholar Richard Lewontin says, "We exist as material beings in a material world, all of whose phenomena are the consequences of material relations among material entities."[17]

The single overriding goal in modern theoretical physics is to finally prove the "Grand Unification Theory" predicted decades ago by Einstein. Most modern-day scientists and philosophers of science are convinced that this theory, when completely elucidated and proven, will not only explain the fundamental forces of nature, but will also offer a complete understanding of the events around us and of our own existence. Achieving this would be, in the words of Stephen Hawking, "the ultimate triumph of human reason—for then we would know the mind of God."[18]

Hawking's fame as a scientist began with a 1970 paper co-authored with mathematician and physicist Roger Penrose, who is the Rouse Ball Professor of Mathematics at Oxford University and is credited with discovering the phenomenon known as "black holes." In *Shadows of the Mind: A Search for the Missing Science of Consciousness,*[19] Penrose brings his considerable talents as a theoretical mathematician and physicist to bear on the dilemma that disturbed Descartes. Penrose agrees with Descartes that some aspects of the human mind, the "What am I?" question, seem beyond scientific understanding, but Penrose says that it is only beyond science *as we know it*. He concedes that human consciousness and subjective experience are beyond computation, but he does not agree with Descartes' fundamental dualism—that there are two aspects, the physical and the immaterial, to humankind. Like other materialistic scientists, Penrose refuses to accept this duality. For him, all reality is material and therefore *must* have a scientific explanation.

In the first portion of *Shadows of the Mind,* Penrose examines human consciousness in terms of its ability to make mathematical computations. He develops an elaborate argument introducing the reader to the complexities of mathematical theory, the intricacies of artificial intelligence, robots, and chaos theory. He concludes, however, "that an essential ingredient is missing from our present-day scientific picture . . . in order that the central issues of human mentality could ever be accommodated within a coherent scientific world-view . . . that this ingredient is itself something that is not beyond science . . . it is an appropriately expanded scientific world-view we shall need."[20]

For Penrose, the desired coherent "scientific world-view" is, of course, materialism. Therefore, the missing ingredient in our understanding of the human mind has to be materialistic, even though Penrose admits that for the time being this missing information "is not possible to simulate by any computational means." He adds, "Some people might rely on a loophole of 'divine intervention' whereby a wonderful algorithm that is in principle unknowable to us has simply been implanted into our computer brains," but Penrose cannot accept such a supernatural explanation.[21]

In the second portion of his book, Penrose illustrates what the missing ingredient to our understanding of the human mind might be. Invoking his extensive experience with quantum mechanics, and speculating on the information-managing possibilities of the micro-anatomy of the neuron, he contends that "some kind of global quantum state must take place across large areas of the brain, and it is within microtubules that these collective quantum effects are most likely to reside." For scientists to comprehend and understand these effects from a materialistic worldview, Penrose proposes an "expanded" way of looking at reality.

Penrose builds his argument in terms of "three different worlds." The world we know most directly he terms "the world of our conscious subjective perceptions," which is composed of feelings, perceptions, memories, fears, love, understanding, knowledge, ignorance, and revenge. Secondly, he acknowledges "the physical world" of objective things. Finally, he comes close to ancient alchemy and proposes a "Platonic world of mathematical forms." For Penrose as a mathematician and physicist, the ultimate understanding of matter, or reality, is the understanding of the mathematical laws (forms) that underlie and control all reality. Understanding of these mathematical forms and their relationship to matter is what scientists need "in order to understand what kind of organization it is, in the physical world, which gives rise to conscious beings."[22]

The question of what gave rise to conscious beings introduces yet another author and another approach to the "What am I?" question. Again the worldview is most assuredly materialistic, but not so much from the viewpoint of neurobiology, biochemistry, mathematics, and physics; it is more from the viewpoint of cognitive science and evolutionary biology. Daniel Dennett is the Director of the Center for Cognitive Skills at Tufts University and author of *Kinds of Minds: Toward an Understanding of Consciousness.*[23] He has also authored *Darwin's Dangerous Idea*[24] and *Consciousness Explained,*[25] both of which are popular expositions of his scientific ideas and philosophy. As a writer, Dennett is an engaging storyteller, though somewhat elusive and clearly skeptical of traditions. As a thinker in his field of cognitive science, he is a thoroughgoing behaviorist. As such he views man as "an organism . . . a machine, producing behavior with a mind-brain as its control system."[26] Like other behaviorists, Dennett is a materialist, "treating human beings as biological organisms and bringing evolutionary theory to bear on our self-understanding." Thus for Dennett, "the theory of evolution will support a radical questioning of traditional attempts to define the essence of man, and in particular such attempts that want to draw a sharp line between our species and our ancestors."[27]

In *Kinds of Minds*, Dennett challenges many traditions. Why do we presuppose that only man and not all living organisms have consciousness? Adopting an "intentional stance," he fails to see what is so special about the human mind except for its highly complex state of evolutionary development. He tells stories of apes and other animals, supposedly to demonstrate how they "think" in much the same way as humans. With his story (quoted from earlier) of the robot named Cog, he challenges the very concept of consciousness and its attribution to humans only. In that story, he leaves the clear implication that with enough time and technological development, "Cog" will be conscious, functioning, and producing behavior in response to "his" environment no differently than would a human.

Dennett proposes that human consciousness and mental ability, our "What am I?" is actually an assemblage of individual mental components built up step by step, layer upon layer, throughout the evolution of the human species. He finds what he calls primitive examples of these functional components in all forms of life, and sees more complex components as well as relationships between them as the various species "climb the evolutionary ladder."

For Dennett, the human mind and its various attributes and functions is simply a product of the natural selection of individual mental functions. These are the functions that won the battle for successful survival:

> A mind looks less miraculous when one sees how it might have been put together out of parts, and how it still relies on those parts. . . . Each component has a long design history, sometimes billions of years long. . . . Mental contents became conscious . . . by winning the competitions against other mental contents for domination in the control of behavior.[28]

In *Kinds of Minds,* Dennett "had to clarify my theory of consciousness, extending it explicitly to other species."[29] For Dennett, the human mind is not so special after all; it is simply a more complex and highly evolved assemblage of functional components, and its more primitive components are generic throughout all living organisms. These components, says Dennett, are so utterly material that one day soon they could be incorporated into a robot that will thereby become "human." In other words, the individual functional components of the human mind are nothing more than physical, material, biochemical, neuroelectric bits. The uniqueness of humankind derives only from the complexity of the assemblage of those bits and their interaction with the rest of the human body and its environment.

THE QUEST FOR A MATERIALISTIC EXPLANATION

These authors represent but a few of the more popular spokespersons of the latest generation of scientists and philosophers grappling with the mind-body problem, the "What am I?" question. The debate centers around the phenomenon of "consciousness," which is deemed to be the essence of "human-ness." This way of thinking is, of course, not new. Descartes and others before him equated human-ness with consciousness. *"Cogito ergo sum"* was Descartes' summary explanation: To think is to be human. For Descartes' successors, simply to be conscious is to be human. There is no longer any real distinction between humans and animals, even between humans and plants. The human being has simply evolved a few more neuroelectric bits and is, therefore, a more complicated apparatus.

The fundamental assumptions of philosophy and science today are very different from those prevalent in Descartes' day. Descartes believed he was "warned" or threatened for even trying to leave God out of his science and philosophy. He believed that he was supernaturally directed to apply his mathematical science exclusively to material things, reserving a place for God in his considerations of immaterial things. Most scientists and philosophers today labor under no such warnings or directions. They reject the notion that the realm of objective scientific inquiry has any limits. They may agree that some phenomena of the human mind *seem* immaterial or difficult to objectify, but they do not accept that there is *really* anything that is immaterial and thus not accessible to science. To these scientists, the idea of mankind being created in the image of God is a primitive joke.

In their knowing, thinking, and experimenting, these scientists see no reason to leave any room for God. That would require acknowledgment of supernatural reality. To acknowledge such a reality would be to violate the fundamental metaphilosophy of science: atheistic naturalism, or materialism. For these scientists, Descartes' dualism is anathema. They see it as retarding science and human progress. In their writings, any evidence of dualism is referred to in disparaging terms; it is treated in the same way that evolutionary biologists treat the concept of creation, namely, as ignorant and sentimental. The following comments are typical:

> Current philosophy of mind has not been dominated by the
> debate between materialists and dualists, for most of the inter-

esting disagreements have been between different factions of materialism. The primary question is really: "In what sense is everything really physical?"[30]

Most of us have dualist tendencies. In our common everyday, non-reflective interactions, most of us act as though we believe that minds are not bodies. We talk about our thoughts coming to us in a moment of inspiration, not about information processing among layers of neurons. . . . Descartes suggested that neither reason nor language—two paradigm mental capacities—were the sort of thing that one could implement in purely physical devices. The advent of artificial intelligence programming, however, suggests that Descartes was probably wrong.[31]

What holds us in dualism's sway is a certain fundamental failure in imagination. . . . A dualist science of mind would not be nearly as advanced as our materialist mind/brain sciences. . . . In sum, there is nothing that even approximates a dualist theory of mind. And without some sort of foundational principles, we can't conceptualize a serious program of dualism. Previous intuitions notwithstanding, dualism is a bust as an explanatory position.[32]

In the same way that evolutionists await the eventual discovery of "missing links" or "transitional forms," neuroscientists await emerging discoveries of neurobiology, biochemistry, physics, cognitive science, and computer science to prove that human consciousness is nothing but matter in motion. This faithful and expectant waiting is really "a form of mysticism—not religious mysticism but materialist mysticism; it reflects an unlimited faith in the power of the materialist approach to understanding man."[33]

Here's how neuroscientist Valerie Hardcastle expresses her expectant faith in the materialistic approach:

I believe that consciousness can be completely explained within the framework of natural science. . . . It is not a radical

claim (contrary to what a skeptic might think) because I identify consciousness with something in our heads. For it is
exactly the sort of claim one must make if one is to be an
earnest materialist. The mind just is the brain (plus maybe
some connections to the environment), so all mental phenomena must be identified with some brain phenomena. For
an already converted naturalist, the question is which phenomena to identify . . . and nothing more.[34]

This insistence upon a materialistic way of knowing permeates
the modern approach to the "What am I?" question. However, it still
creates some real problems for materialists, who "encounter great
difficulties when they try to objectify the internalized functions of
the mind that have no behavioral manifestation."[35] In other words,
materialists must account for attributes of the mind that *seem* intangible and immaterial. What could be the physical explanation, for
instance, of our ability to maintain a unified conscious experience
such as who we are in space, time, story, and environment? How can
"intentionality" (the content or meaning of our thoughts, feelings,
and actions) be explained? How do we pay attention to some things
and ignore others? Why do we see a human face on the surface of
the moon? Why are some perceived objects or situations "familiar"
and others not?[36] What could possibly be the physical explanation
"of the perception of time, especially the representation of the temporal order of events"?[37]

One important and longstanding philosophical dilemma for the
materialist assertion that all attributes and functions of the mind are
physical centers on the inherent dissimilarity between material
brain and immaterial consciousness, between physical events and
seemingly non-physical ideas.[38] This dilemma is stated clearly in the
following question: How can immaterial thoughts be the product
of, or cause reactions in, material objects such as our bodies?
Granted that something material cannot cause or influence something that is immaterial, and vice versa, the least difficult position for
a materialist to take is that there is nothing immaterial after all.

Another dilemma facing the thoroughgoing materialist is one of moral philosophy. If the human mind and consciousness are truly only material, if we are only matter in motion (with our thoughts, feelings, and behaviors really only determined by our inner and outer environment), then how can humans aspire to what is called "free will"? The deterministic view "holds that with respect to his beliefs, thoughts, decisions, and actions, man has no choice. Given the conditions of his environment and his genes at any given time, only one alternative is possible. In sum, man has no control over his destiny; he is totally controlled by conditioning and physiology."[39] Even while endorsing materialism, some recoil at such radical determinism. They point out that the determinist is "claiming to offer logical arguments in order rationally to persuade his audience of his view, even as he claims that his audience consists of robots who have no choice about their beliefs."[40]

Numerous difficulties face a thoroughgoing materialist as he tries to explain the human mind or consciousness. The problems stem from the difficulties in proposing and sustaining any purely physical explanation of such things as perceptions, emotions, expectations, memories, thoughts, preferences, and ideas. The responses to those problems are also numerous.

The extreme materialist may assert that an immaterial consciousness does not really exist—we are our bodies and nothing more; there is no mind-body dilemma because the two are the same. Consequently, death of the body is, at the same time, death of the mind. Other materialists assert that mind or consciousness and its apparent attributes and functions are simply different terms for what are actually only physical things after all. Another materialist answer to the apparent difference between mind and body is that the concept of mind or consciousness is just another label for neural events, an "epiphenomenon" of normal human brain function.[41] All of these materialist approaches agree that, as science advances, the different terms of identification will disappear.

The adoption of materialism as a sole explanatory method and conclusion in the study of psychology "goes back to the turn of the century when, motivated by the desire to look scientifically respectable, psychologists adopted the model of physics. Their central fear was that any other model would smack of bad science at best and religious mysticism at worst."[42] Therefore, even though science is not yet able to completely explain consciousness and the human mind, "materialistic mysticism" sustains the faithful. Waiting upon the next advance in neurochemistry, PET scanning, computer science, and such, they wait to close the gap between what is known today and what they believe to be just over the horizon.

A special issue of *Science* magazine typified this optimism as it highlighted recent mind science advances in a section titled, "The Science of the Mind." In introducing the section, the editor proudly summarized forty years of scientific endeavor. She noted that in 1956 it was predicted that,

> Human experimental psychology, theoretical linguistics, and computer simulation of cognitive processes were all pieces of a larger whole and that the future would see progressive elaboration and coordination of their shared concerns.

The editor then asserted that this prediction had come to pass:

> Numerous interrelated disciplines are now engaged in the attempt to understand the mechanisms underlying normal and abnormal mental processing. The boundaries between these disciplines (which now include anatomic and computer studies of neural circuits, animal and human lesion studies, neurophysiology, neuropsychology, neuroimaging, neuropharmacology, and experimental cognitive psychology) have become increasingly less distinct. The remarkable progress that has been made in recent years is beginning to generate excitement outside of the scientific community because of its relevance to our daily lives in shedding light on normal cognitive functions (such as language, memory and planning) and on brain related diseases (such as schizophrenia and Alzheimer's disease).

In addition to that roster of scientific disciplines that are currently attacking the mind-body problem, the editor adds that "genetics has also become another piece of the cognitive neuro-science whole."[43]

The articles in the special issue of *Science* speak to the latest research on working memory, visual perception and processing, acquisition and use of language, the neural basis of grammar, and the neurochemistry of prediction and reward.[44] In an article subti-tled, "A Project for a Scientific Psychopathology,"[45] famed psychi-atric researcher Nancy Andreasen predicts that soon a totally brain-based, materialistic understanding of all mental illnesses can be achieved. Her subtitle recalls another such optimistic, but failed, attempt a century ago in Freud's "Project for a Scientific Psychology."[46] Andreasen notes that Freud "abandoned both the Project and neuropsychiatry during the *fin de siecle 1900's*"; however, she adds with great optimism that his "project is slowly being achieved." She attributes this "fruition" to the "maturity of the tech-niques of neuroscience as well as the convergence of efforts from multiple domains."

In 1996 the proceedings of the First Tucson Discussions and Debates were published as *Toward a Science of Consciousness*. The book includes fifty-five scientific papers from the speakers at what is intended to become a regular scientific meeting concerned with cognitive science. The papers cover the same cross-discipline map that the editor of *Science* magazine extols: philosophy, cognitive sci-ence, medicine, experimental neuroscience, neural networks, sub-neural biology, quantum biology, nonlocal space and time, hierarchical organization, and phenomenology.[47]

The pursuit of a materialistic understanding of the human mind, the relationship between mind and body, and ultimately the answer to the question What am I? is a preoccupation of the inter-national scientific community. It is conducted at tremendous expense. Its claims of progress are regularly and widely advertised. The entire endeavor is fueled by grand and optimistic promises: the elimination of mental illness; personal well-being and prosperity; an absence of personal dissatisfaction, guilt, or shame; and even world peace. Better living through chemistry for all mankind would seem to be just around the corner.

Meanwhile the question What am I? remains unanswered, at least by scientists and philosophers whose philosophy is materialism. Their hopeful search for the completely materialistic understanding of the human mind remains decidedly unfinished. Each of the authors reviewed above proposes paths along which the faithful should proceed. Coincidentally, the path suggested by each author relates to his or her own field of expertise—neuroanatomy, quantum physics, neurochemistry, or cognitive science—with evolution as the common foundation. Their hopeful style of writing and seemingly plausible suggestions impart an air of optimism to work that is entirely speculative and devoid of any substance warranting such optimism.

THE FUTILITY OF THE QUEST

These contemporary thinkers are foundationally wrong, and their great error is the error of which Descartes was warned in his "triple dream" of 1619: They are committed to a purely materialistic, monistic explanation of the universe. By unswervingly subscribing to atheistic naturalism, they deny the existence of God and of supernatural reality. On this course they are determined to advance, like the builders of the Tower of Babel.

We should expect that ardent scientists will be claiming more and more to have discovered how matter in motion in our brains, bodies, and environment are systematically related to our thoughts, feelings and behaviors. Objective science has learned much about the wondrous material creation of the human nervous system and its related organs. However, given their anti-religious mindset, their progress will be no different from that of evolutionary biology and paleontology. Theorists will claim to have found evidence, things will appear to be explained, and processes will be supposedly replicated in a laboratory. For those determined to "know the mind of God," the goal will seem forever just at hand.

However, the goal will not be achieved. Man will completely know neither the physical nor the immaterial. He will be forced to fabricate evidence, as was the case with evolutionists in the past.

Mankind has been duly "warned and threatened" that their attempts to eat of this tree of knowledge will be thwarted; this quest will forever be interpreted as rebellion by the Creator of all things, material and immaterial, visible and invisible. As we have seen, the Bible records what happened when mankind first ate from this forbidden tree:

> And the LORD God commanded the man, "You are free to eat from any tree in the garden; but you must not eat from the tree of the knowledge of good and evil, for when you eat of it you will surely die." (Gen. 2:16-17)

> "You will not surely die," the serpent said to the woman. "For God knows that when you eat of it your eyes will be opened, and you will be like God, knowing good and evil." (Gen. 3:4-5)

> "Have you eaten from the tree that I commanded you not to eat from?" (Gen. 3:11)

> "Cursed is the ground because of you . . . for dust you are and to dust you will return." (Gen. 3:17, 19)

> So the LORD God banished him from the Garden of Eden. . . . After he drove the man out, he placed . . . cherubim and a flaming sword flashing back and forth to guard the way to the tree of life. (Gen. 3:23-24)

The human quest for divine knowledge and power manifested itself again at Babel, and once again God treated it as rebellion:

> "Come, let us build ourselves a city, with a tower that reaches to the heavens, so that we may make a name for ourselves. . . ." The LORD said, "If as one people . . . they have begun to do this, then nothing they plan to do will be impossible for them. Come, let us go down and confuse their language so that they will not understand each other." So the LORD scattered them

from there over all the earth, and they stopped building the city. (Gen. 11:4, 6-8)

God always reserves to Himself the prerogatives of divine power and knowledge:

The heart is deceitful above all things and beyond cure. Who can understand it? "I the LORD search the heart and examine the mind." (Jer. 17:9-10)

Modern scientists and philosophers, however, do not accept these divine limits to knowledge of the human mind. Their philosophy of atheistic naturalism requires obedient perseverance toward the goal in spite of the "warnings and threats." They refuse to hear a God who has already answered man's "What am I?" question. They abhor His answer that we are fallen, rebellious creatures under the wrath of a holy and perfect Creator.

Because he is created in the image of a wise and merciful God, man is allowed to discover much of the workings of God's created order. However, instead of standing in awe of the Creator and glorifying Him, man glorifies himself:

They neither glorified him as God nor gave thanks to him, but their thinking became futile and their foolish hearts were darkened. Although they claimed to be wise, they became fools. . . . They exchanged the truth of God for a lie, and worshiped and served created things rather than the Creator—who is forever praised. (Rom. 1:21-22, 25)

If man's achieving a grand unified theory of the mind is made impossible by the Creator of the mind, and yet persistence in this goal is required by the current philosophy of science, what may be the outcome of this quest? An interesting foretaste of what may be the outcome has already been offered in the heady disciplines of theoretical physics and cosmology. Theoretical physics and cosmology are scientific and philosophical fields concerned with questions such as, What is the universe? How does it work? Where did it come from? *A Brief History of Time* is the title of an unpredictably popular book by Stephen Hawking, surely the most prominent theoretical physicist and cosmologist of our time. Hawking's book brought home to the public as never before the issues and goals of modern science at its most esoteric heights. In this book, Hawking introduces the reader to the search for the unified theory of the four fundamental forces by which he believes every operation of the material universe will be understood, and by which we will come to "a complete understanding of the events around us, and of our own existence." In explaining and offering this hope, Hawking is certain that mankind will solve the riddle of the existence not only of the universe but of himself as well. For Hawking, and for his enthusiastic readers, this "would be the ultimate triumph of human reason—for then we would know the mind of God." By knowing and completely understanding God, these scientists certainly mean also that they would have the power of God.

Hawking and his colleagues have been persistent, and the successes of their quest have been regularly reported in the popular media. With reassuring frequency, supercolliders discover new subatomic particles essential to the understanding and proof of the Grand Theory. The relationship of these discoveries to the proof of the "Big Bang" theory has also been regularly asserted by these scientists. All available evidence seems to suggest that the universe and all of the laws of physics and mathematics began at one point in time, in one unimaginable explosion of energy and mass. But why? What was there before? No scientist or philosopher of science can answer those questions, and most do not even try. Could there have been a time before the big bang, before the point of "singularity" when all the mass in the universe to come was compressed into one infinitesimally small point, during which time the laws of science did not yet exist?

The nature of that question and its possible answer veers "dangerously" close to the supernatural and is truly beyond the laws and explanations of science as we know it. But any entertainment of supernaturalism as an option is unacceptable to atheistic naturalism; therefore, a natural and atheistic explanation must be found. In response to that dilemma, Hawking and others now propose a "quantum theory of gravity," involving "imaginary time" in which "the distinction between time and space disappears completely." In so doing, Hawking takes physics into an entirely speculative realm beyond existing possibilities of evidence, proof, replication, and confirmation. As he defines this new speculative realm as science, it takes on all the usual characteristics of myth:

> The quantum theory of gravity has opened up a new possibility, in which there would be no boundary to space-time and so there would be no need to specify the behavior at the boundary. There would be no singularities at which the laws of science broke down and no edge of space-time at which one would have to appeal to God or some new law to set the boundary conditions for space-time. . . . It would be neither created nor destroyed. It would just BE.[48]

Even though this theory is untested, unproven, and seemingly unverifiable, it has attracted wide positive acclaim among scientists and philosophers of science. This is surely due to the desire of such people for Hawking's theory to provide a materialistic solution to questions related to the immaterial. They like the theory because it seems to answer questions about the immaterial without resorting to the supernatural. This explanation solves for the theoretical physicist and cosmologist the same dilemma that needed solution for the scientists attempting to explain the human mind and consciousness: What may have seemed immaterial, intangible, and supernatural actually is not; all that is and ever was, is really just matter in motion.

Rather than acknowledge defeat, fall on one's knees, and admit that God has placed a limit to man's knowing, the scientist of today remains stiff of neck, autonomous, and assured—even while looking God in the face. Carl Sagan comments, in the introduction to *A Brief History of Time:*

> The word God fills these pages. Hawking embarks on a quest to answer Einstein's famous question about whether God had

any choice in creating the universe. Hawking is attempting, as he explicitly states, to understand the mind of God. And this makes all the more unexpected the conclusion of the effort, at least so far: a universe with no edge in time, no beginning or end in time, and nothing for a Creator to do.[49]

Stephen Jay Gould, proud defender of evolutionary science, had this to say on the occasion of Carl Sagan's death:

Carl also shared my personal suspicion about the nonexistence of souls—but I cannot think of a better reason for hoping we are wrong than the prospect of spending eternity roaming the cosmos in friendship and conversation with this wonderful soul.[50]

Such a surge of emotion coming from neuroelectric bits! But not a hint of acknowledgment of a Creator in a position to judge Stephen and Carl; for Gould, even if they are wrong, it won't be a lake of fire—but rather roaming in friendship and conversation. Therein lies the rub; a Creator implies a Judge.

If modern scientists are correct in their view of man, then Ernest Hemingway was far more in touch with reality than are any Gould or Sagan. To Hemingway, life was "just a dirty trick,"[51] so he blew his evolved mass of neuroelectric bits into nonfunctioning bits with a shotgun.

As our sophisticated scientists continue in their determination to build "a tower that reaches to the heavens," we who believe God's Word can be assured that God will soon say, "Let us go down . . ." (Gen. 11:4, 7).

May we humble ourselves, recognize the philosophy at the heart of modern science, and wait upon the Lord.

"This is the one I esteem: he who is humble and contrite in spirit, and trembles at my word." (Isa. 66:2)

SIX

AUGUSTINE'S "ANTI-PSYCHOANALYTIC INFLUENCE"

One of the most interesting aspects of Sigmund Freud's rise to fame is the ease with which he assembled his ideas and promulgated them, and the enthusiasm with which his ideas were greeted by the people of his time. The people of Europe were looking for solutions to the "degeneration" so obvious all around them. They were eager for any ideas that might provide an answer to their dilemma. Accustomed to the many scientific discoveries of their day, they were quite naturally drawn to any proposed solution that carried the imprimatur of science. The ideas of Darwin and his followers had tempted the people with alluring notions of natural selection, environmental determinism, and above all, the promise of human-controlled improvements of the human species. The way was paved for the advent of the Freudian promise, and there was no effective or substantial resistance to that promise.

The church in Europe was weak and spineless in the face of the alluring Freudian onslaught. It had already capitulated to scientific positivism, Darwinism, and the attacks of the philosophers, writers, artists, and lyricists of the late nineteenth century. Rather than rely on and speak out for the Word of God on such issues, the church doubted that the Word was really of God. Lacking trust in the Bible's authority, the church merely re-dressed the world's words in religious garb.

The situation remains the same today. Rather than stand as a bulwark against ideas that strike at the fundamental doctrines of the Christian faith, the church has syncretized those worldly ideas and integrated them into its own ministry. A two-millennia history of pastoral counseling solidly grounded on Scripture, and exampled by stories of its application by innumerable saints down through the ages, has been jettisoned in the name of psychotherapy. With little fanfare, seminary after seminary, Christian college after Christian college has abandoned curricula in pastoral counseling in favor of the worldly concoction of insight-oriented psychotherapy, decorated with religious-sounding vocabulary and justified by Christian-sounding motivational claims. Thus, a century after Freud, the counseling practiced by the church is hardly distinguishable from the therapy practiced by the non-Christian world. The fundamental ideas are the same; the techniques are the same; the outcomes are the same.

There was a time, however, when the church challenged fundamental ideas about man, and the challenge was so meaningful that its effect was felt for a thousand years. Augustine was the right man at the right time, as he unfolded from Scripture the truth of God against ideas falsely called wisdom or science.

Aurelius Augustinus (A.D. 354–430) was born and raised in Thagaste, in the North African nation of Numidia (present-day Algeria). Born of an intemperate pagan father and a devout Christian mother, Augustine undoubtedly heard the Gospel early in life, but at first he resisted it. Instead, he pursued a life indistinguishable from the lives of his young, well-to-do pagan friends. As a boy he apparently exhibited considerable academic proficiency, and was therefore afforded an excellent education by his ambitious parents. His academic success earned for him the support of a wealthy patron, who paid for his further education at a prominent school in Carthage. Having enrolled there at age seventeen, Augustine performed well and became a top student in rhetoric.

At Carthage, however, Augustine was easily drawn to the sensual life. He took a mistress, fathered a son out of wedlock, and immersed himself in the theater. Bothered by the Christian teaching and example of his mother, he began to feel guilty about his life of idle pleasure. Searching for something better, he read Cicero and became enamored of the quest for truth and wisdom. He became involved in gnosticism as practiced by a cultic group known as the Manichees. He was powerfully attracted by the allure of the Manichees' apparent intellectualism and inclusion of Christian-sounding concepts. Young Augustine committed himself to the life of a philosopher, and soon became a highly regarded teacher of rhetoric, first in Carthage, later in Rome, and finally in Milan, Italy.

In Milan, Augustine studied classical philosophy and was much influenced by the writings of Plato and his followers. He was especially attracted to those aspects of Plato's writings that seemed to be speaking to some of his own moral and philosophical concerns, especially his nagging concerns about God. In his autobiographical *Confessions,* Augustine stated that he could agree with Plato, "who said that the true God is at once the author of things, the illuminator of truth, and the giver of happiness."[1]

At this same time Augustine came under the influence of Ambrose, Bishop of Milan, and his associates. Under deep conviction concerning his sin nature as well as specific past sins, Augustine was converted to Christ and was baptized by Ambrose on Easter day, 387.

The next year Augustine returned to his hometown, where he established a community of disciples, serving as their teacher and spiritual leader. At this time he also began serious writing, combining what he had learned from classical philosophy with the truth revealed in Scripture. Out of this came a body of work almost all of which is preserved intact and is read and studied to this day. Augustine's writing is greater in volume and is generally considered greater in importance than that of any other post-Apostolic ancient author.

In the beginning of his writing career, Augustine wrote on complex philosophical and doctrinal subjects, always from a scriptural perspective. The problem of the existence of evil, the acquisition and importance of language, and the process of teaching and learning were among his earliest subjects.

Augustine's fame grew as a powerful expositor and interpreter of Scripture. In 391 he was called by a congregation of believers at Hippo to be their presbyter, and five years later was appointed Bishop of Hippo. In that capacity he served as pastor, teacher, and writer for the rest of his life. He died in 430 in Hippo, while that city was under siege by the Vandals.

Augustine relied on Scripture as he addressed the classical questions of philosophy: Who is God? What is the soul? What does it mean to exist? How do we know we exist? What is time? Yet, he is not generally remembered as a great philosopher. He is remembered as a defender of the church against false teaching and unscriptural doctrines. Among the doctrinal issues he tackled were the incursion of pagan, gnostic ideas into the teachings and practices of the church; unscriptural teaching about human free will versus divine sovereignty; claims that man is born innocent as opposed to being born a sinner; confusion about divine foreknowledge and predestination; and whether or not we can do good apart from God's enabling grace.

Augustine had a massive, decisive, correcting, and protecting effect on the beliefs, teachings, and practices of the church, and on all of Western society, throughout the medieval period. Within months of Augustine's death Hippo was conquered by the Vandals, and Augustine's parishioners and students either fled or were killed. Two centuries later the same area was conquered by the followers of Mohammed, who control it to this day. Augustine and his parishioners may have perished, but Augustine's legacy lived on in his writings, in his arguments for the faith.

This bulwark stood against the onslaught of false teaching for a thousand years. Only after the Roman Catholic Church allowed Augustine's doctrinal bulwark to deteriorate did the ancient ideas against which Augustine had argued flourish again, refashioned in modern garb. Augustine's arguments against these ancient heresies were reinvigorated and reapplied, outside of the Roman Church, through the efforts of Calvin, Luther, and the other Protestant Reformers. But even this reinvigoration of Augustine's arguments began to wane in the Protestant churches in another 400 years, and it was these same ancient ideas against which Augustine had fought, once again allowed to flourish, that set the intellectual, cultural, and religious stage for the eventual development of Freud's psychoanalysis.

Historian Hanna Arendt calls Augustine "the one great thinker who lived in a period which in some respects resembled our own more than any other in recorded history."[2] During Augustine's peak years, the great Roman civilization was crumbling all around him; are we not in similar ways witnessing the crumbling of our own culture? Every day we see advanced atheistic materialism masquerading as science, deconstruction and disavowal of absolute truth posing as philosophy, New Age occultism offering transcendent experiences, and psychologized Christianity offering a false gospel.

In the following three chapters we will explore three prominent ideas from the ancient world against which Augustine successfully battled. These were Pelagianism, gnosticism, and some aspects of Platonism. Even though Augustine seemingly vanquished the threat of these three ideas against the church 1,500 years ago, the ideas remained, as if in waiting, for a time when Augustine's influence would wane. We will hear a respected historian of psychoanalysis lament the influence of Augustine as one of the great "anti-psycho-analytic forces in Western culture"—ironic evidence of how desperately the church needs an Augustine today.

SEVEN

~~~

PELAGIAN ROOTS; AUGUSTINE'S ANSWER

As the Christian church grew in size and influence, the need for clear, concise, and understandable expressions of its doctrines became obvious. It became clear that unless the church assiduously maintained belief in, and adherence to, "certain specific and well-defined teachings, it will gradually dissolve, and in any case cannot be considered a Christian community."[1] Christianity is a revealed religion, the substance of which was "once for all entrusted to the saints" (Jude 3) and recorded in Scripture. Over time, theologians have progressively helped us understand what was proclaimed to the first believers by Jesus and the apostles and faithfully recorded in Scripture. These theologians have clarified and codified an authoritative or "orthodox" body of doctrine. This clarification has always been occasioned by honest questions, challenges, and differing interpretations of Scripture. Some of these different views and interpretations have been of such error, have been so intolerable, and have been so destructive of the truth of the Gospel that they have been called heresies. One such doctrinal controversy, of particular interest in understanding modern psychotherapy, involved the errant teaching of a monk named Pelagius.

Pelagius was the clerical name taken by a man from the British Isles who was perhaps Welsh and perhaps originally named Morgan. He was born in the middle of the fourth century, became a simple monk, studied Greek theology, and by the year 409 had moved from the distant edge to the very center of the Roman Empire, into Rome itself. "He was then at the height of his creative powers, a man of culture and character, sensitive to the moral corruption of the times and seeking both reform and the propagation of Christianity."[2] In 409 Pelagius published his *Defense of the Freedom of the Will*. In this and other writings he advocated man's ability to improve himself and his world, with or without God's involvement. Here are examples of Pelagius' views as quoted by Augustine:

> We have implanted in us by God a possibility for acting in both directions (toward good or evil). . . . But that we really do a good thing, or speak a good word, or think a good thought, proceeds from our own selves. . . . Nothing good, and nothing evil . . . is born with us, but is done by us . . . with a capacity for either conduct.[3]

Pelagius did not emphasize trust and obedience or the life of faith as much as he embraced monkish legalism, self-discipline, asceticism, and self-created righteousness. As historian Philip Schaff explains, "Faith with him, was hardly more than a theoretical belief; the main thing in religion was moral action, the keeping of the commandments of God by one's own strength."[4] His beliefs about the nature of mankind are further revealed in a letter he wrote to a well-known and virtuous nun. This letter made Pelagius the focus of widespread controversy:

> As often as I have to speak concerning moral improvement and the leading of a holy life, I am accustomed first to set forth the power and quality of human nature, and to show what it can accomplish.[5]

Living in Rome, with all of its corruption both secular and clerical, Pelagius taught that people could and should improve themselves, that they could repair their own corrupted morals as well as those of society. In that corrupted environment, Pelagius and his views became popular among Christians and non-Christians alike, and he gained growing numbers of adherents. Two of his strongest followers and spokesmen were Coelestius, a prominent lawyer, and Julian, Bishop of Eclanus. Pelagius and Coelestius traveled to North Africa in 410 in an apparent effort to meet and dialogue with Augustine, who was by then bishop of Hippo and already an outspoken critic of Pelagius. Augustine was, however, occupied in Carthage and never actually met Pelagius. From North Africa Pelagius traveled eastward to Jerusalem, while Coelestius went to Carthage, where he tried to sway believers to Pelagian views and sought to become a presbyter of the church. This occasioned bitter dispute. In 412, a council of the church in Carthage, presided over by Augustine himself, charged Coelestius with advocating the following erroneous beliefs of his mentor Pelagius:

1. Adam was created mortal, and would have died, even if he had not sinned.
2. Adam's fall injured himself alone, not the human race.
3. Children come into the world in the same condition as Adam was before the Fall.
4. Humanity neither dies in consequence of Adam's fall nor rises again in consequence of Christ's resurrection.
5. Unbaptized children, as well as others, have eternal life.
6. The law, as well as the Gospel, leads to the kingdom of heaven.
7. Even before Christ, there were sinless people.

Because he refused to recant these views, Coelestius was excommunicated by the Carthage council. By 414 Pelagius was in Jerusalem and was gaining many adherents. The Eastern church had not yet grappled with the mysterious relationship between divine sovereignty and human free will, though in the Western church Augustine and others had been writing on these complex subjects for some years. The controversy between Pelagius' supporters and his critics waged back and forth, pitting theologians of the East against those of the West, until 418, when Pope Zosimus, on the advice of Augustine and 200 other bishops, issued an encyclical pronouncing anathema against Pelagius and Coelestius. Anyone who might support Pelagius or his views "was to be deposed, banished from his church, and deprived of his property."[6] Such was the zeal of the early church in establishing true doctrine and eliminating error.

Following this papal condemnation, Pelagius, Coelestius, and Julian fled to Constantinople, where they were welcomed by Nestorius, a patriarch of the Eastern church. Nothing definitive is known of the activities or fate of either Pelagius or Coelestius beyond the year 429. Julian supposedly died about 450 in Sicily. In 431, the Third Ecumenical Council of Ephesus officially rejected Nestorius and condemned Pelagius and Coelestius along with him. In spite of this, the views of Pelagius smoldered along until specifically condemned by the church at the Council of Orange in 539. In condemning Pelagianism, that council affirmed the "position on sin and grace which had been so sharply and so unyieldingly formulated by Augustine" more than a century before.[7]

For the two decades during which Pelagius and his disciples tried to advocate his errant doctrines, his chief adversary was Augustine. Much of what we know today of the views of Pelagius is contained in the body of Augustine's writings against them. What we understand today of sin and grace, human freedom, and God's sovereignty was unfolded from Scripture by Augustine in his battle against the Pelagian heresy. It was upon the work of Augustine that Pope Zosimus, the Council of Ephesus, and finally the Council of Orange depended for clarification and condemnation of Pelagianism. It is upon that body of work and out of those early church controversies that we have today the established doctrine of original sin, and what understanding we are able to have of human free will and its relationship to divine sovereignty.

It is important that modern-day Christians understand the views of Pelagius, why they were considered heretical by the early church, and why they should still be considered heretical wherever they appear today. Pelagius was unable to comprehend and unwilling to accept the mysterious relationship between the apparently independent ability of humans to make choices and decisions—to choose to do good or evil, to love or to hate—and what Scripture says about the omnipotence and omniscience of our eternal, sover-

eign Creator God. Pelagius reasoned, from a purely human perspective, that if God is truly sovereign then humans must be mere
robots. And if humans are mere robots, then the bad things they do
makes God the author of evil. Pelagius solved that dilemma by reasoning that humans must have sufficient freedom of their own will,
enough autonomy, to be able on their own to choose good and avoid
evil. Pelagius saw pagans doing "good" works; thus he reasoned that
humans must have within themselves an inherent capacity to do
good that does not spring from or depend on God's involvement in
any way.

Pelagius' conclusion that the human will is free led him also to
conclude that sin is the result of a defect in this will, an error, a
wrong choice, rather than the product of an inherent proclivity
toward sin. He emphatically denied the doctrine of original sin and
the teaching that the sin and guilt of Adam was applied to all
mankind. He thus argued that babies are born innocent and at birth
are like Adam was before he chose to sin. He saw man as having a
need, as well as the ability, to define his own self, to create his own
moral and ethical values. He saw education and training as important in this process, and extended this to his claims that man could
build upon this inborn force for good to transform society, reverse
corruption, and create a kind of paradise on earth.

For Pelagius, God's involvement in the life of man is to lovingly
assist him—to work with him—in man's own personal and societal
quest toward self-fulfillment, peace, and happiness. Having given
the natural capacity for good to all people, God's involvement was
not absolutely required for these achievements; His involvement
merely gave them more "vigor."[8] For Pelagius, God's grace is
intended for all mankind, who "are able to attain unto faith and to
deserve God's grace" by good works and keeping the commandments.[9] Thus for Pelagius, acts of love and the personal development of one's self became the meaning and purpose of life. God's
involvement was a matter of contract or choice in which a person
might make a "commitment" to God, might "consider" His will,
and might "appreciate" His help. Pelagius put his hope in mankind
first and in God only secondarily. Pelagius agreed that only the faith-

ful can go to heaven, but one is defined as "faithful" by virtue of intelligence, choice, commitment, willpower, and works, rather than by trusting in Christ.

At least fifteen of Augustine's collected works were occasioned by the accelerating heretical influence of Pelagius. Much of his concern resulted from his receipt of numerous letters and inquiries from believers confused by Pelagius' teaching. As Schaff explains, while Pelagius wrote and taught in defense of the freedom of human will, Augustine demonstrated from Scripture and from reason that the human will is impotent and in bondage to sin:

> If human nature is uncorrupted, and the natural will competent to do good, we need no Redeemer to create in us a new will and a new life, but merely an improver and ennobler; and salvation is essentially the work of man. The Pelagian system has really no place for the ideas of redemption, atonement, regeneration, and a new creation. It substitutes for them our own moral effort to perfect our natural powers, and the mere addition of grace as a valuable aid and support.[10]

During medieval times some tried to accommodate the views of Pelagius and Augustine. "Semi-Pelagianism" and "Semi-Augustinianism" are names given to this effort, which was encouraged by the understandable attractiveness of the Pelagian idea that man is naturally good and can improve himself—as opposed to the "morally and emotionally . . . dreadful" Augustinian explanations of predestination and of the human will being in bondage, totally unable of itself to freely choose good and avoid guilt.[11] The Augustinian view prevailed for the most part in the church and in European culture until the Enlightenment.

In a highly regarded paper first published in 1952, Silvano Arieti, an enduring icon of the psychotherapy community, speculated as to why it took until the late nineteenth century for someone like Freud to appear on the scene and originate psychoanalysis. Arieti credits three "anti-psychoanalytic" forces in Western culture as preventing the earlier advent of psychoanalysis. The first of these forces, according to Arieti, was the emphasis on rational, logical thinking as espoused by Plato and his student Aristotle, "which diverted the interest of the people from the irrational, the specific and the subjective . . . enough to prevent dynamic psychiatry for twenty-five centuries."[12] The second of these "anti-psychoanalytic" forces was "the suppression of the sensory and the emotional," by which, for the most part, Arieti means unrestrained sexual pleasure. This "thirty-five-century long suppression of emotion and sexual pleasure" he credits originally to the Jews and laments the fact that it was taken up as a moral tenet of Christianity. Finally, Arieti credits Augustine's ideas about sin, his "moral evaluation of behavior" from a sin-perspective, with forestalling Western man "from studying the psychological, nonjudgmental motivation of phenomena."[13] In other words, Arieti is telling us that the "anti-psychoanalytic" influence of Christianity is what held back the invention of psychoanalysis! He notes several times in his paper that, as the influence of the church in Europe waned after the Renaissance and during the Enlightenment, interest in the irrational, the speculative, and the subjective increased. Attitudes relaxed against sensuality and freedom of sexual expression. The "obsession about sin" dissipated and was progressively replaced with the nonjudgmental psychological understanding of human motivation and behavior. "That emotional insight which was lost twenty-five centuries ago, has now to be recaptured. At the same time, the . . . focus of attention is shifted from the judgmental point of view to that of . . . inner feelings . . . to see the world not from a point of view of what is right or wrong, of the shoulds and should-nots, but from the point of what . . . feelings really are, once they are divested of this authoritarian ethic."[14] For Arieti and for Freud and for their followers, this is progress!

Arieti is surely correct in concluding that the waning influence of orthodox, historic Christianity has allowed the development of new, unscriptural ideas about people and their problems. Following the Renaissance and during the Enlightenment, the rigor of Aristotle's logic and its emphasis on orderly, rational thinking was progressively replaced with subjective, speculative, introspective thinking, especially in "nonmaterial" areas such as the study of the human mind. Where there had been control over sexual expression, freedom of expression became increasingly permitted and encouraged. And most pertinent to the focus of this chapter, the ancient and alluring views of Pelagius—that man is born good, not born in sin—crept again out from under the once protective but now waning influence of Augustine.

PELAGIANISM'S ROMAN CATHOLIC AND ARMINIAN PATHWAYS TO THE PRESENT

Until about 590, the debate between the views of Augustine and those of Pelagius was one of the most important issues facing believers. Even though the views of Augustine and the actions of the early church leaders against Pelagianism would seem to have vanquished Pelagian influence, remnants of his attractive heresy survived into medieval times. From 590 until 1517, when the Reformation began, the development of Christian doctrine was almost exclusively the province of the Roman Catholic Church. During this time the Roman Church established the doctrines of purgatory, prayer to Mary, saints, and angels, canonization of saints, celibacy of the priesthood, saying the rosary, transubstantiation, confession to priests, and the various official sacraments. Other controversies took place around the subjects of worshiping images, the split between the Eastern and Western churches, predestination, atonement, and the authority of the pope. These years also saw the establishment of professional theological schools ("scholae") and professional theologians ("scholastics"), who emphasized rationalism and the methods of philosophy as the preferred way of defending the faith. Theology, as a result, came to be more of a rational, philosophical enterprise than an explaining of what Scripture had to say on particular subjects. Important for our considerations here was the progressive movement on the part of the church and its scholastics away from the views of Augustine. Increasingly, man was viewed by "rational" theologian-philosophers as "cooperating" with God in the process of salvation and sanctification. The role of works or good deeds became increasingly important. The gradual adoption of the seven official sacraments especially tended to establish human endeavor as the key to the Christian life:

> During the medieval period, the Roman Catholic view of anthropology emerged—man originally possessed a righteousness that was supernaturally endowed; he was not morally neutral. As a result of the Fall, man lost his supernatural righteousness, but he did not lose his natural abilities. The result was not total depravity but rather moral neutrality out of which man had the ability to cooperate with God in salvation.[15]

As time passed, the Roman church moved increasingly toward Pelagianism. It concluded that human will was not destroyed by the Fall: Mankind could choose on his own to do good, he could choose to cooperate with God in salvation. Most Catholic theologians agreed that God's grace was required for salvation, but it was a grace variously defined and understood. The emphasis was on man freely being able to commit himself to the faith, accept the gift of God's grace, and cooperate with God in producing good works. In this system, assurance of salvation, often called "eternal security," was unattainable; such assurance had to be "re-obtained" over and over again by sacraments and works.

During the sixteenth century, the Roman Church was challenged by those within its own ranks who sought to call it back to its historical foundations in Scripture. These theologians, who would become known as the Protestant Reformers, did not intend to divide but rather to repair the church. A central concern of the Reformers was the degree to which the church had adopted a Pelagian view of man, free will, original sin, and the means of justification and salvation.

In the face of these attempted reforms, the Roman Church convened the Council of Trent (1545–1563). Rather than consider and positively address the Protestant concerns, this council solidly affirmed and established as Roman Catholic exactly those positions on grace, the authority of Scripture, the sacraments, the authority of the pope, the church as God's kingdom on earth, and the liturgy of the Mass, that had incited the Reformers in the first place. This council and its edicts solidified Roman Catholic theology and church practice for the next 400 years.

In 1962, the 400-year reign of Trent was overturned by the Second Vatican Council. This council was called in response to those within the Catholic Church who advocated the use of modern philosophical approaches to theology, a greater emphasis on layperson advocacy and leadership, a change in the liturgy of the Mass, the inclusion of other faiths in the Roman camp, and an emphasis on individual religious liberty. In many ways, as a result of Vatican II, what was once a concise theology and practice has become, for Catholics, an uncertain and highly relativistic religion. Unchanged, however, is the long-held emphasis on human endeavor in salvation and on our ability to choose, of our own initiative, to do good and to commit our lives to God. Such theology is based on the ancient Pelagian view of original innocence. The stream of Pelagianism runs deep and straight in Roman Catholic theology and church practice. This is the view that inspires Catholic missionary endeavor and its "dialogue" with other faiths and even the un-faithed. Through the doctrines and practices of the immensely influential Roman Catholic Church, it can only be concluded that the heresy of Pelagius has found an especially effective pathway from ancient times into our present times and thinking.

Another pathway that the Pelagian heresy took to our present time was through the teaching and influence of the Dutch theologian Jacobus Arminius (1560–1609) and his numerous followers. Having studied under Calvin's successor Beza at Geneva, Arminius became most famous for advocating a position on human free will versus divine sovereignty distinctly different from, and seemingly in reaction to, that of John Calvin. Arminius taught that we have the ability to choose between good or evil, with or without God's involvement. Like Pelagius, Arminius believed that anything less than such an understanding of human free will would necessitate man being a "robot" and God therefore being "responsible" for evil in the world. Arminius and his followers teach that only Adam, not all mankind, was made guilty by Adam's sin, but that all people "receive a sinful disposition or a tendency to sin as an inheritance from Adam."[16] They teach that "God bestows upon each individual from the dawn of consciousness a special influence of the Holy Spirit, which is sufficient to counteract the effect of the inherited depravity and to make obedience possible, provided the human will cooperates, which it has the power to do."[17] Arminians hold that God gives each person "the ability to turn to God in faith and repentance, and in fact influences the sinner to do this unless he or she specifically resists it."[18] For Arminians, then, people may be born with a tendency toward sin, but over and against that tendency every person has a "special influence" on his free will that allows and encourages him to choose goodness over evil.

From Holland, the views of Arminius spread to Switzerland, Germany, England, and America. John Wesley is credited with establishing Arminian views in England and being responsible for their spread to America. Arminianism is today a position formally held by many evangelical Christians and unofficially practiced by many others:

> Among denominations in contemporary evangelicalism, Methodists and Nazarenes tend to be thoroughly Arminian, whereas Presbyterians and the Christian Reformed tend to be thoroughly Reformed. Both views are found among Baptists, Episcopalians, dispensationalists, Evangelical Free Churches, Lutherans, the Churches of Christ and most charismatic and Pentecostal groups.[19]

> We shall probably not be wrong if we suggest that most modern-day Protestants . . . are consciously or unconsciously more Pelagian than Augustinian, more Arminian than Calvinistic.[20]

WHY THE ISSUE OF PELAGIANISM IS SO IMPORTANT

The culture of a people is greatly shaped by its dominant religious beliefs. Throughout much of the history of Europe, its culture was shaped by historic, orthodox Christianity—for the most part the Christianity explicated by Augustine. During and since the Enlightenment, the dominant religious beliefs of Europeans have shifted progressively from historic Christianity to what today might be considered the "replacement religion" of humanism, with its fundamental beliefs in utilitarianism and pluralistic relativism: Something is good if it works well for the greatest number, and what is true for you may not be true for me, but tolerance is the highest virtue. This same development has taken place in America, although perhaps delayed in its progression by the forestalling effects of Protestant Christianity, which were more long-lived and vigorous in America than in Europe.

The religion of a people can also be greatly shaped by its culture, but only if that religion has lost its vigor. Historic Christianity, first in Europe and later in America, has not only been shaped by but has actually been discarded by those cultures—but only after and because it lost its vigor. The history of the discarding of the historic Christian faith in Europe and America makes interesting if not disconcerting reading and is well delineated by others.[21] In general, however, the reasons for the discarding of the faith are today no different from what they have been from the beginning. The once seemingly faithful are simply quite willingly led astray by attractive ideas and promises, by false but alluring teachers, by false but convincing signs and wonders, by "godless chatter and the opposing ideas of what is falsely called knowledge [or science]" (1 Tim. 6:20). The seemingly faithful formerly guarded what was entrusted to them by adhering to and vigorously defending the fundamentals of the faith; by firmly upholding and seriously studying Scripture as inspired, authoritative, and sufficient; and by speaking out the truth of the Gospel to the unsaved, into the culture and against its sins. As time passed, however, they willingly gave themselves over to other attractive but false ideas, and in the process lost their connection with the true faith.

One of the most attractive ideas of all is that we humans were actually born innocent, with all the natural potential to become happy, successful, and peaceful people, and that we would *be* so had we not been victimized by our environment. Our troubles and troublesomeness are necessarily the responsibility of someone or something else. The achievement of personal happiness, then, lies at the end of a personal endeavor toward righting those wrongs done to us by others. Ultimately, however, all of this succession of attractive ideas rests upon the assumption that we were originally innocent or at least morally neutral, capable of choosing good and possessing a free will. Whether this idea has come down to our time through Protestantism in its Arminian form, through Roman Catholicism, through the teachings of other religions and philosophies, or simply through the absence of clear teaching from a vigorous Christian church, makes little difference. These assumptions of original innocence, ability to choose good, free will—and their paradoxical accompaniment, the rationale of environmental determinism—are the assumptions, the beliefs, that serve as the foundation of the entire insight-oriented psychotherapy industry today.

Christians should not be confused or misled on these issues. Scripture clearly teaches the doctrine of original sin. Those who call themselves Christians and who do not accept the doctrine of original sin are taking a name upon themselves that has no real meaning. To deny this fundamental understanding of human nature is to deny who God is and what Jesus did for us on the cross. To deny the doctrine of original sin is to strip God of His attributes. To deny original sin is to deny the Messiah His identity and purpose. If we are actually only victims and not sinners, then we do not need a savior. If we are originally innocent or neutral, if we can do good without God, then we can eventually become God. If we can simply choose to commit ourselves to God in a contract, then God is a liar, Scripture is false, Jesus was a lunatic, and we are totally on our own.

This is the fundamental approach of insight-oriented psychotherapy: We are innocent victims. We are on our own. "If it's going to be, it's up to me."[22]

EIGHT

❧

GNOSTIC ROOTS; AUGUSTINE'S ANSWER

In modern-day insight-oriented psychotherapy, participants focus on themselves, their own "stories," their own emotions, their own feelings. The therapy is directed toward self-validation, self-actualization, self-development, and self-cure. It requires the participation of a therapist, who affirms, accepts, clarifies, and encourages the client toward self-understanding and the achievement of a better, more effective, more independent "higher self," with an expected state of pleasure, devoid of guilt and shame. The achievement of this "higher" state of emotional existence is possible, according to psychoanalytic theory, because man is born not only with a "clean slate" but also with "a spark of the divine," a natural predisposition toward love and goodness. This higher self may have been inhibited, oppressed, abused, malnurtured, or neglected, but it is never fully extinguished.

The achievement of self-actualization or the higher self does not come easily. Psychotherapy involves work and struggle. Step by step, clients resolve "conflicts" within themselves between their inherent goodness and the inhibitory effects of the body and world in which they live. As they resolve conflicts within themselves they move to higher levels of awareness and mastery. Uncomfortable realities must be acknowledged and then mastered. New skills must be acquired. Traumatic experiences from the past must be resurrected, re-experienced, relived, sometimes re-remembered, and "worked through." All of this is necessary on the personal path toward enlightenment and self-actualization. The therapist assists in this quest by drawing from a well of supposedly scientific and certainly secret wisdom. He is an exalted member of a select and elite group of "professionals," able to understand what the troubled client has not been able to understand, and to bring light where there has been darkness, doubt, and despair.

Ever since the Fall, mankind has desired to know everything. Man naturally seeks to explain all that he perceives. He demands to understand his reality fully and tends to have no respect for limits placed upon such understanding. The more mysterious the perception, the more man endeavors to derive his own explanation. Elsewhere we have observed the desire to "know the mind of God" as the ultimate quest of admittedly atheistic, naturalistic science. The greater the mystery, the greater will be fallen man's desire to know and the more fervent will be his effort to do so:

> "For God knows that when you eat of it your eyes will be opened, and you will be like God, knowing good and evil." (Gen. 3:5)

Being like God, knowing good and evil, having all the answers: This is the essence of the desire. From the dawn of creation, the desire for human solutions has tempted mankind to stray from simple faith, simple trust, and simple obedience.

From the earliest days of the church there has existed a tendency to follow unbelievers in placing more importance on human knowledge and human endeavor than on revealed knowledge. The Christian heresy known as "gnosticism" is a theological system that asserts that "over and above the simple Gospel, which is all the ordinary spirits can understand, there is a secret higher knowledge reserved for an elite."[1] Whereas that other great tendency among believers, to see salvation as available through good works and keeping of the law, "was more of a practical than a theological problem for the early church," this overemphasis on knowledge "produced one theological problem after another . . . [and] . . . has continued to reproduce itself within Christianity and reappears from time to time in new guises."[2]

GNOSTICISM IN ANCIENT TIMES AND IN THE EARLY CHURCH

Already widespread throughout the Greek and Roman Empires prior to the time of Christ, gnosticism affected all religious, intellectual, and philosophical aspects of the ancient world and challenged and invaded the early church from its surrounding culture. The widespread attractiveness and enduring presence of gnosticism can be traced to its two most fundamental aspects: It claimed to offer secret wisdom explaining the most profound mysteries of life, and it claimed that this secret wisdom was available only to an elite group of intellectuals. The presence of gnosticism in the earliest days of the church is evidenced by the fact that the apostles themselves wrote against the incursion of gnostic teachings. Paul deals with gnosticism in his two letters to the Corinthians (e.g., 1 Cor. 1:26-27) and in his letter to the Colossians; the apostle John deals with it in his first letter.

The early Church Fathers Justin and Irenaeus considered Simon the Sorcerer (Acts 8:9-25) to be the forefather of gnosticism in the church. The early church historian Eusebius of Caesarea (ca. 264–339) agreed, and mentioned Menander, a successor to Simon the Sorcerer, who in turn had his own two disciples named Saturninus and Basilides, who established "ungodly heretical schools" in Syria and Egypt respectively.[3] But the first gnostics may have appeared long before the time of Christ, "on the fringes of Judaism."[4] The few actual gnostic writings available today and the abundant early church writing against gnosticism point to the presence of and influence of Old Testament texts and errant Jewish interpretations of those texts in the early development of ancient gnosticism. Other religious traditions also played a part in the origin of gnosticism. Even more powerful an influence was Greek philosophy. "The Platonic dualism of spirit and matter, soul and body, God and world, good versus evil, also had considerable importance for Gnosis."[5] In the Greek Empire after Alexander, such religious and philosophical ideas spread far and wide along with Greek culture and language. As the Empire spread, it "conquered" local religions, often by mixing them with those of the Greeks. Gnosticism seemed to grow in this syncretism and was in key ways characterized by the principal religious beliefs and practices of those times. One of those beliefs was that redemption from the troubles of this earthly life is available through "traditional but often reinterpreted cultic practices, faith, knowledge, wisdom, i.e., intellectual attitudes."[6]

During the first two centuries after Christ, as the church focused on the simple preaching of the Gospel and the building up of its numerous new members, many of the more intellectual Christians were seeking ways to relate their faith to the mysteries of life:

> Gnosticism was a response to the widespread desire to understand the mystery of being: It offered detailed secret knowledge of the whole order of reality, claiming to know and to be able to explain things of which ordinary, simple Christian faith was entirely ignorant. It divided mankind into various classes, and reserved its secret wisdom for those who were recognized as belonging to the highest, most spiritual class, a religious elite.[7]

Gnosticism found in early Christianity an easy target. The canon of Scripture had not yet been established or even widely circulated. There did not yet exist a well-developed body of church doctrine. As a result many of the terms, concepts, and even practices of the faith could be expanded upon and reinterpreted in terms of the gnostic system which was, in contrast, already well-established and widely influential. Terms and concepts such as creator, logos, redeemer, salvation, sanctification, eternity, and the Spirit "could all be detached from their historical roots in the life and teachings of Jesus and the apostles, and interpreted as universally valid philosophical and religious ideas."[8] Gnosticism's claim of a "revealed" truth was resonant with the beliefs of early Christians, helping to ease its incursion into the church. Early Christians were attracted to self-denial and personal discipline. These practices were advocated by gnostics, who explained them with the attractive dualistic idea that flesh is evil and spirit is good. As a result of these superficial similarities between Christianity and ancient gnosticism, increasing numbers of early church leaders began to adapt Christian doctrine to the gnostic system and to teach this heretical adaptation to all who were interested.

Gnosticism's incursion into the early church was so persistent and subtle, as well as so destructive, that it occasioned what may be considered the first significant and comprehensive statements of Christian doctrine. In the years 180–189 Irenaeus wrote his five-volume work, *The Unmasking and Refutation of Falsely So-Called Gnosis:*

> Thus we see that one of the earliest significant works of Christianity was the direct result not of any desire to produce a comprehensive theology, but grew out of the necessity to deal with a dangerous and persistent heresy. The fact that [it] is so comprehensive is due in no small measure to the fact that the heresy against which it speaks was not limited to a partic-ular point of doctrine, but was an alternative vision of reli-gious reality spanning a wide range of doctrines.[9]

Gnosticism seized upon an opportunity to fill a vacuum in the early church. Where the early church had not yet grappled with cer-tain questions of its followers and its challengers, where it had not yet begun to fully and sufficiently unfold from Scripture its teach-ing as to the "mysteries" of life, there gnosticism entered with its own brand of alluring and attractive answers. Answers from Scripture were yet to be provided in some areas, and whenever "Christian thinkers fail to do this, or do an inadequate job of it, gnosticism will almost invariably arise in some variety of reincarna-tion."[10] I would argue that, into a similar religious vacuum, late in the nineteenth century, Freud entered with his own reincarnation of gnosticism. Psychoanalysis had its own secret wisdom revealed to an elite, who then were able to provide through "knowledge" and techniques the answers to the mysteries of the degeneration of earthly life, thereby bringing redemption.

Ancient gnosticism appealed to man's ever-present desire to know, on his own terms, the answer to all of his questions. It claimed to fully explain the origin of the cosmos, the present condition of man, how man can obtain redemption from his present state, the course of that redemption, the role of a redeemer, and what the future holds for man and the cosmos. The central myth of gnosticism involves the presence in man of a "divine spark" or spirit, which has fallen from the divine world into, and suffers in, the corrupted material world—and which can be restored to the divine world. This process of restoration takes place only through the acquisition of "knowledge" (gnosis), which leads from a lower state of existence to a higher state of blissful reunion with the eternal cosmic principle.

Ancient gnosticism was essentially "dualistic." It conceived of all reality as composed of two fundamental principles, good and evil, which were constantly either in balance or in conflict with each other. As such it conceived of the material world as evil and dark and in conflict against "a higher world which . . . culminates in the assumption of a new otherworldly and unknown God, who dwells beyond all visible creation and is the real lord of the universe."[11] While Christianity often speaks of a conflict between flesh and spirit, evil and good, this conflict is not for Christianity the ultimate and fundamental explanation of the nature of all reality. Ancient gnosticism could not accept God as Creator of man, of both his body and his spirit. It could not accept that man, both in his body and in his spirit, is in rebellion against God. It could not accept a single, spiritual God, who purposely created all reality as an entity distinct from Himself but with which He is personally involved and over which He is all-sovereign.

The term gnosticism derives from the word *gnosis,* which derives from the Greek word meaning knowledge or understanding. The "knowledge" of interest to gnostics was far beyond mere factual, intellectual, philosophical, or religious information. It included all of that, but more importantly it was a kind of knowledge that had a life-transforming, redeeming effect. The content of this redeeming knowledge was certainly religious, historical, mythological, philosophical, highly intellectualized, and truly esoteric, but its difference from other knowledge was in its effect. This knowledge (gnosis) had the power to release man from bondage, to redeem him.

This knowledge was provided through some kind of mysterious revelation. It was not merely gathered or learned in any conventional sense, but was made available through heavenly mediation to those who are elect and capable of receiving it. This process was understood as mysteriously uniting the ultimate knower and giver of the knowledge ("God" in Christian gnosticism), the means of knowledge (gnosis), and the divine substance (spark) deposited within every human being. "He who in this manner shall have gnosis knows whence he has come and whither he goes."[12] "He who has the gnosis is free. Ignorance is a slave."[13] "If anyone has gnosis, he is a being who comes from above."[14]

The difference between the redeeming gnosis of ancient gnosticism and the redeeming faith of Christianity is dramatic and total. "Union" with God through knowledge is as different from reconciliation with God through the Messiah as black is different from white. No wonder these teachings occasioned such zealous opposition from the apostles and early Church Fathers.

For the gnostic, ancient or modern, man is the center of all history, and in him all that is important finds meaning and expression. Man exists, however, in a material world and in a physical body that is corrupt and corrupting. His heart "is the abode of evil spirits who prevent its becoming pure, and instead treat it disgracefully through 'unseemly desires'; it is comparable to an inn, which is full of filth and dissolute men."[15] For the ancient gnostic, man was composed of both a good and an evil nature, and his observable identity was the outward result of the conflict between these two natures. In the person who had not yet received gnosis, the evil nature was always in ascendancy. Only by the receipt of gnosis could anyone achieve victory over the evil nature and begin taking on the characteristics of the good nature always within him. That good nature always within him is the deposit of the divine spark, the substance of the higher God from which every person descended in the first place. Through gnosis and then through the practice of asceticism, a small divine spark could become more and more powerful and predominant in the observable identity of the redeemed person.

For ancient gnosticism, the fact that every person has within him a spark or a divine substance indicates that he has "a kinship of nature between the highest God and the inner core of man."[16] The presence within all people of this divine substance also guarantees that redemption through gnosis or knowledge is possible. It is through that divine substance or spark that the gnosis made the redeeming connection between mankind and God. This "doctrine of the God-man" was a central gnostic tenet. One aspect of the God-man is the idea that man has within himself a substance of a God and has therefore a "supramundane" relationship with God. This supramundane relationship with God accords man the exalted metaphysical status of a heavenly being who has fallen and has been dispersed into the earthly world, waiting for redemption through gnosis.

According to ancient gnosticism, man should not think of himself as a lesser or merely created being as over and against an infinite and separate eternal God. He should think of himself as a God-man who is involved in a struggle to get back to his rightful (if temporarily disrupted) exalted state of union with God. Redemption or return to that exalted state is a promise central to gnostic thinking. The attainment of gnosis, of self-recognition of the divine spark within, leads to deliverance from worldly corruption and salvation from the force of evil within the human heart. Gnosis is the means, redemption is the promise, and reunion with God is the ultimate manifestation of that redemption. Throughout gnostic literature, self-knowledge is equated with gnosis:

> Examine yourself and know who you are and how you were and how you shall be. . . . You have already come to knowledge, and you will be called "the one who knows himself," for he who has not known himself has known nothing. But he

who has known himself has already come to knowledge concerning the depth of the ALL.[17]

According to gnosticism, ignorance or lack of gnosis prevents redemption. Hippolytus explains the gnostic hope in this quote from agnostic writers called the Peratae, whom we know about only through his work:

> If any of those who are here is able to comprehend that he is a character of the Father brought down from above and put into a body here, . . . entirely like the Father in heaven, so will such a one ascend to that place. But he who does not receive this teaching nor recognize the necessity of becoming is like an abortion born by night and will perish by night.[18]

Redemption is not automatic for everyone, according to the gnostics. Gnosis must be received, ignorance must be conquered, and gnosis "must be accompanied by a way of life which matches the acquired condition of 'one redeemed.'"[19] Having received the gnosis, the ultimate self-recognition, the gnosis-redeemed person is then able to act and live in accordance with his exalted destiny and become free of the world's corrupting influences.

As ancient gnosticism began to invade early Christianity, it tried to transform Christ into a gnostic-style redeemer figure. The concept of a redeemer is not constant throughout the highly variable world of ancient gnosticism; however this concept did exist just prior to the time of Christ. These gnostics taught that a person could not discover redemptive gnosis simply on his own, but rather that he needed some kind of granted, revelatory, redemption experience, process, or person that would show him his "calamitous situation" as well as "the possibility of deliverance."[20] Only this kind of "call" to the divine spark already present within every person could awaken the "sleeping soul" and initiate its quest for the higher self:

> Still are you asleep and dreaming. Wake up, turn about, taste and eat the true food! Impart the word and water of life!

Cease from evil desires and wishes and the (things) which are unlike (you).[21]

Therefore he who has knowledge is the one who comes from above. When he is called, he hears, answers and turns to him who calls him, ascends to him and knows how he is called. Since he has knowledge, he fulfills the will of him who called him.[22]

In this redeemer role can be fitted such varied conceptions as "the call" of gnosis upon a sleeping soul from "outside the cosmos,"[23] wisdom (sophia), understanding (nous), insight (epinoia), power of thought, "the illuminator," a "guide," a "redeemed redeemer," various historical or biblical characters, the Sorcerer, Zoroaster, Buddha, even a gnostic Jesus. "The ancient idea of the 'redeemer' corresponds more to the concept of 'liberator' or 'deliverer,' and this actually fits the gnostic 'redeemer' figures also. They are those who for the first time show to men the way to liberation from the cosmos."[24] Once redeemed by gnosis, and once this redemption is proven by actions characteristic of one who is redeemed, a person can become a "redeemer figure" or guide, a "herald of gnostic wisdom."[25] Such a guide could deliver the gnosis to the unredeemed, as a call to his divine spark, and in this way continue the work of redemption among humanity:

I, the understanding, am near the pious, good, pure, pitiful, reverent ones and my presence becomes aid, and at once they perceive the all . . .[26]

I will be saved and I will save. Amen. I will be redeemed and I will redeem. Amen.[27]

While the moral and ethical aspects of living advocated by ancient gnostics were diverse and fluid, ranging from libertinism to asceticism, the majority advocated asceticism. The early Church Fathers in general favored abstemiousness as the desired evidence of the Spirit-led, obedient Christian life. They saw it as the observable results of the desire to obey God. As a result, the early church was an easy target for invasion by gnostic ideals such as abstinence and self-control. The asceticism and abstinence of ancient gnosticism "became a popular bridge which facilitated the incursion of gnostic ideas into the Christian communities."[28] This was true even though the gnostics saw such asceticism as a way "to keep the soul free for its spiritual quest," rather than as evidence of a desire to obey God.[29] Underscoring all such practices for gnostics were the fundamental notions that gnosis, the redeeming knowledge, could be obtained through such practices; that redemption could be assured by such knowledge; and that the after-death ascent of the soul could be facilitated by certain practices in this life.

Gnostics advocated exercising control over supposedly evil bodily passions, pleasures, and feelings. The asceticism of ancient gnosticism could be extreme by modern standards. Some gnostics saw marriage and procreation as evil. Animal foods were to be avoided. The Law of the Old Testament was to be followed literally. Fasting and feast days were considered necessary for redemption. Renouncing the world, relinquishing possessions, and living by strict rules of community were all required by most gnostics. Gnosticism "leaves the decision to do what is right to human endeavor and promises a reward for those who make the effort and punishment for those who are negligent."[30]

Ancient gnosticism taught that redemption, enabled through the "call" of gnosis and then assured by "redeemed" behavior, was realized upon death. At the moment of death there began the "ascent of the soul." This upward ascent would supposedly retrace the downward original fall of the soul that placed God-men on earth in earthly bodies. The way of this ascent was a struggle, as figures and forces of evil tried to impede the pathway. Many gnostic groups advocated magical rituals and ceremonies to aid the deceased traveler on his way. Others advocated techniques and practices conducted in this life to ease one's own ascent after death. The emphasis on works and techniques, rituals and sacraments found favor with some early Christians, who decided that the gnostic approach was a more fully developed form of the Christian life.

GNOSTICISM IN AUGUSTINE'S DAY AND IN PSYCHOTHERAPY TODAY

Throughout history, philosophers and religious thinkers have been tempted to characterize man and his troubles in a gnostic manner. Man has a divine spark somewhere deep within him; he is essentially good, though thwarted. The environment, the world, the family, even the physical body are essentially bad. The bad somehow easily overpowers the good inner nature of man, and he is then troubled or causes trouble. The troubled person is therefore always a victim, and knowledge is the key to his redemption. The therapist occupies the role of redeemer. With enough effort and knowledge, the struggle can be won and the higher self can be attained.

Augustine describes the attraction of the Manichean form of gnosticism in his early life:

> It gave joy to my pride to be above all guilt, and when I did an evil deed, not to confess that I myself had done it. . . . I loved to excuse myself, and to accuse I know not what other being that was present within me but yet was not I.[31]

The intellectual aspects of gnosticism fed Augustine's pride; gnosticism was complex compared with the simplicity of the Christian Gospel, and its attribution of sin to something other than the self assuaged his agony over his own personal sinfulness. Augustine eventually realized, however, that the teachings of the Manicheans were unsatisfactory, illogical, anti-scriptural, and heretical. Credit for this realization must go, to a significant degree, to his ever-watchful mother, who constantly solicited him toward the truth of the Gospel. He was also influenced by friends who helped him see that gnostic astrology was a false science. Finally, he was disillusioned by the moral impurity of the supposedly purified Manichean teachers and leaders.

The Manichean sect of gnosticism was founded by a Persian named Mani (born c. 216), who early in life became convinced that he was a prophet of a new religion:

Wisdom and deeds have always from time to time been brought to mankind by messengers of God. So in one age they have been brought by the messenger called Buddha to India, in another by Zoroaster to Persia, in another by Jesus to the West. Thereupon this revelation has come down, the prophecy in this last age, through me, Mani, the messenger of the God of truth to Babylonia.[32]

Mani traveled throughout Asia and the Orient. On these travels he gathered religious and philosophical ideas. He wove these into existent gnostic ideas, adding them to ideas and language he borrowed from Christianity. As such, he was able to found a particularly successful and attractive brand of gnosticism offering revelation, salvation, moral virtue, "truth," and human excellence. This was all based on a Christian-sounding religion of nature and human endeavor.

Mani himself did not fare so well. In 276 he was crucified by priests of Zoroaster in Persia who were, to say the least, unimpressed with his ideas and apparent success.

The gnostics historically, and the Manicheans especially, were eager to explain the mystery of the existence of evil in a world over which God was supposedly sovereign. Typically they would try to preserve their understanding of God's character by proposing that there exists in the world a second cosmic principle—evil, or "darkness"—a force that is against God. But as Irenaeus pointed out two centuries before Augustine, when he was combating the gnostic heresy and its notion of God versus evil:

> If God permitted the creation of [evils] because powerless to prevent them, He were not omnipotent; but if he had the power to prevent and did not, He were a deceiver and hypocrite, the slave of necessity.[33]

For Augustine, and for believers today, the answer to the mystery of the existence of evil in the world lies in simply accepting God's revealed Word:

Why did God permit men to sin? you ask me; and I answer you: I can't say at all, I only believe He had reasons for doing it, reasons worthy of His infinite wisdom, but past my understanding.[34]

We humans, however, prefer not to have anything beyond our understanding, so the gnostic notion of evil existing in opposition to good, of evil being apart from and outside of good, persists even to this day. Today, however, it persists especially in the world of psychology with its conception of all human troubles coming from outside of the self.

This modern concept of man-as-victim, of evil existing outside of the naturally good self, was quite familiar to Augustine as well. As we have heard Augustine say, there was a time in his pre-Christian life when he loved the idea that his sinfulness was not of himself but came from some other source. It was this alluring, conscience-dulling aspect of the gnostic and Manichean system that was so attractive to the young pagan Augustine, just as it is attractive to people today. Augustine, however, came to understand the deception of Manicheanism:

Sinning takes place only by the exercise of the will . . . no one compelling.[35]

God is not the progenitor of things evil. . . . Evils have their being by the voluntary sin of the soul to which God gave free will.[36]

It was I who willed, I who was unwilling. It was I, even I myself. . . . Therefore was I at war with myself, and destroyed by myself.[37]

It is not some other "force" that is responsible for the sins we commit, but we ourselves. "The soul who sins is the one who will die" (Ezek. 18:20). Today the therapy client enjoys the idea that his troubles are not "him" but are the responsibility of someone else.

But Christians, recognizing the fallen nature of the human heart, should not toy with such ideas.

Another gnostic concept popular today, though revised and refined, is the useful and attractive conception of the "higher" and "lower" self. "Lower self," "id," "bad self," "neurotic self," or "injured inner child" are terms used in the therapy world to give definition and delineation to the bad effects of the past and the resultant troubles in the present. The lower self is defined as separate from the higher self, the "innocent" or "healthy" self. The modern therapy client will never admit that badness or "lower-ness" is a part of his own true nature, so he gives all of it a different name, origin, and location. The lower self is treated as if it is a material thing that can be off-loaded with proper knowledge and technique. But as Augustine argued, and as Scripture teaches, man has only one self. The one self of man is inherently sinful, given to trouble, and to the causing of trouble. There is no "other self" or "ego-alien" force or substance that is separate in any way from the one true self. There is neither higher self nor lower self; there is only self. Scripture does not allow me to claim a higher self capable of independent goodness or a lower self causing me to have troubles or to make trouble for others.

This is not to say that people with troubles or people who cause trouble for others do not suffer or have personal pain. This should be obvious to all of us, not only from our own experience and self-examination, but from our observation of those around us. Similarly, to disavow "victimhood" is not to say we are blind to the fact that individual lives have difficulty. We are all in many ways shaped by our past, burdens do weigh us down, habits are not easy to break, and memories can be exceedingly unpleasant. But the solution to these realities of life can never be gnosis and gnostic techniques. Salvation through knowledge and technique is an empty promise; perfection is not available through human endeavor. Such promises are alluring, ensnaring, prideful, vain, and pseudoscientific. They are empty of the truth of the Gospel and the enablement of the indwelling Holy Spirit. The ancient gnostics and their modern-day heirs, the psychotherapists, teach a gospel different from that presented in Scripture. They present an unbiblical view of our human problem and offer an unbiblical solution. They see our problem as the thwarting of our innate goodness by a hostile and responsible environment; the solution they offer is insight and effort.

It would be hard to imagine a society more given over than our own to the quest for self-improvement. We scan the horizon and find countless fitness centers, palm readers, self-development seminars, health food stores, road-obstructing joggers, exercising anorexics. There are countless ways for people to exercise their body and their willpower on a frantic, zealous, quasi-religious quest toward the higher self. Ideas that begin as reasonable practices of preventative medicine become techniques of zealous self-punishment and self-control that rival the bizarre rituals of asceticism railed against by Augustine 1,500 years ago.

According to this gnostic view of life, fat is evil, caffeine is evil, sugar is evil, and calories are evil. The simple pleasures of life are considered slothful and indulgent. Self-control, dietary control, muscle-building, vitamins, meditation—these are ascetic steps toward personal perfection. These become the steps of human endeavor toward the higher self. These are too often works toward a false salvation, a false redemption. These are, in God's eye, filthy rags of pride, vanity, and self-assurance.

In a world awash in the concepts and practices of insight-oriented psychotherapy, it is not at all difficult to discover evidences of its roots in ancient gnosticism. Whether it be traditional psychotherapy, self-actualization, self-empowerment, attainment of mastery, the achievement of security and significance, or the acquisition of deep insight, there is a quest for what might be called a higher self. Be it through psychotherapy, assertiveness training, self-help books, meditation, nutrition, the pursuit is the same: The client is involved in a struggle against those forces from past or present that impair his or her ascent to a higher, happier, more satisfied, more successful, more handsome self. The client is convinced that there is indeed a goodness innate within him. The expression of this "light" has been blocked, oppressed, impaired, hurt by those outside—the forces of evil or "darkness." The client fights against these obstacles (traumatic experiences, neglect, abuse, molestation, deprivation) in order to free his potential for open expression. He understands that his troubles, or the things he has done that have troubled others, are not really "him," not really a product of his true self. They are the bad effects of the corrupting world upon his otherwise innocent, pure, good, loving, "divine spark" real self. It is the corrupting effects of the environment that are responsible for the troubles and the troublemaking. The responsibility lies elsewhere, outside of the psychotherapy client—who seeks only to understand and define his higher self.

Another influence of ancient gnosticism on insight-oriented psychotherapy is evidenced in the fundamental belief that something akin to gnosis is required for the successful attainment of the higher self. Psychotherapists call this special redemptive knowledge self-understanding or insight. The attributes of insight are closely associated with a high degree of intelligence, since it is information of an esoteric sort. Insight is referred to as "deep," as if to say it is somehow profound, penetrating, clarifying, revelatory, and prophetic. It is a special kind of knowledge in that it has special power in the life of the suffering therapy client; it is capable of providing redemption from the suffering. It is a kind of knowledge that is revealed by the redeemer-therapist. It is a kind of knowledge that is highly personalized, totally unique, and not at all subject to external comparison or validation. It cannot be understood by the outsider nearly as well as it can be understood by the client and the therapist.

The redeemer-therapist of psychotherapy correlates with the redeemer figure of ancient gnosticism. Therapists today are uniformly regarded as members of an elite corps, specially gifted, specially trained. They are regarded as having special powers, garnered through training or by their own success in the struggle for attainment of the higher self. The therapist of today is assumed to possess a special kind of knowledge about the inner workings of his clients that gives him amazing abilities to "interpret" the phenomena of their lives, to interpret their dreams, even to read their minds. Having arrived at the higher state of self-understanding and mastery over the "dark forces" of his own past, the modern-day therapist is assumed to have the special ability to "redeem" others. He is assumed to have in his possession the gnosis, the secret knowledge of redemptive power. For a fee, and with many sessions, that therapist is capable of offering to the fortunate client this gift of redemption. If the client is intelligent enough, wealthy enough, well-insured, persistent, obedient, and faithful to the therapist-redeemer, he too can ascend to the higher self and perhaps become a therapist-redeemer himself!

Ancient gnosticism was a thoroughly humanistic approach to life. Its promise was based on human wisdom and human endeavor. It exalted man to the status of a God-man. It posited that within man was the divine. It advocated techniques and practices of living and thinking and feeling that could be mastered by man as long as he had the required gnosis. These attributes of ancient gnosticism survive powerfully today in insight-oriented psychotherapy, for which self-cure is a fundamental "pillar." Even though a therapist or "redeemer" is usually required for a successful therapy effort, the real change comes from the client's changed behavior, thinking, and feeling. These changes are what he does for himself, to himself. The insight or gnosis is necessary, but the effort on the part of the client is the key to attainment of the goal, to reaching the higher state of personal development and self-actualization.

The ultimate promise of ancient gnosticism was reunion with the ultimate cosmic principle; for Christian gnosticism this was called reunion with God. Being like God, becoming a god, being restored to godhood, were various articulations of the gnostic redemptive promise. Reincarnated today in the therapy industry, this same old promise is held forth—that man can and will become what he was always intended to be: exalted above pain, guilt, or shame; free of troubles; free of suffering; in charge; powerful; self-actualized, safe, and secure; restored to Eden.

NINE

❧

PLATO'S FAITH IN REASON; AUGUSTINE'S FAITH IN GOD

The success of insight-oriented psychotherapy is said to depend on the development of "insight," defined as a reasonable, acceptable, intellectual understanding of the causes of one's mental and emotional problems. Psychiatry textbooks define insight as a process "by which the meaning, significance, pattern, or use of an experience becomes clear" or understandable.[1] Simply put, insight supposedly provides the why behind the what of a person's mental and emotional problems. The promise that psychotherapy can discover the why of a troubled life is its chief and most attractive product.

Freud did not actually use the term insight; rather, he described the curative process in psychoanalysis as "riddles to be solved whose solution might be accepted by the sufferer."[2] Like so many of the terms and concepts used in psychotherapy, insight lacks a clear, concise, agreed-upon definition. The definition we have noted would not be accepted by all therapists. This lack of agreement does not, however, prevent the vast majority of insight-oriented therapists from using the term. Today even the average person on the street uses the term as if it did have some widely accepted definition.

One author states that insight "represents a complex and important tool which the patient acquires during analysis and which he must put to use in his efforts at resolution of his previously unconscious conflicts."[3] The leading textbook of psychotherapy fails to provide a single, clear definition of insight.[4] The principal American textbook of psychiatry, on the other hand, states honestly: "Insight is not fully understood. . . . Despite its presumed potency as a therapeutic agent, neither the role nor the function of insight in psychoanalysis is definitive."[5]

Aside from the fact that there is no agreed-upon definition of insight, insight-oriented psychotherapists are uncertain as to whether or not the truthfulness (the "veridicality") of the client's achieved insight, or what they might refer to as "self-understanding," is even necessary to therapy's claimed effectiveness. We have elsewhere referred to current psychotherapeutic literature's brazen resistance to any suggestion that the therapist has a responsibility to confirm the truthfulness of a client's "personal narrative."

Two principal notions about insight are, however, generally believed by therapists. The first is the notion that mere intellectual self-understanding, knowing *why,* is of little or no real value to the client unless he applies this understanding toward "working through" or self-correcting his thoughts, feelings, and behaviors. The second widely accepted notion about insight is that even valiant efforts at self-correction will be of little or no lasting value without their being informed and guided by insight. Although there is considerable confusion among psychotherapists about what insight really is and how it supposedly supports cure, most therapists believe that, without the acquisition of insight, there can be no progress toward the resolution of problems. For the practitioners and clients of psychotherapy, insight is something that cannot be defined, but without which change cannot take place! Freud stated, "We have no other means of controlling our instinctual nature but our intelligence . . . the psychological ideal [is] . . . the primacy of intelligence."[6] For Freud, and for all practitioners of psychotherapy who strive to provide insight for their clients, the goal of therapy is for the client to achieve mastery over his instincts, neuroses, and conflicts through his intelligence. The ideal result for psychotherapy is for reason to overpower the unreasonable, the rational to overpower the irrational. Only in this way can the client control his passions, his conflicts, his own unknown demons. This can only occur once those passions and conflicts have been made known and understandable—then the will can conquer them.

How far back can we trace this idea that intellectual self-understanding is absolutely required for self-change? How did we get the idea that it is possible for humans to obtain truthful, meaningful self-understanding?

Previously we have referred to a 1952 paper by Silvano Arieti, in which he comments on three "anti-psychoanalytic cultural forces" in Western civilization that for literally thousands of years augured against the development of insight-oriented psychotherapy.[7] Arieti believed that Freud's great "advance" in his "discovery" of psychoanalysis was forestalled by these three forces. These forces, according to Arieti, were: a general avoidance of the "sensory and the emotional"; an overconcern with "morality"; and a preference for "rational, objective thinking."

By avoidance of the sensory and emotional, Arieti was principally referring to the general tendency in Western culture to avoid free, unrestrained expression of sexuality in action or intellectual discussion. As long as Western culture placed restraints upon open expression of sexuality, there was no place for a man like Freud or the expression of Freud's ideas about sexuality.

By an overconcern with morality, Arieti was referring to the tendency of Western culture to assess human behavior from the standpoint of absolute truth rather than in a relative and subjective way. As long as Western culture relied on a value system that clearly delineated the "what" of life as either sin or righteousness, and subordinated any concern about the "why" to the biblical doctrine of the Fall, there was little room for Freud or his ideas.

The third anti-psychoanalytic force in Christianized Western civilization, lamented by Arieti, was a "rational objective thinking [which diverted] the attention of Western man from the irrational, the specific and the subjective [and thus] delayed the birth of psychoanalysis for twenty-five centuries."[8] Arieti was referring here to what he described as an unfortunate Western preference for "rational thinking" as over and against "a general interest in the irrational impulses of men, in uninhibited emotions, and a concern for the individuality of man's thinking."9 Obviously for Arieti, for Freud, and for those who uphold the industry of insight-oriented psychotherapy, it is the irrational, the uninhibited, the unbridled individual who is the more fertile area of interest.

The point that Arieti was trying to make in his seminal article was that finally, in the late-nineteenth century, "pro-psychoanalytic cultural forces" came to the fore and anti-psychoanalytic forces shrank to the background, making it possible at long last for someone like Freud to offer psychoanalysis to the waiting and deprived world. The pro-psychoanalytic forces, according to Arieti, were Darwinism, Existentialism, Romanticism, and Expressionism. The major *anti*-psychoanalytic force in Western culture was Christian doctrine. Arieti additionally postulated (partially incorrectly, I will argue) that the anti-psychoanalytic cultural force of rational, objective thinking was actually Platonism as it was maintained and strengthened by Plato's student Aristotle and then supposedly transmitted to Western culture by the Christian church.

Anywhere that Christianity began to lose its vigor and its influence, pagan ideas and philosophies came forward and began to exert their influence on the culture. The waning influence of Christianity in the West generally and in Europe specifically provided a cultural, artistic, scientific, and philosophical environment that was fertile for Freud's ideas. One of Freud's most fundamental teachings was that man *could* acquire reliable, truthful self-understanding, that the application of this self-understanding *could* bring about self-change, and that this self-understanding was absolutely *required* for self-change. I would agree with Arieti that only after Christianity had sufficiently waned could this Freudian idea of insight be proposed and widely accepted.

Arieti is surely accurate in seeing the acceptance of Freud's psychoanalytic theories, including his ideas about the possibility, efficacy, and necessity of insight, as dependent firstly upon tolerance for the "sensory and the emotional." Secondly, Freud's acceptance did require a deemphasis of sin and righteousness as categories of understanding human behavior. And thirdly, it required an acceptance of the irrational, the uninhibited, and the individuality of subjective experience. Freud was the right man at the right time. His ideas found just the tolerance needed for them to flourish in *fin de siecle* Europe.

According to Arieti, the previous emphasis in Western culture on the rational, objective, logical pursuit of knowledge had actively opposed any emphasis on experience, feeling, transcendence, and subjectivity. He traces the origin of this emphasis back 2,500 years to a shift in ancient Greek philosophy. For this twenty-five centuries of rational, objective thinking, and its woeful forestalling of the advent of psychoanalysis, Arieti blames Plato. He blames Plato for his philosophical contributions, and he then blames the church for supposedly adopting, transmitting, and maintaining Plato's ideas, causing them to influence Western civilization at large.

THE ANTI-PSYCHOANALYTICAL SIDE OF PLATO

Plato (428–347 B.C.) was an Athenian and a member of a noble and politically well-connected family. He was highly educated, well traveled, well read, and well versed in the intellectual concerns of his times. He was highly patriotic and would willingly have carried on the tradition of his family by becoming a statesman in service of his country. Plato became troubled, however, by what he considered the deterioration of Greek culture. He was especially troubled by the Athenian democratic system, the decline in learning, and the loss of the "historic clarity of Greek thought," accompanied by shameful public and private morals.

Plato came under the influence of the famed teacher-philosopher Socrates and accordingly became passionately interested in philosophy. He studied it with special emphasis as to its impact on personal and governmental conduct. "Socrates is said to have been the first who directed the entire effort of philosophy to the correction and regulation of manners, all who went before him having expended their greatest efforts in the investigation of physical, that is, natural phenomena."[10] Socrates applied his philosophy to "the obtaining of a blessed life," and he believed that man could come to understand "the causes of things . . . by a purified mind . . . the purification of life by good morals in order that the mind, delivered from the depressing weight of lusts, might, with purified understanding, contemplate that nature which is incorporeal and unchangeable light where live the causes of all created natures."[11]

When Socrates was condemned to death and executed in 399 B.C. (by taking the poison himself) for his supposedly corrupting ideas and for his refusal to worship the accepted gods, Plato left Athens in disgust. When he returned in 387, he had become broadly acquainted with ideas from other lands and schools of thought. Having become deeply committed to philosophy and its teaching, he founded his Academy and taught there until his death in 347. One of his most famous pupils was Aristotle, who came to the Academy at age seventeen. The Academy continued to function as a school of learning and philosophy until it was, like other such schools in Greece, abolished by the Emperor Justinian in A.D. 529.

It is generally accepted that Plato has been a significant—some would say the most significant—contributor to what is referred to as Western civilization. "Among the disciples of Socrates, Plato was the one who shone with a glory which far excelled that of the others, and who not unjustly eclipsed them all."[12] Alfred North Whitehead, the philosopher known for his "process theology," in a "spirit of rampageous over-generalization," once said that "the safest generalization of Western thought is that it consists of a series of footnotes to Plato."[13] However overstated it may be, Whitehead's assessment does reflect the lasting influence of a man who lived 2,500 years ago.

Plato assembled his body of philosophy in his *Dialogues*. The work of Plato and his Academy, and the effect it had on his many students, reestablished the historic clarity of Greek thought and also worked to turn aside many of the cultural practices alien to Plato's sensibilities. "Plato was the culmination of several centuries of Greek speculation and he took full advantage of the insight which his predecessors had developed,"[14] says an introduction to a collection of his works. The principal Greek view upon which Plato built his philosophy was the fundamental notion that the world and all reality is a dynamic system, organic and alive; that it is orderly; and, most importantly, that it is capable of being fully understood by human reason and intellect. Plato, like the Greek philosophers who came before him, was convinced that the world perceived by our senses is but a superficial and changeable manifestation of the permanent, unchangeable, ultimate nature underlying and ordering all reality. Plato accepted these ancient Greek notions and built upon them a view of the world that survives to our present day. For Plato, the world—because it is pervaded by this ultimate nature, reason, logos—is by definition thoroughly intelligible. For Plato, man— because he is of the same substance as the world—is *also* by definition thoroughly intelligible by man.

Arieti's crediting Plato as being an originator of anti-psycho-analytic cultural forces through rational, objective thinking is correct. Plato was not at all a mystic like some of the Greek philosophers who came before him. He was dismayed to see the mystics increasing in number around him. He had no respect for reliance upon subjective experiences, feelings, or irrational styles of thinking and knowing. He despised the mystic's use of apprehension, flashes of insight, feelings, denial of rational order, and subjective emotionalism. For Plato, the key to understanding both the world outside and the soul inside was the severe use of logic. Plato urged disciplined, intellectual discourse, and lively criticism of competing ideas. He believed that only a disciplined intellect could ever hope to know the true meaning of reality that is concealed behind, but gives expression to, its superficial appearance. Plato would be pleased to be credited with forestalling irrationality and subjectivity for 2,500 years!

For Plato, the highest purpose for any one person was to use his powers of reasoning, his own intelligence, and the more advanced intelligence of others to search beyond the mere appearances and perceptions of reality in order to find the permanent principles that order all reality. This search would give reality a meaning and purpose. Plato spoke of these permanent principles with various terms, such as Forms, Ideas, Reason, Intelligence. Whatever the term, these permanent guiding principles represented the only real truth that existed for Plato. To discover these truths was to apprehend the divine.

Plato acknowledged that human intellect is faulty and not wholly responsible and trustworthy. He was convinced, however, that by intelligence and discipline and with the help of one who already knows, these human limitations could be overcome. Through the disciplined use of intelligence and careful reasoning, Plato asserted that man can come to understand the "form" behind the "content" of reality. He saw this as the logos, the divine, the changeless principles behind all changeable experience. Through intellect and reason, man can become wise and even divine.

"Inquiry," said Plato, "when not disciplined by one who knows, is futile."[15] Plato embodied this belief by his use of the "Socratic method" of dialectical discussion between one who knows (the teacher) and one who does not yet know (the student). He sought to "purge the student of his false beliefs and participate with him in a cooperative search for truth and understanding."[16] Questions and answers, propositions and responses—this was Plato's method for the disciplined discovery of truth. In his *Dialogues,* Plato recorded these sessions and not only offered the words of those dialogues as the content of his philosophy, but offered the form, the method of those dialogues as a sure way to knowledge. He was convinced that the world and the human soul were intelligible by this method. He did not conclude this because the method was effective, but because he believed that there was an ultimate intelligence behind all reality. That is what made reality intelligible for Plato. His goal was the acquisition of this understanding, the "march of the soul in pursuit of knowledge . . . to the essential nature of each thing."[17]

For Plato, the same truths that explained and ordered material reality explained and ordered mankind as well. In the same way that he saw the truths behind material reality as intelligible by man, so also he saw the truths behind the immaterial as intelligible by man. In these truths, according to Augustine, could "be found the cause of existence, the ultimate reason for the understanding, and the end in reference to which the whole life is to be regulated."[18] In this sense, Plato's philosophy developed its own psychology of man.

Plato's psychology rested upon his understanding of the human soul (psyche). He understood the human soul to be a bridge between the ultimate principles (the explaining and ordering permanent truths) and the physical human body. He saw the soul as being immortal like the ultimate principles, but also as being temporal as the physical operator of the mortal human body. For Plato, a person's soul was the activating principle of his life; the soul was the source of life. As such, Plato saw it as man's natural duty to tend the soul and make it as perfect as possible. By tending and making perfect, he meant the disciplined use of intelligence in order to *understand* reality in a rational manner, and the use of this understanding to *control* thoughts, feelings, and behavior.

According to Augustine, Plato taught that,

> Minds defiled by earthly desires [would never be able to] raise themselves upward to divine things [which could, however] be comprehended by a purified mind; and therefore that all diligence ought to be given to the purification of the life by good morals, in order that the mind, delivered from the depressing weight of lusts, might raise itself upward by its native vigor to eternal things, and might, with purified understanding, contemplate that nature which is incorporeal and unchangeable light.[19]

According to Plato, this "march of the soul" was of vital, eternal importance. He asserted that the soul was eternal, that it continued to exist in an afterlife, and that it could even be reincarnated.[20] "It can have no escape or security from evil except by becoming as good and wise as it possibly can. For it takes nothing with it to the next world except its education and training, and these, we are told, are of supreme importance in helping or harming the newly dead at the very beginning of the journey there."[21] "We should make all speed to take flight from this world to the other world, and that means becoming like the divine so far as we can, and that again is to become righteous with the help of wisdom . . . to know this is wisdom and excellence of the genuine sort."[22]

The acquisition of intelligence and of understanding of the true, ultimate principles of reality and of the human soul was salvation, according to Plato. "It is wisdom that makes possible courage and self-control and integrity or, in a word, goodness."[23] "Wrong, arrogance, and folly are our undoing; righteousness, temperance, and wisdom our salvation."[24] Only by this acquisition of wisdom can a person master himself and make himself better. "The cause of all change lies within themselves, and as they change they move in accord with the ordinances and laws of destiny."[25]

According to Augustine, "Plato determined the final good to be to live according to virtue, and affirmed that he only can attain to virtue who knows and imitates [the ultimate principle]—which knowledge and imitation are the only cause of blessedness."[26] Plato sums it up this way: "To act beneath yourself is the result of pure ignorance, to be your own master is wisdom."[27]

Plato was definitely an "anti-psychoanalytic cultural force" from Arieti's perspective in that he was opposed to the irrational, the subjective, and the undisciplined approach to knowledge. It is true that his preference for rational, objective thinking did survive, especially as it was further elaborated and perfected by his chief student and exponent, Aristotle. It is also true that this Platonic preference for rational, objective thinking, especially as codified by Aristotle, was incorporated by the Western church in its approach to theological inquiry. It could be said that this rational, objective style of thinking was transmitted by the church to Western civilization at large, since Scripture does not support irrationality. Arieti is correct in his understanding of this aspect of Platonism as a powerful "anti-psychoanalytic cultural force," and in his understanding that this force was influential for the next twenty-five centuries.

THE *PRO*-PSYCHOANALYTICAL PLATO
ENCOUNTERS AUGUSTINE

What Arieti did not seem to see, however, was just how *pro-psychoanalytic* Plato actually was in his insistence that "wisdom [is] our salvation."[28] Arieti seems to have missed the similarity of that assertion of Plato to the assertion of Freud that "We have no other means of controlling our instinctual nature but our intelligence. . . . The psychological ideal [is] . . . the primacy of intelligence."[29]

So what happened to Plato's pro-psychoanalytic notion of wisdom as salvific? Had that notion survived from the time of its birth through the succeeding centuries, surely it would have spawned a powerfully attractive psychology long before the nineteenth century. Long before Freud, there surely would have developed a veritable industry of tending the soul and making it as perfect as possible. There would have developed centuries ago a cadre of professional "ones who know" to guide troubled souls along the way to enlightenment and self-mastery. This, however, did not happen. This outcome was prevented because Augustine encountered Plato and confronted from Scripture those Platonic beliefs that were unscriptural.

The chief assertion that Augustine challenged was Plato's confidence that human reason could save. Prior to his encounter with Plato's philosophy, Augustine, while a student at Carthage, had been infatuated with gnosticism as a means of pursuing truth. When he left Carthage and moved to Milan in 386, he was loosed from this influence and discovered the truth of Scripture. He retained, however, his interest in philosophy and employed it throughout his long life in a persistently well-reasoned defense of the faith. Augustine commended the teachings of his predecessors and helped to transmit much of that classical heritage to the West. Among those whose influence he commended the most was Plato. Much of what Augustine wrote about the nature of God, the soul, and learning was improved by its conversation, comparison, and contrast with Plato's views on the same subjects. "It is evident," said Augustine, "that none are nearer to us than the Platonists."[30] "Their gold and silver was dug out of the mines of God's providence which are everywhere scattered abroad."[31] In *The City of God,* Augustine refers to Plato as "justly esteemed as the noblest of the philosophers."[32] But on the question of whether it was through faith or through reason (wisdom) that people could come to salvation or could know the divine, Augustine vehemently disagreed with the ancient master of pagan philosophy:

Unless you believe, you will not understand.[33]

. . . the higher light, by which the human mind is enlightened, is God.[34]

Augustine obviously had the highest regard for the abilities of human intelligence and the powers of human reasoning. Understanding fallen human nature, however, Augustine was fully aware that human intelligence and reason was clouded. Because of the Fall, man's ability to reason is distorted and limited. Only through faith and by the grace of God can a redeemed person have any apprehension of true wisdom. Only the redeemed person and his redeemed reason and intelligence can begin to appreciate something of the divine.

Augustine said of the Platonists that, "the light of our understanding, by which all things are learned by us, they [the Platonists] have affirmed to be that self-same God by whom all things are made."[35] But he also knew that Plato and his followers did not recognize the true God of Scripture, nor did they recognize "the grace of God in Jesus Christ our Lord."[36]

Augustine argued that human reason is never completely free from the bias and influence of our fallen, sinful nature. He insisted correctly that one must believe before one can understand. He asserted that our will, our desires, our affections, our interests have primacy over our ability to know or understand anything. Only faith, which alone can purify the will, can enable us to know truth. Without faith, according to Augustine, we will never understand the ultimate truths of life. Without God, the answers to the difficult questions are simply not available to us. As Augustine quoted from Scripture so often in his writings, "Blessed are the pure in heart, for they shall see God."[37] And as he stated elsewhere,

Will you be able to lift up your heart unto God? Must it not first be healed, in order that you mayest see? Do you not show your pride, when you say, First let me see, and then I will be healed?[38]

Augustine knew that "faith is in some way the starting point of knowledge," and that to search for the divine, as the Platonists put it, or for ultimate truths, apart from faith is "a puffed-up and vain science."[39] As such he warns us,

> . . . to return and begin from faith in due order: perceiving at length how healthful a medicine has been provided for the faithful in the holy church, whereby a heedful piety, healing the feebleness of mind, may render it able to perceive the unchangeable truth, and hinder it from falling headlong through disorderly rashness, into pestilent and false opinion.[40]

Augustine knew from personal experience how sinful he was, and how long he had searched everywhere but in Christ for the answer to his anguish: ". . . by believing might I have been cured, that the eyesight of my soul being cleared, might some way or other have been directed toward thy truth . . . which could no ways be healed but by believing."[41]

Only by first believing the Gospel, by receiving faith, by receiving an appreciation of Scripture and the guidance of the Holy Spirit, may any person achieve any real understanding of himself, of his world, or of God. Plato argued the opposite—that by the powers of human reasoning and intelligence a person could come to understand himself, his world, and the divine. The Platonists, said Augustine, were too vain to admit that they must first believe in order to understand.[42] "The proud scorn to take God for their master, because 'the Word was made flesh and dwelt among us.' So that, with these miserable creatures, it is not enough that they are sick, but they boast of their sickness, and are ashamed of the medicine which could heal them. And, doing so, they secure not elevation, but a more disastrous fall."[43]

Concerning the Platonic ideal of self-mastery through self-understanding, Augustine said that it was by first believing that man gained his freedom. Faith, and the understanding that comes with faith, renders unnecessary the relentless and futile search for self-understanding. By believing, a person is freed from the pursuit of vain and fleeting philosophies and fads. This is because through faith the person receives an understanding of his life and his world from the perspective of a sovereign Creator God. He is given absolute and eternal standards of life and godliness that are not subject to change and decay. Plato's goal of self-mastery or self-sufficiency was anathema to Augustine. For Augustine, as it should be for Christians today, the goal was submission to the higher will of God as revealed through Scripture. Self-mastery, self-sufficiency, and self-actualization are contradictory to the ideal of humble submission to God.

Augustine argued that the Platonists wanted to know the divine without really trusting in the one true God. People may be willing to consider God intellectually, but they are not naturally willing to give over their own self-control in submission and obedience to Him. Augustine knew that the best of human minds were corrupted human minds, turning ultimately away from God and toward self.

The Platonists would not agree. They saw the human will as subservient to reason. They saw man as capable of discovering the divine, the truth, through his own reason. They saw that capability as being produced or increased by intellectual discipline, asceticism, self-control, mastery over passions, and by instruction from "one who knows." They refused to believe that only through faith in God's revealed Word could people become wise. They refused to accept, as Augustine did, that he who would save his life must lose it (Matt. 10:39).

From the truth of Scripture, Augustine argued forcefully against the Platonic reliance on reason and forcefully in favor of reliance on God through faith. Because of that truth and the victory of that truth, in large part through Augustine's efforts, no Platonic psychotherapy developed; no elite group of "ones who know" arose in Western civilization for another 1,400 years. Because of the truth of Augustine's argument, there was truly a powerful anti-psychoanalytic cultural force in Western civilization.

CONCLUSION TO CHAPTERS 6–9

In chapters 6–9 we have explored three heretical assaults upon the early church and have learned of Augustine's able defense against those heresies—his "anti-psychoanalytic influence" on Western civilization.

Pelagius would not accept the mystery of God's sovereignty as it relates to human free will. He thought that belief in God's sovereignty reduced man to the status of a robot. He tried to recast God as a kindly helper and to recast mankind as being originally innocent. For Pelagius, sin was a "mistake" and was the result of external influences. Man was fully capable of doing good on his own, able to enter heaven on his own merit.

The gnostics assaulted the early church with alluring claims that secret knowledge, special practices, and the help of an elite redeemer/guide could kindle the divine presence in each human. Individuals could raise themselves from their lower self to a higher self and experience union with the divine.

Plato lent to the early church a preference for rational, objective thinking. Along with that, however, his philosophy also offered the false gospel that people could—with their own purified intellect and the help of "one who knows"—come to know the ultimate principles that guide and order their life and world. The gospel of Platonism was that human wisdom alone could bring salvation.

Considering these ideas, ranging in age from 1,500 to 2,500 years, it is evident that the foundations of psychotherapy were established long ago in Western civilization. The alluring ideas—that man is an innocent victim, that he can reliably understand his own soul, that special knowledge or special techniques supply this understanding, that a redeemer/therapist with secret gnosis or wisdom can help gain this understanding, and that enlightened self-discipline can lead to a blessed life—are ancient, attractive, and enduring.

Even though each of these ideas suffered defeat under the pen of Augustine and the authority of the early church, it was obviously not a permanent defeat, for all of these ideas are alive and flourishing today in modern psychotherapy. This resurgence is greatly strengthened as the church has adopted these ideas into its own amalgam of "Christian psychology." If Augustine were among us today he would surely set his mind prayerfully to pen and his voice to pulpit, fighting these ideas and their spokespeople. Surely his ardor would be against those who have tried to "integrate" these ideas into the church through Christian psychology. An interested reader may taste some of Augustine's passion in these areas, and even recognize its pertinence to issues with us today, by examining his disputations against Porphyry. Porphyry was a man of Augustine's time who claimed to be a Christian but espoused Platonism and other pagan philosophies and constantly tried to integrate them into Christianity. Here is a sample of what Augustine had to say to Porphyry:

> You drive men, therefore, into the most palpable error. And yet you are not ashamed of doing so much harm, though you call yourself a lover of virtue and wisdom. Had you been true and faithful in this profession, you would have recognized Christ, the virtue of God and the wisdom of God , and would not, in the pride of vain science, have revolted from His wholesome humility. . . . You say that ignorance, and the numberless vices resulting from it, cannot be removed by any mysteries, but only by the Father's mind or intellect conscious of the Father's will. . . . But that Christ is this mind you do not believe; for Him you despise on account of the body He took of a woman and the shame of the cross; for your lofty wisdom spurns such low and contemptible things, and soars to the exalted regions. But He fulfills what the holy prophets predicted regarding Him: "I will destroy the wisdom of the wise, and bring to nought the prudence of the prudent." For He does not destroy and bring to nought His own gift in them, but what they arrogate to themselves, and do not hold of Him. And hence the apostle, having quoted this testimony from the prophet, adds, "Where is the wise? where is the scribe, where is the disputer of this world? Hath not God made foolish the wisdom of this world? For after that, in the wisdom of God, the world by wisdom knew not God, it pleased God by the

foolishness of preaching to save them that believe. For the Jews require a sign, and the Greeks seek after wisdom; but we preach Christ crucified, unto the Jews a stumbling-block, and unto the Greeks foolishness; but unto them which are called, both Jews and Greeks, Christ is the power of God, and the wisdom of God. Because the foolishness of God is wiser than men; and the weakness of God is stronger than men." This is despised as a weak and foolish thing by those who are wise and strong in themselves; yet this is the grace which heals the weak, who do not proudly boast a blessedness of their own, but rather humbly acknowledge their real misery. . . .

But in order to your acquiescence in this truth, it is lowliness that is requisite, and to this it is extremely difficult to bend you. . . . Is it not because Christ came in lowliness and ye so proud? . . . Are ye ashamed to be corrected? This is the vice of the proud. It is forsooth, a degradation for learned men to pass from the school of Plato to the discipleship of Christ, who by His Spirit taught a fisherman to say, "In the beginning was the Word, and the Word was with God, and the Word was God. The same was in the beginning with God. All things were made by Him; and without Him was not anything made that was made. In Him was life; and the life was the light of men. And the light shineth in darkness; and the darkness comprehended it not."[44]

In a word, "The proud scorn to take God for their master."[45]

THE EFFECTS OF THE PSYCHOTHERAPEUTIC ETHOS

Introduction to Section Three

In Section 1 we defined and described the fundamental pillars of insight-oriented psychotherapy. We contrasted those pillars with Scripture and saw the contrast to be stark and undeniable. The body of theory defined by the pillars of psychotherapy is not only unscriptural but constitutes a false gospel. Psychotherapy offers a view of man, his problem, and its solution that is the exact opposite of what Scripture reveals. Bearing this out, we looked at some of the consequences of this false gospel upon the clients of psychotherapy and upon our culture as a whole.

This section continues and expands upon that theme: the consequences of insight-oriented psychotherapy. Chapter 10, "Caring for Souls: Then and Now," draws a sharp contrast between the ministry of Christians counseling other Christians as understood and practiced by the Puritans 300 years ago and the professional practice of Christian psychological counseling today.

Chapter 11, "Jane's Story: Modern Psychotherapy vs. Truth," examines a basic mortal flaw in the fundamental pillars of insight-oriented psychotherapy and shows how this flaw harms those who seek its help. We will see that psychotherapy rests upon a concept of "psychic reality" that in no way, shape, or form has any connection with objective, observable, verifiable, accurate, "witnessable" reality. Worse yet, this view of psychic reality is so widely accepted by the customers as well as practitioners of psychotherapy that there no longer exists any responsibility on the part of therapists to verify the "personal narrative" of a paying customer.

Chapter 12, "Recovered Memory Therapy: Have We Recovered from It?" spells out the dramatic and real-life consequences of a system of therapy with an unbiblical view of man and an untruthful concept of truth. The now-departing Recovered Memory Therapy debacle could never have taken place if truth really mattered to the therapists and clients involved. The only reason Recovered Memory Therapy is now passing from the scene is that truth has begun to matter to families falsely accused (even falsely jailed), to the lawyers who took up their causes, and to the courts that are handing down the malpractice awards.

TEN

🙰

CARING FOR SOULS:
THEN AND NOW

In what has been termed the Great Commission, Jesus told His disciples,

> "All authority in heaven and on earth has been given to me. Therefore go and make disciples of all nations, baptizing them in the name of the Father and of the Son and of the Holy Spirit, and teaching them to obey everything I have commanded you. And surely I will be with you always, to the very end of the age." (Matt. 28:18-20)

Surely the Puritans were correct in understanding "teaching them to obey" as including what they called "the cure of souls."

From the beginning of the church, and at any time when it functioned with serious attention to Scripture, caring for souls has been one of its hallmarks. One might say that this remains true today, but today's version of this activity is usually called "counseling." *Sola Scriptura* is no longer the foundation of this counseling, and many sources other than Scripture are relied upon as authoritative.

The cure of souls has become a highly technical and costly enterprise within the church. It is characterized by an abundant literature, various competing schools of thought, and an ever more elaborate range of techniques and specialized methods. Statements of the goals and objectives of "soul care" usually resonate with contemporary cultural issues and trends. Because many in the church no longer see the Bible as sufficient for the care or cure of souls, a vast literature on counseling has been added to Scripture. This extrabiblical literature supposedly supplies insight, guidance, methods, and rationales that the counselor is unable to obtain from Scripture alone. Since they are presented as science, most Christians seem to accept these modern approaches and are often offended at the simplistic notion that such methods should be tested against Scripture.

Increasingly, as we have noted, Christian counseling takes on the professional trappings of secular psychotherapy with its specialized training and certification, malpractice coverage, office shelves full of books and journals, national meetings, ads in the yellow pages, and appointments with fees attached. It is not easy to determine whether such practices have come from heretical theology in our seminaries and pulpits, or whether heretical theology is flooding our seminaries and pulpits due to the tremendous popularity and financial gain of these practices. Regardless of whether the chicken or the egg came first, heresy permeates the church in its care of souls.

NOW: HARVARD UNIVERSITY, 1996

In a *Christianity Today* article titled "A Generation of Debtors,"[1] Andy Crouch tells of his ministry as a staff member with InterVarsity Christian Fellowship at Harvard University. Crouch's view of God, man, and ministry sounds more Freudian than biblical, and sadly his view is not unique within the evangelical church today.

Crouch's student counselees exhibit feelings of guilt, addictive sexual relationships, low self-esteem, disrespect for parents, cynicism, depression, anger carried inside for years, eating disorders, drug abuse, alcoholism, compulsive shopping, and "emptiness under our feet." Crouch says these are typical Harvard students, and they certainly match the concerns that Christians everywhere are bringing to their counselors as we approach the millennium.

Crouch does not hesitate to reveal his views as to why the students have these difficulties. Using his own personal experience rather than Scripture as his base, he elaborates on the personal narratives of the students with whom he works: Lisa's low self-esteem is caused by her grandfather failing to pay for her Harvard education because she is female (he paid for the education of Lisa's brother). Paul has a pattern of addictive sexual relationships because his "parents were busy and successful entrepreneurs who had made little time for him when he was in high school." Paul still feels guilty about sexual relationships because he has not yet experienced a forgiveness by God that he could "quite believe." Karen has had "anger carried inside for years" because her father left her mother when Karen was three years old.

In addition to such etiologies, Crouch says that all "Generation Xers" are owed "debts that will never be paid." These debts that "loom over their future" include the national debt, lack of true family, parents emotionally absent though physically present, feelings of emptiness, and "never experiencing love and acceptance from their fathers, *at least in a way that they could receive it*" (italics mine). Crouch describes these things as the "core experiences of pain of this generation which are lodged at the heart of who they are, in the innermost chambers of their identities and memories; and like the core of an apple, they contain the seeds of their actions, attitudes, hopes, and fears."

Crouch reveals much of the deviant theology guiding modern "Christian" counseling when he says of his counselees and of himself: "In these students, I see myself . . . and a whole generation. Each is bright, likable, and deeply broken. Each shares a toxic intersection of brokenness and sin." There is no indication, however, that Crouch or his students are broken by their own sin; they are broken, rather, by the imperfections of their environment, by someone else's sin.

The article quotes Jungian analyst Jeffrey Satinover, once a professing Christian but now involved in orthodox Judaism: "The only way for people to find release from these addictive patterns that entrap us is to find healing for some core experience of pain that the sin has tried to address." Crouch follows this Jungian doctrine in advising his counselees to pray "for healing of core experiences of pain . . . and . . . for God's power to forgive those who had done them wrong." He goes on to say that the church must offer these Generation Xers a forgiveness *"to feel and experience,* not just talk about" (italics mine). He wants the church to offer a Holy Spirit "coming in power . . . who fills the absences of our lives" and who brings "the real presence" of God.

Crouch describes a counseling session where Karen is able to say, "Daddy, I forgive you," and to "confess her own guilt in giving anger a dominant place in her heart." The focus is then further on Karen's feelings as she experiences "a river of love flooding the room . . . so tangible that no one spoke for several minutes." Others of his student counselees "moved into inner cities and traveled to the poorest parts of the world, *not primarily to help,* but to be where Christ is" (italics mine). The purpose even of their good works is self-centered, and this seems completely acceptable to Crouch. He says, "There our emptiness is mysteriously transfigured into forgiveness, healing, and resurrection."

This InterVarsity campus staffer is all too typical of modern Christian counselors in viewing people and their problems in terms of the fundamental beliefs undergirding insight-oriented psychotherapy. This view so permeates our culture that even Christians who carry their Bibles to church every Sunday seem oblivious to its unbiblical nature, especially when it is presented with such emotion and apparent compassion. To Crouch and Satinover, the "bright, likable, and deeply broken" students at Harvard were derailed from happiness and psychological health by their unfriendly environments and bad parenting.

Though Scripture warns us clearly against accepting an accusation (e.g., of bad parenting) unless verified by two witnesses, this is apparently of no concern at all to Crouch and Satinover. There is no suggestion that they even think about it. They are so permeated with psychoanalytic doctrine that they would likely be shocked at any suggestion that they should check with parents or grandparents before accepting the "personal narratives" of these students.

There is not the slightest indication in the article that Crouch and Satinover see these students as born in the line of Adam, with a natural inclination toward sin. Instead, they view them as victims of other people and even of the national debt! The Freudian pillar of environmental determinism is obvious in Crouch's descriptions of his students, and it is clearly to Freud that Crouch turns rather than to Scripture when he strategizes his interventions. Crouch may be quite unaware of this, but that does not change the consequences of his unbiblical doctrinal base. It is not surprising that the student named Paul does not quite believe that God has forgiven him.

Crouch seems to really believe that the thoughts, feelings, and behaviors of his students are determined by "inner core experiences of pain lodged at the heart of who they are . . . containing the seeds of their actions, attitudes, hopes, and fears." He states that our past experiences "entrap us" and "have power over us." The fundamental pillar of psychic determinism is clearly at play here.

Crouch seems almost to cast himself in the role of a typical psychotherapist, able to discover the unconscious causes of his clients' problems: "Over the course of several conversations, I was not surprised to learn that his parents were . . ." He sees the gaining of insight into the heart, into the core experience, as "the only way for people to find release." He apparently believes he has discovered the "why" of the students' troubled lives. The bad experiences stored in the "core" need to be remembered, re-experienced, and "worked through" before they can be "released." This is clearly the Freudian doctrine of gaining insight into the unconscious.

We should not be surprised that this doctrinal foundation leads the students into the ancient gnostic pursuit of a personal state of insight and individualized ecstasy. This has become so acceptable in the modern church that believers who fail to pursue such insight are viewed as negative and lacking in joy. The goal of the Christian life has become a mystical, highly emotional, highly personalized experience of the sort sweeping the church in Third Wave Pentecostalism, such as manifested in the "Toronto Blessing." The students say, "I need that kind of cleansing . . . to feel and experience . . . to forgive myself . . . to fill the absences." The goal differs little from that of the New Age movement! The biblical command to walk by faith and not by sight seems rather boring and lacking in excitement; it fades as meaningless when compared to the intense experiences associated with the new doctrinal base.

Someone may ask, "Might not the New Age movement and secular psychotherapy have some usable new ideas for Christians, allowing for the fact that they leave Jesus out of their techniques? After all, they are attempts to meet felt needs, and isn't that what the church should be doing?" One Christian psychologist writing during the 1970s suggested that Christian psychology is biblical in "plundering the Egyptians" for such valuable nuggets. Isn't it likely that God allowed Freud to discover such important facts about our emotions so that the church could be equipped to meet the felt needs of the twentieth century? After all, it took time for the church to come to understand that God brought the universe into existence through evolution! Do we want to treat Freud and Jung the way Galileo was treated? Never let it be said to the modern church that theology might conflict with science!

Or could it be that real Christianity is radically different in every way, contradicting not only Freud and Darwin, but also the counseling methods Crouch describes? After all, the Israelites were not told to plunder the *pagan religion* of the Egyptians.

What does the Bible say about caring for souls? The Bible reveals that our felt needs are not our real needs. David felt that he needed Bathsheba; God said David's "need" actually amounted to "despising the word of the Lord" (2 Sam. 12:9). Simon the Sorcerer felt the need to lay his hands on people and give them the Holy Spirit; God called Simon's felt need "wickedness . . . full of bitterness and captive to sin" (Acts 8:22-23). Saul felt the need to murder the Lord's disciples; God called it persecution of Him (Acts 9:4). Peter felt the need to separate himself from the Gentiles; Paul said Peter's anti-Gentile inclination was "hypocrisy . . . not acting in line with the truth of the gospel" (Gal. 2:13-14).

Scripture is filled with such examples. To set a goal of meeting felt needs is to divert people away from facing their real need. To assume that a felt need is the real need is cruelty in the name of compassion, and it is from the Father of Lies. The Bible is clear that man's real need is for redemption from sin. It never suggests that we need to be saved from the sin of our environment or from the sin of another individual. As we have seen, God forbids the blaming of parents and grandparents for one's own sin: "The soul who sins is the one who will die" (Ezek. 18:4).

Think again about those Harvard students. It is likely that Lisa really does believe she has low self-esteem because of her grandfather, that Paul really does think his parents gave him too little time, and that Karen really does feel angry that her father left her mother. Instead of taking Scripture to show these students that these things are not the real problem, Crouch views it as a great achievement to have brought out these complaints against these families. On the basis of his supposed discovery of the core experience of pain, he pursues a mystical experience for the students in hopes of showing them "God's presence."

If this campus ministry staffer truly believed Scripture, he surely would direct the students to it, helping them see that their real problem is their own rebellion in the face of a loving Creator. He would show Lisa that she actually has self in far too high a position; Paul that he has too little time for anyone but self; and Karen that God would have her be thankful that her mother didn't leave when her father did. He would take these students to Jeremiah and Ezekiel and show them that God takes very seriously the blaming of parents. He would point them to Deuteronomy 24:16, where God says, "Fathers shall not be put to death for their children, nor children put to death for their fathers; each is to die for his own sin."

If obedience to Scripture is a priority for the campus minister, he will point students to Ephesians 2:10: "For we are God's workmanship, created in Christ Jesus to do good works, which God prepared in advance for us to do." He will show new believers that their service to God is in response to His love and is for His glory, rather than being the route to self-fulfillment as they are able to "be where Christ is." These are not minor differences; these are radical differences. Christ has promised He will never leave the one who trusts in Him; a Christian need not seek to live among the poor (or the rich) in order to "be where Christ is."

Still, some will say, "But it works! I feel better now. My grades are better. Now instead of 'sexual addiction,' I'm a good liver. I pray, fast, owe no debts, pay my tithe, and give alms. I never miss a large group meeting, and I'm helping the poor since I see Christ in their eyes" (my paraphrase from *Pilgrim's Progress*). Bunyan rightfully named the man Ignorance who said that. Bunyan said to him, "I fear however you may think of yourself, when the reckoning day shall come, you will have laid to your charge that you are a thief and a robber, instead of getting admittance into the city."[2]

Christian psychology's problem is primarily a theological problem. Though the doctrine of psychotherapy is heretical, we cloak it in "Jesus-words" with an appearance of compassion, add a few tears, and accept it as "Christian." Jesus is increasingly presented as a cosmic therapist with supernatural powers. The scriptural presentation of the Son as the "heir of all things," through whom God "made the universe," and who is the "radiance of God's glory and the exact representation of his being, sustaining all things by his powerful word" and providing "purification for sins" (Heb. 1:2-3) has disappeared in today's church under the determination to meet felt needs. The biblical Jesus just doesn't suit our felt needs, so we will make a Jesus in our own image. In the words of theologian Joseph Hartunian,

> Before, religion was God-centered. Before, whatever was not conducive to the glory of God was infinitely evil. Now, that which is not conducive to the happiness of man is evil, unjust, and impossible to attribute to the deity. Before, the good of man consisted ultimately in glorifying God. Now, the glory of God consists in the happiness of man. Before, man lived to glorify God. Now, God lives to serve man.[3]

THEN: MASSACHUSETTS BAY COLONY, 1630–1775

Caring for souls in the modern church bears little resemblance to the care traditionally given by the churches that grew out of the Reformation. This becomes apparent especially as we look at soul care as practiced by the Puritan Christians of colonial America. In our efforts to build a god in our own image, we have magnified the errors of the Puritans and have ignored them as unloving radicals dressed in black who placed scarlet *A*'s on the bosoms of unwed mothers. But the Puritans were not the only Christians who have at times forgotten the Bible's teachings about love. Today's church would do well to take Scripture even half so seriously as did the Puritans, and in so doing to review the scriptural definition of love.

"Puritan" was a pejorative name given these children of the Reformation in England, ridiculing their efforts to purify themselves and the Anglican church. During the reign of Charles I, Anglican Archbishop Laud tried to purge the country of dissenters such as the Puritans. *Foxe's Book of Martyrs* contains the stories of many believers who died for the testimony of Christ during this purge. John Bunyan was imprisoned for twelve years for preaching without a license, and during his imprisonment wrote his classic *Pilgrim's Progress*. Between 1629 and 1641, some 80,000 of these beleaguered Puritans left their island home for other parts of the globe in search of religious freedom; some 21,000 settled in Massachusetts.

These immigrants intended to establish in the new world what they called a "Bible Commonwealth." As recorded by historian David Hackett Fischer, John Winthrop arrived in 1630 to be governor of the Massachusetts Bay Colony and promised the people, "We shall build a city upon a hill, the eyes of all people are upon us."[4]

As Puritan immigrants came to America and sought to join local Puritan churches, they had to pass a rigorous examination of their beliefs and manner of living. Those who did not join a local church were banished to other colonies or sent back to England.[5] The Puritans' relationships with each other reflected their Christian commitment. Far from the independent individualists so often portrayed in history books, they formed tightly woven communities more interested in living for God's glory than in seeking political independence. Political scientist Barry A. Shain, in *The Myth of American Individualism*, observes that modern historians, desirous of fulfilling "the contemporary need for appropriately secular foundational myths," characterize these early Americans as "predominantly individualistic or, for that matter, classically republican." However, says Shain, any honest examination of Puritan letters, sermons, legal documents, and other publications reveals that they had a "Protestant communal vision"[6] rather than the individualism we try to ascribe to them.

Once they landed on America's shores, these immigrants worked to preserve the values and way of life they had known in England. They sought to work out their salvation in this life "with fear and trembling" (Phil. 2:12). The faith that united and guided them was the historic Christian faith of the Reformation. They accepted Scripture's teaching of human depravity and were convinced of mankind's natural inclination toward evil. They believed that only the atonement provided by Christ, and the indwelling of the Holy Spirit which followed upon that, could save us from a life of ever greater depravity. These believers had no optimistic illusions about man having an inner core of goodness and innocence. They accepted Scripture's presentation of the Christian life as a battle against sin and its instruction that church leaders as well as the general "priesthood of believers" were to help one another in the struggle.

The Puritans understood it to be their individual and corporate duty to "love each other in a godly way, to be serviceable to one another, to lovingly give, as well as lovingly take admonitions."[7] These were people who, in Shain's words, "believed it was the legitimate and necessary role of local religious, familial, social, and governmental forces to limit, reform, and shape the sinful individual. Moreover, it was assumed that these intermediate institutions would have to act restrictively and intrusively (if not coercively), for in no other way would the recalcitrant and naturally deformed human being take on a godly and publicly useful shape."[8]

Of particular interest in our present study is how and why the Puritans cared for their own souls, the souls of their brethren, and the souls of the nonbelievers around them. Family life was of utmost importance to the Puritans. They thought in terms of covenants and contracts pertaining to the roles and responsibilities of husband, wife, and children in a family unit, "the root whence church and commonwealth cometh."[9] They established a variety of community and church institutions to preserve the strength and integrity of the family as part of the larger community. However, the family was not considered to be utterly independent. If a father would not or could not maintain order in his own home, community leaders would become involved even to the extent that his children might be placed in other "more orderly" families, where they could be forced to "submit to government." "Tithingmen" were legally empowered to "take charge of ten or twelve families of [their] neighborhood, to diligently inspect them."[10]

Individuals were not allowed to live alone. The Puritans believed that a person living alone would be "subject to much sin and iniquity which ordinarily are the companions and consequences of the solitary life."[11] The law in Massachusetts in 1648 stated that stubborn and rebellious sons over the age of sixteen who refused to obey or who struck or cursed their father or mother could be subject to the death penalty.[12] The Puritans refused to tolerate any marital disharmony or physical abuse between husband and wife. At the slightest visible upset, neighbors, tithingmen, the church, and even the local government reacted swiftly and decisively to restore peace and good relations. Sexual activity outside marriage was similarly confronted and punished—as zealously as it was encouraged inside marriage. Rates of prenuptial pregnancy in Massachusetts were among the lowest in the world during the seventeenth century; three towns reported no cases at all between 1650 and 1680.[13] Child-rearing for the Puritans was similarly based on the Bible. Since they believed that infants were born with a natural inclination toward sin, they considered the "breaking of the will" an important goal.[14] This was to be done in love, however; these were not homes of cold and indifferent abuse.

The Puritans put their beliefs into action in communal worship, where they would confess sins publicly, participate in corporate prayer, and listen to sermons designed to convict them of sin. Shain says, "In New England, churchgoers listened to somewhere around fifteen thousand hours of sermons in a lifetime, and their extant handwritten notes offer persuasive evidence that they understood and retained much of what they had heard."[15]

These Puritans were concerned as well about the "cure of souls." The manner in which they conducted their lives, both privately and in community, reflected this caring for their own souls as well as the souls of others. At issue were the most fundamental beliefs of Christianity: the salvation of the lost soul and sanctification in the believer's life.

Such concern for the "cure of souls" has been present among believers from the very beginning of the church. From the time of the Reformation, soul care involved not only outward sins but more importantly the inward person and the state of his soul. Believers were to care for one another not only in a physical but also in a spiritual sense.[16] Confession continued to be an important part of the Christian life in these Reformation churches, but it was freed from its medieval sacramental and clerical aspects. Believers were encouraged to confess their sins to one another, as a priesthood of all believers (James 5:16; 1 Pet. 2:4-10). The Bible, now widely available, was seen as the sufficient and authoritative source of truth for this priesthood. The Puritans "read the Bible as an authoritative guide to morality and used as their elementary school primer the Westminster 'shorter Catechism' of reformed doctrine."[17] Confession, repentance, admonition, encouragement, and restoration all were a part of the "cure of souls." Following the teaching of John Calvin, church leaders were taught to place the care of souls among their primary responsibilities before God:

> The office of a true and faithful minister is not only publicly to teach the people over whom he is ordained pastor, but as far as may be, to admonish, exhort, rebuke, and console each one in particular.[18]

The Puritans adopted this Reformation teaching, tried to rely on Scripture alone, emphasized the grace of God, and stressed the believer's responsibilities. Believers were led toward earnest devotion, prayer, and self-examination, as a part of growth toward Christian maturity. All this was done for the purpose of glorifying God. As the Puritan writer Jonathan Mitchell stated, "A Christian may and ought to desire many things as means, but God alone as his end."[19]

As we have seen, the Puritans of Massachusetts were not a people who strove for autonomy and individualism. Among them there was a "near universal condemnation of the aspirations of the liberated self. Their understanding of the concepts of self and family are in tension with the ethical and political claims of modern individualism."[20] These people believed that their brethren, "joined together in community and in congregation, were also needed to assist one another in walking in the path of righteousness."[21] The sermons these people heard spoke to them of the responsibility of a true believer to come alongside his neighbor and care for his soul, to put self last, to put God first, and to put the needs of fellow believers above one's own needs. They were taught to sacrifice individuality for the good of the community of believers. In the words of three Puritan leaders:

> Live not for yourselves, but the Publick. . . . Let your own Ease, your own Pleasure, your own private Interests, yield to the common Good.[22]

> The welfare and happiness of such a community, or body, is to be valued above and preferred to the happiness of an individual.[23]

> The source of all of man's unhappiness is his selfishness.[24]

To these early Americans, the attainment of private and public virtue involved a continual battle to overcome the natural human inclination to personal and public sin. Because of their knowledge of and belief in Scripture, they knew that autonomy and individualism was "the root vice."[25] They knew that what God required was "the total denial and suppression of the self in subservience to God and the public good." They knew that "the very Habit and gift of Faith is of an Emptying Nature, emptying the soule of all confidence in itself and in the Creature and so leaving and constituting the soule as an empty vessel, empty of its own worth."[26]

For the Puritans, the care of souls grew naturally out of their desire to obey God's Word. It was active, involved, widespread, intrusive, and sometimes coercive. Every effort was made to be true to Scripture both in doctrine and in practice. Soul care was conducted "under the guidance of pastors . . . and within the mutual ministry of the saints one to another, for the purpose of building up the body of Christ through mutual encouragement, admonition, confession, repentance, forgiveness, restoration and counsel."[27]

Before we dismiss the Puritans as "witch-burners," we need to recognize that "now we see but a poor reflection" and "now I know in part" (1 Cor. 13:12). Before we banish the very idea of this "cure of souls" as too invasive into our privacy as independent, democratic Americans, we need to recognize the increasing invasion of our homes by the government and the courts in the name of saving our children. Before we bow to the "secret knowledge" of the Christian psychologists, we need to bow before the Word of God.

CARING FOR SOULS

I have presented in this chapter two approaches to caring for souls. Surely there is a stark contrast between the theology of the Massachusetts Bay Colony in the seventeenth century and the theology of InterVarsity at Harvard in 1996. Though separated by nearly four centuries, the contrasts represented are vitally important for the church today. The approach taken at Harvard presents a heavy veneer of compassion—but is it truly compassion? The approach taken in the Bay Colony strikes us as too harsh, too invasive—but is it? The doctrines underlying the two approaches are radically different. Which one is according to Scripture? Which one comes from a loving Creator who knows me far better than I know myself? That is the real issue.

Four centuries ago, caring for souls was the expected fruit of a Christian life, and the written Word was authoritative and sufficient. The importance of this aspect of the Christian life to the Puritans is evidenced in their extensive works of writing, preaching, and teaching on the cure of souls. These works were produced to guide and encourage the faithful in caring for their own soul as well as the souls of one another. Richard Baxter's *A Christian Directory* is a typical and especially thorough example of such writings.[28]

The Puritan efforts at soul care differ from the multitudinous psychological and Christian self-help books published in our time in that they strove to rely solely on Scripture and to care for souls without influence from human sources of wisdom or insight. The Puritans accepted the teaching of Scripture that out of the human heart come our sinful choices. They attended to the sinful thoughts and behaviors of themselves as well as others through attention to the spiritual condition of the heart. They were convinced that only through mastery and application of the Word could the sinful heart be conquered by the Holy Spirit so that a genuine cure of the soul would result.

The subtitle of Baxter's *A Christian Directory* is: *A Sum of Practical Theology and Cases of Conscience. Directing Christians How to Use their Knowledge and Faith; How to Improve all Helps and Means and to Perform all Duties; How to Overcome Temptations, and to Escape or Mortify Every Sin.* This work is actually an unusually thorough Bible study, leading the reader through "Private Duties," "Family Duties," "Church Duties," and "Duties to our Rulers and Neighbors."

Baxter states his purpose as follows:

1. To direct ungodly minds, how to attain to a state of grace.
2. To direct those having saving grace how to use it; both in the contemplative and active parts of their lives; in their duties of religion, both private and public; in their duties to men, both in their ecclesiastical, civil, and family relations. And, by the way, to direct those that have grace, how to discern it, and take the comfort of it; and to direct them how to grow in grace, and to persevere unto the end.[29]

A Christian Directory and other such books provided readers advice, counsel, wisdom, confrontation, teaching, and encouragement for seemingly every life situation. They are intensive devotional studies of Scripture and its application to real life. They are powerful examples of *Sola Scriptura* applied to life itself.

The article "A Generation of Debtors," quoted earlier in this chapter, is an example of how today's church cares for souls. It reveals that concern for the soul remains an aspect of the Christian life, but that the attitude of *Sola Scriptura* no longer prevails. Today, we rely on many sources in addition to Scripture, and these additional sources soon eliminate Scripture. The modern example at Harvard clearly evidences the deadly intrusion of the fundamental doctrines of insight-oriented psychotherapy into the Christian caring for souls. It evidences as well the *extrusion* of Scripture from the thinking of even the seriously committed Christian leader.

Since Jay Adams published *Competent to Counsel* in 1970,[30] there has been a slowly growing awareness of the need for the church to undertake the biblical care of souls. This has been turned into action only where *Sola Scriptura* still has meaning. Since 1970, books and articles have been published attesting to the danger posed by integrating popular and academic counseling psychology into Christian counseling.[31] Counseling psychology's claim to be an exact science has been refuted more than once. Psychotherapy's claim to be effective and reliable has been found wanting. Books have been written describing the flawed and anti-scriptural theories that undergird the practice of counseling psychology. A growing number of individual practitioners and theorists of secular counseling psychology and of integrated Christian psychology have been examined and their inconsistencies with Scripture detailed and exposed. Several works have also been published (from a solely scriptural basis) on specific counseling issues.[32]

More recently, work has been published warning of the growing number of self-styled counselors calling themselves "biblical," of the dangers of Christian counselors taking on the professional trappings of the insight-oriented psychotherapy industry.[33] The allure of the Freudian edifice, its ideas, and its practices is a powerful temptation. Most Christian counseling has been rendered impotent by succumbing to this temptation under the guise of "integration" and the tempting notion that "all truth is God's truth," ignoring the reality that all that man considers truth is not necessarily true from God's perspective, however much we might think it ought to be.

The church is called to evangelize the world with the demands of the Law and with the good news of the Gospel of Jesus Christ. This is the first and foremost message of the church to every living soul. The church is called then to care for the souls of believers. From the moment of salvation, true believers will progress in sanctification. Life for the believer can surely be likened to a pilgrim's progress. The wicked heart of the Christian is covered with the robe of Christ's perfect righteousness; however, the struggle against sin will continue until the day of glorification of this mortal body. God's Word and the Holy Spirit are our provisions for this struggle; however, the organized church and other believers are expected to be in the battle with us,

> . . . to prepare God's people for works of service, so that the body of Christ may be built up until we all reach unity in the faith and in the knowledge of the Son of God and become mature, attaining to the whole measure of the fullness of Christ. (Eph. 4:12-13)

> But one thing I do: Forgetting what is behind and straining toward what is ahead, I press on toward the goal to win the prize for which God has called me heavenward in Christ Jesus. All of us who are mature should take such a view of things. . . . Join with others in following my example, brothers, and take note of those who live according to the pattern we gave you. . . . Our citizenship is in heaven. And we eagerly await a Savior from there, the Lord Jesus Christ, who, by the power that enables him to bring everything under his control, will transform our lowly bodies so that they may be like his glorious body. . . . That is how you should stand firm in the Lord. (Phil. 3:13-15, 17, 20; 4:1)

The Reformers studied Scripture and taught the church the doctrine of the priesthood of all believers. Christians no longer participated in the unscriptural sacramental and clerical practices that had evolved in the Roman and Eastern churches. Equipped with the written Word of God, empowered by the Holy Spirit, and aided by the organized church, one believer could hear the confession of another, could come alongside him, speak from Scripture, and encourage him toward maturity and fullness in Christ:

> All believers are competent to minister to one another in the Body of Christ by grace through faith in God and His Word. They are saved by grace through faith, and they are to live and minister to one another by grace through faith. After they believe God for salvation through the death and resurrection of Christ, they are to continue their walk in the Spirit through the life of the resurrected Christ living in them. As they live by faith, they are competent to minister God's grace to one another, believing that God is sovereign and true to His Word that He has given them.[34]

> His divine power has given to us everything we need for life and godliness through our knowledge of him who called us by his own glory and goodness. (2 Pet. 1:3)

God equips all believers for their part in the care of souls. He does not use members of an elite corps who claim secret knowledge. He needs neither the bearers of training certificates nor those with worldly seals of approval:

> Brothers, think of what you were when you were called. Not many of you were wise by human standards; not many were influential; not many were of noble birth. But God chose the foolish things of the world to shame the wise; God chose the weak things of the world to shame the strong. He chose the lowly things of this world and the despised things—and the things that are not—to nullify the things that are. (1 Cor. 1:26-28)

God does not require that we be eloquent or smooth in our

delivery of the message. Believers are to care for souls whether they are rhetoricians or marble-mouths. It is what they believe, and what supernatural power works through them, that counts—rather than the style of their delivery or the extent of their training in therapeutic techniques:

> I did not come with eloquence or superior wisdom as I proclaimed to you the testimony about God. . . . I came to you in weakness and fear, and with much trembling. My message and my preaching were not with wise and persuasive words, but with a demonstration of the Spirit's power, so that your faith might not rest on men's wisdom but on God's power. (1 Cor. 2:1-5)

> May the God of hope fill you with all joy and peace as you trust in him, so that you may overflow with hope by the power of the Holy Spirit. I myself am convinced, my brothers, that you yourselves are full of goodness, complete in knowledge and competent to instruct one another. (Rom. 15:13-14)

All believers are called to care for souls. They are not in the church for themselves or by themselves. If they are resting on the truths of Scripture and if they ask God for love for others, then the grace of God will work through them.

Believers who care for the souls of others are not responsible for the outcome; their task is simply to obey as God's servants. The agent of change is the Holy Spirit, not any human being:

> Therefore confess your sins to each other and pray for each other so that you may be healed. The prayer of a righteous man is powerful and effective. (James 5:16)

> Each one should use whatever gift he has received to serve others, faithfully administering God's grace in its various forms. If anyone speaks, he should do it as one speaking the very words of God. If any one serves, he should do it with the

strength God provides, so that in all things God may be
praised through Jesus Christ. (1 Pet. 4:10-11)

As they care for each other's souls, believers "fulfill the law of
Christ":

Brothers, if someone is caught in a sin, you who are spiritual
should restore him gently. . . . Carry each other's burdens, and
in this way you will fulfill the law of Christ. (Gal. 6:1-2)

The law of Christ is the body of teaching Christ gave to the church.
Caring for souls is a response to the command to "Love your neighbor as yourself" (Matt. 19:19). The apostle John clearly stated that
this love is a mark of the genuine Christian:

For anyone who does not love his brother, whom he has seen,
cannot love God, whom he has not seen. (1 John 4:20)

If we are to trust and obey Christ's teachings, we are to care for
souls. This is not a task to be relegated to "professionals," and it is
not a task to be casually dismissed. There is no evidence in Scripture
that only a few are called or "gifted" for this responsibility. We may
well enter upon this duty with fear and trembling, recognizing the
seriousness of the challenge before us. However, obedience is the
issue, not "success" as the world defines it.

As Paul discusses the role of Christians as comforters, he
addresses issues fundamental to the care of souls:

Praise be to the God and Father of our Lord Jesus Christ, the
Father of compassion and the God of all comfort, who comforts us in our troubles, so that we can comfort those in any
trouble with the comfort we ourselves have received from
God. . . . If we are distressed, it is for your comfort, . . . which
produces in you patient endurance of the same sufferings we
suffer. . . . Just as you share in our sufferings, so also you
share in our comfort. . . . On him we have set our hope that

he will continue to deliver us, as you help us by your prayers.
(2 Cor. 1:3-4, 6, 7, 10-11)

Paul assumes that suffering is a normal part of the Christian life. He accepts it as real and as having purpose. This causes Paul to praise God, acknowledging Him as the only source of true comfort in the face of suffering. Paul shares his suffering as well as his joy with other believers. Caring for souls means not only comforting fellow believers but also encouraging them, through faith, to "patient endurance of the same sufferings." Caring for another's soul often includes sharing the comfort God has given you amid similar sufferings. To confine all talk of one's suffering to the closed office of a counselor is to miss opportunities for caring for each other's souls. We are called to encourage, exhort, and comfort each other; never is it to be a one-way encounter where the person behind the desk is paid to do the encouraging, exhorting, and comforting.

Care for the unsaved soul is manifested in a single activity: the relentless presentation of the Law and of the Gospel of Jesus Christ in word and deed. Only by grace through faith are we saved. Only in salvation can we receive the true comfort of God in our suffering. Chapter 1, part 1 of Baxter's *A Christian Directory* is titled, *"Directions to unconverted, graceless Sinners, for the attaining of true saving Grace."* The first order of business in caring for the unsaved soul must be to point him to the righteous demands of his Creator and to the cross of Jesus Christ as payment for his failure to meet those demands.

The Law must be presented first, for unless the individual despairs of his ability to keep the Law, the provision of a Redeemer is meaningless. When he does despair of his inability to keep the Law, and recognizes that he is a sinner in the hands of an angry God, then the true Gospel can be presented; otherwise, that soul cannot be "cured." We must not present a Freudian gospel overlaid with evangelical terminology; care must be taken to present the Gospel of which Paul was not ashamed, since only that Gospel "is the power of God for the salvation of everyone who believes" (Rom. 1:16).

The Freudian gospel may give a temporary experience of ecstasy, even of security, but it is an illusion. Flee from presenting the therapeutic Jesus with cosmic power to raise people's self-esteem and bring them to their godlike potential. Such a gospel is from the Father of Lies. Present the Jesus of Scripture in all His humility and all His glory, in all His love and all His justice.

Providing advice and counsel for the problems experienced by an unbeliever can be a dangerous pursuit. Making them feel better can lessen their realization of their need for a Savior. It is wrong to present the Gospel as something that "works for me; you should try it too," or to offer "biblical principles", as a ladder of virtues by which to build a better life. The counselee will either eventually reject such counsel as one more failed method or delude himself into thinking that he has achieved the successful, happy life through this system of works. Either way, the man is doomed (Eph. 2:8-9; 1 John 5:5).

Caring for souls is not an enterprise characterized by elaborate techniques, steps, strategies, secret insights, incisive interpretations, or sudden profound realizations:

> Preach the Word; be prepared in season and out of season; correct, rebuke and encourage—with great patience and careful instruction. (2 Tim. 4:2)

> All scripture is inspired by God and profitable for teaching, for reproof, for correction, and for training in righteousness, that the man of God may be complete, equipped for every good work. (2 Tim. 3:16-17, RSV)

> These, then, are the things you should teach. Encourage and rebuke with all authority. Do not let anyone despise you. (Titus 2:15)

> . . . train the younger women to love their husbands and children, to be self-controlled and pure, to be busy at home, to be kind, and to be subject to their husbands, so that no one will malign the Word of God. (Titus 2:4-5)

Do not rebuke an older man harshly, but exhort him as if he were your father. Treat younger men as brothers, older women as mothers, and younger women as sisters, with absolute purity. (1 Tim. 5:1-2)

If your brother sins, rebuke him, and if he repents, forgive him. (Luke 17:3)

Correct, rebuke, encourage, teach, train in righteousness, and exhort. These are the actions of the believer caring for the soul of another believer. With Scripture as the authoritative and sufficient benchmark, the priesthood of believers is not only *called* to care for souls, it is *competent* to care for souls.

Churches claiming Scripture as their authority should not be filled with people coming to the worship service while their family problems go quietly to the professional counselors or to the forever multiplying "support groups." Techniques, support groups, cell groups, efforts at "community" will offer nothing but a temporary and gasping illusion of comfort. The underlying theology is erroneous, not just the methods. The error is a fatal one, and no amount of funding or strategic planning will change the destructive end toward which it plunges.

ELEVEN

JANE'S STORY: MODERN PSYCHOTHERAPY VS. TRUTH

In the summer of 1990, Jane, a housewife in a small town in central Ohio, gave birth to her third child. With that birth she had three daughters—a newborn, a three-year-old, and a six-year-old. Jane was thirty-four years old, in good health, and happily married to Dave, her high school sweetheart. Theirs was a complementary, loving relationship. He was quiet and methodical while Jane was extroverted and given to wide mood swings in response to her life experiences. Jane was the outgoing "character" of the two; she was talkative, gaining attention from others with her appealing humor.

This last delivery had been complicated. Labor was difficult and prolonged, with much exhaustion. The baby was healthy, but Jane was really "wiped out." She and her husband were a bit downhearted when their child was another girl rather than the hoped-for son, but those feelings were replaced quickly with genuine affection for the new baby. Jane, however, did not seem to spring back to her old self. She regained her functioning but became easily tearful. Little things seemed to overwhelm her, and she unloaded her feelings on her husband like a torrent when he came home from work. This worsened so much that Dave became irritable and frustrated, seeing his wife as incessantly "whining." She was sad, saw every demand as overwhelming, cried easily, was tired all the time, and complained constantly.

At the urging of their family physician, Jane and Dave saw a local psychiatrist. Dave just wanted Jane to "get well." He hoped that the doctor would give her some pills. At the conclusion of the session she was diagnosed as having "postpartum depression," given an antidepressant, and referred to a local social worker for "supportive psychotherapy."

Jane dutifully reported to her therapist every week over the next month without really feeling any better at all. Her psychiatrist had increased her medication dose, but all she gained from that was a dry mouth and some dizziness. She did not experience the promised elevation of her "depression." She told her therapist about her life, her upbringing, her marriage, and her friends. She really had no complaints and described herself as very fortunate to have had such a "wonderful life." She extolled her now deceased parents and praised her husband, but felt bad because she was "letting them down."

Jane's therapist finally asked her, "If everything in your life is so wonderful, then why are you depressed?" Now Jane felt as though she was disappointing her therapist, and she resolved to be a "better patient." Her therapist then told her that sometimes there are things locked in the depths of the mind that control our present lives, that we cannot find and change without specialized help. The therapist taught Jane, in a simplified way, about the "unconscious" and "repression." She said that with help, one can unlock the secrets of the unconscious, can know it, and by sheer determination can control it. The bad can be replaced with good, and thus a miserable life can become a happy one . . . with some professional help. She explained that often there are things in the unconscious that one does not want to know, some really bad things that might lie hidden, but that must be brought out if one is to "get well." These bad things do leave a trail of hints in our everyday life that can tip off a therapist to the "real problem."

Jane began to feel excited because she could see that her therapist was no longer seeing her as uninteresting or nonproductive, but

as somebody with a really interesting past "just below the surface."
The therapist began to ask more pointed but seemingly unconnected questions: Did you ever act like an adult when only a child?
Were you ever self-conscious about your body? Did you ever have
nightmares or sleeping problems? Were you ever defiant or compliant to an extreme? Did you tend to have older friends? Do you
always try to please others? Have you had a sense of overwhelming
responsibilities? Have you ever had low self-esteem? Did you ever
do too well or too poorly in school? Was your father overly protective? Do you act differently around different people? Have you ever
felt or dreamed that a "black cloud" was over you?

Jane's therapist said she was aware that her questions seemed
unconnected; she assured Jane that the questions were from published lists of "tip-off" questions, "proven" as indicators of
repressed problems that could be negatively influencing one's present life. Jane was impressed with her therapist's resolve to get to
the "core" of her problem. She resolved to make every effort to
comply. She was informed that she gave enough positive responses
to the tip-off questions that the therapist was sure that she was
repressing memories of traumatic experiences. Furthermore, they
were the cause of her seemingly hopeless case of depression and
must be retrieved.

The therapist was, however, worried that she might be getting
beyond her own expertise with Jane's case. Who knows what might
be discovered, and could she handle it? She had read accounts of
patients recovering some pretty awful stuff and was not sure she was
experienced enough to "work through" all of that with Jane.
Privately she wondered if Jane's father might have been something
other than the respected farmer, family man, and church elder that
everyone in town had always thought he was. A good exterior can
cover up a foul interior. Was she (the therapist) ready to be the one
in that small town to expose something so terrible?

The therapist attended a professional meeting of family therapists in a nearby city. She listened to a lecture on the recovery of
repressed memories of child abuse. The featured speaker was well
known for his pioneering work in this area. He gave a fascinating

lecture that seemed to be speaking directly to the therapist and to her patient Jane. After the lecture, she approached the doctor in the hall and briefly presented Jane's case to him. She especially recounted the positive answers to the tip-off questions and the seemingly "wonderful" past the patient insisted was hers.

The psychiatrist told Jane's therapist that he and his associates had recently opened a special inpatient unit at the university hospital for the treatment of patients with problems stemming from the repression of past abuse. This was the answer! The therapist called Jane at home from the hotel and excitedly asked her to come to the conference to meet this "specialist." Jane rushed to the conference and had a brief interview with the doctor. She was admitted to the special inpatient unit the next week and stayed there continuously for the next forty-one months.

Once on the unit, Jane found that she was going to be the doctor's private patient. She was more than a little pleased, because the other people on the unit were seen individually by residents and other "lesser" staff. She was especially grateful that her health insurance included full coverage of inpatient psychiatric care.

Jane gave her all to the therapy. Her doctor was interested not so much in what she remembered but in what she did not remember. He told her that she may have to go through some "deep water" before she got better. He also told her that what she would discover might be "pretty awful," but that she had to trust him and "hang in there." His questions were pointed and probing. When she could not find what he was looking for, he gave her "homework" to search her mind, her past, and her dreams for the missing information.

Jane worked hard. The doctor warned her again and again of what might be forthcoming and helped her anticipate what she would find and how she should handle it. Fragments began to emerge. There *were* times that her father did in fact lose his temper. There *were* spans of time that she could not account for. There was a time when she felt a presence in her bedroom at night. She did have some nightmares about fires. There were times that she seemed familiar with places she did not remember having been to.

There were times that she was accused of doing things or saying things she "knew" she had not done or said. Her doctor was pleased with her for remembering these "fragments." He didn't seem surprised that some of these memories were associated with fear or anguish. Nothing about her seemed to surprise him. He seemed "able to read her mind."

Jane seemed to have difficulty putting the fragments together. The doctor suggested some explanations from his experience with other similar patients. "My father abusive toward me? Never!" But the more she did her homework, the more it seemed to make sense and to fit with the doctor's theory. Fitting the fragments together was not easy for Jane; she required a lot of help. Her doctor used hypnosis repeatedly and discovered many things about her past. After such sessions, she would be distraught at the revelations. She began to have doubts about her treatment and questioned whether or not such things had really happened to her. The formerly compliant patient became resistant and sometimes argumentative. Her doctor saw it as a sign that her past experiences were unusually traumatic, and thus resistance was to be expected. The abrupt and unpredictable switching of his patient from compliant to resistant and back caused him to explore other past behaviors like that. He talked with Jane about previous lapses or gaps in her memory and whether she ever slipped into fantasy life or pretended to be another person. Jane did have a rich fantasy life as a child and, yes, there were times that she was accused of doing something that she didn't think she had done. *Maybe I did switch to another personality, an alter, to enjoy something or escape something,* Jane thought. During a hypnotic therapy session "Edith" was discovered. Edith was the first of more than thirty-five distinct "alters" that were "discovered" by the doctor and Jane over the next year. These alters were fascinating to the doctor and frightening to Jane when she heard about them. Even more scary were the stories they "told" the doctor and the staff about their combined past.

By asking questions, by anticipating the answers, by preparing Jane for the answers, by teaching Jane about how her mind worked and how it controlled her present, by hypnotic suggestion, by "flooding therapy" (tying the patient down in a seclusion room and yelling the "truth" in her ears until she collapses in acceptance), by simulation sessions (acting out what happened and looking for signs of familiarity or its tricky reverse—revulsion—to prove its truth), by rewarding her for making progress and secluding her when she became resistant, by listening to every "alter" and writing down its every word . . . the full story emerged. Using the theories and practices of modern psychotherapy, the doctor was able to piece together the fragments until a plausible, coherent "personal narrative" was created that not only explained Jane's presenting complaints but also fitted nicely with his theoretical position and practice specialty.

Jane, the psychiatrist decided, had been raised by parents who led a satanic cult. Most of the people in her town were in it. Her father and others raped her regularly during these "services." Many others were abused. Women in town bred babies to be sacrificed. These services were held at night in the church basement. Jane herself had bred babies before she was married. She or her alters had abused her own children and allowed them to take part in the rituals. She had kept this from her husband. In her altered states, she had done many awful things.

As these "memories" were "recovered," Jane required more and more psychotropic medication to control her moods and anxiety. She became a "zombie" on the unit and was obsessed with killing herself.

Because of Jane's "discoveries," it was decided that her two older children needed intensive treatment. They were admitted to the inpatient children's unit of the same hospital and remained there for the last twenty-one of their mother's forty-one months of hospitalization. During their stay, they were seen in individual therapy and play therapy, where they would be exposed to toys and dolls to assess their familiarity and past experience with physical and sexual abuse, satanic rituals, weapons, and instruments of torture.

Dave was at home during all this time. He worked at a large corporation with excellent medical insurance and therefore had to stay on the job to keep the insurance policy. He took care of the baby with the help of his sister. He was initially incredulous at his wife's case, but as it developed he gradually assumed it must all be true. Jane's parents had both died in the first year of his and Jane's marriage. He had never known them well. Jane's only sister had died "of natural causes" when Jane was only six years old. Dave had moved to the town only a few months before he met Jane in high school and was not in any position to deny what the professionals at the university hospital were telling him about the family.

Early in the course of Jane's treatment, Dave would question the validity of her recovered memories. He was repeatedly assured by the doctor and the staff that her recollections were accurate because they were in fact productions of her repressed unconscious and as such were valid and meaningful. He was repeatedly asked, "Why would she make it up?" His protest that there was no evidence to substantiate the recollections was met with various facile explanations, including the claim that abuse like hers is always well covered and evidence is never found. One of his protests included the fact that the church had never had a basement!

In the thirty-sixth month of Jane's stay at the hospital, she was really no better. She was switching from one alter to another. She required lots of medication. She received lots of attention from the staff. She was also seen daily by a resident who said he loved her and wanted to see her even after he was no longer assigned to the unit. At about this time, a new psychiatrist came to work on the unit. He began to work with Jane to help her alleviate the guilt over what she had done in the past. During sessions of deep hypnosis, which he called "seances," he tried to help her make contact with the spirits of the sacrificed babies so that she could obtain the names and addresses of their "parents," in order to make some kind of expiative contact with them. He was unable, however, to conjure up the identities of the victims or their street addresses and blamed Jane for lack of cooperation.

In the thirty-eighth month of Jane's hospital stay, a medical student was assigned to the unit for a three-month rotation through clinical services. He took an interest in Jane and her case. Though he had no psychiatric experience or expertise, he reviewed Jane's voluminous chart and concluded that it was her care that was insane, not Jane. He began to talk with her and eventually discussed his conclusions with Jane's husband. Initially his efforts were fruitless, and Jane accused him of trying to set her back and of having been sent from the "coven." She reported him to the staff, but they did not believe her, assuming it was another "alter" playing games as always. After the student finished his rotation on the unit, he continued to visit Jane and her husband occasionally.

Meanwhile, the staff on the unit seemed to be losing interest in Jane. She was no longer making progress, and since she was approaching the $1.5 million limit on her insurance, they were thinking of sending her to a state hospital. This reality shocked Jane, who saw herself as a model patient who was there to get well. The last visit by the medical student before his graduation was the point at which Jane and her husband both became convinced that they had been led down the garden path of false memories. A few days later Jane and Dave signed out of the hospital with their two daughters, against medical advice.

The family returned home and took up their daily responsibilities. There has been no subsequent counseling, medication, or accusations. Jane leads a normal life as wife and mother and occasionally speaks in public about her experiences to warn others of such risks.

NEW DEFINITIONS OF TRUTH

Jane's story is true, except for the names of people and places. And over the last several years her story in its essence has been repeated often enough that more than 12,000 sets of parents have joined an organization called the False Memory Syndrome Foundation. All of these parents tell essentially the same story: One of their children (a daughter in 94 percent of the cases) went into insight-oriented psychotherapy for some problem; their complaints were vague and common, such as depression, lack of fulfillment, lack of achievement, marital disharmony, weight problems, and the like; the therapist eventually suspected that there were some repressed traumatic experiences that needed to be exposed; through a series of questions and tip-off signs this hypothesis was "confirmed"; then, through a process of anticipative questioning their daughters had vivid, clear, emotional recollections of past abuse. At the suggestion of the therapists, every one of these daughters then confronted their parents with charges of past abuse; the parents all denied those charges; they all were then told that they were "in denial" and were therefore barred from any further contact with their daughters until they were ready to confess.

All of these parents report that their daughters have drifted away from them into a replacement world of therapy, survivor groups, and ceaseless "recovery" of more and more memories of abuse and abusers.

Why wouldn't a psychotherapist try to *confirm* the recollections of his client, especially when they allege criminal abuse at the hands of another identifiable person? This is certainly the standard practice in working with children. The merest mention of abuse of any conceivable kind sends the therapist to the telephone to report the perpetrator to the authorities. State laws demand this and grants the reporting therapist total immunity from claims of libel or slander. Those who knowingly fail to comply with this reporting requirement can lose their professional license. This is not at all the case, however, in the conduct of individual or group psychotherapy with adults. The response of a typical therapist to this question might startle one who does not understand the theories and resultant practices of modern American psychotherapy. A typical therapist simply does not see confirmation of historical data as his professional, moral, or ethical responsibility. He does not see reporting of accused abusers as his civic responsibility. He is not at all burdened by questions regarding the absence of witnesses or physical evidence. The use of the information for purposes of redress is someone else's business. The typical therapist is concerned only with the acquisition of information from the patient's mind. The goal is to develop a rationale by which the patient may understand his or her life and problems. The goal is to develop "insight." The only thing deemed important is what the patient feels or believes. The goal is to develop the patient's personal narrative or story, in hopes of making sense of his or her life. In the business of insight-oriented psychotherapy, this constitutes "psychic reality." As Ellen Bass and Laura Davis wrote in their book *Courage to Heal,* "If you think you were abused . . . then you were."[1]

In the years during which Freud assembled his theory of the mind, there was considerable optimism among scientists. They believed that they were on a course of progress in which no aspect of reality would be beyond human understanding. Their optimism was fueled by the many obvious material signs of scientific advancement; these were the years of the industrial revolution and of numerous discoveries in all fields of science. Empiricism—the view that our only source of knowledge is the observation and measurement of material data—was the method by which they believed they would reach their goal of thoroughly knowing and controlling reality. This epistemological optimism was grounded in the belief that there is an objective reality "out there" that we can discover and know with absolute certainty.

As discussed in chapter 1, this was the time during which Darwin's theory of evolution of the species through environmental determinism or natural selection was published and began to have significant influence. Darwin's contribution to Freud's theory, however, goes well beyond the fundamental idea of environmental determinism. Of equal import is the widespread acceptance of a historical epistemology without which Darwinism could not have been accepted, and without which Darwinism never could have had its far-reaching influence on science in general and on psychology in particular. When the "historical" methods of knowing traditionally used by anthropologists, paleontologists, and embryologists were placed on a par with the methods of knowing traditionally used by mathematicians and physicists, the definition of "science" was significantly broadened. Freud could have successfully assembled his theory of the mind and of psychoanalysis only during a time when the very concept of what is science had already been broadened. Freud was a physician who always thought of himself as a scientist. He knew that if his goals were to be achieved, his contribution must be accepted as a "science." But it was only in the broadened concept of science of Freud's day that psychoanalysis could claim to be a science.

The expanded epistemology of science that allowed Darwin's theory to be termed scientific was much advanced by Darwinism itself. Strict definition of concepts, rigorous experimentation, use of measurable and objective data, and falsifiability had been the traditional methods of empirical scientific investigation. These methods were not entirely rejected, but the acquisition of knowledge based on such things as similarity, tradition, belief, authority, and association was added to the traditional empirical methods. As such, not only was the very definition of science expanded, but the concept of scientific proof had to be expanded as well. To the traditional methods of empirical proof, such as reproducibility and competitive replication of experimental results, were added plausibility and desirability of outcome. These became acceptable ways for "scientists" to "prove" that their assertions were in fact "truth."

Prior to this time, it would not have been possible for an investigator of the human mind such as Freud to identify himself or his pursuit as scientific. Freud himself recognized a distinction between "human concerns and natural objects."[2] Natural or material objects had been the traditional domain of empirical scientific inquiry. Such objects could be measured, weighed, and manipulated in accordance with the known laws of the material universe. "Human concerns," questions of the mind and the meaning of life, had been the domain of philosophers and theologians.

During the same years that the epistemology of science was being expanded, the belief in the supernatural was receding in importance and influence. Darwin's decisive role in this marginalization of the supernatural was his presentation of the first theory of evolution completely devoid of the God of Scripture or even of an "intelligent designer." Theologians of that time offered little or no resistance, and the relentless momentum began toward a completely atheistic and naturalistic metaphilosophy of science. Today this momentum appears to be maximized, with God having been totally rejected from science.

An expanded definition of science, an expanded epistemology of science, an expanded repertoire of proof-methods, and an absence of God and the supernatural: These were the nutrients in which Freud's ideas took root; this is the pseudoscientific base of the insight-oriented psychotherapy industry as we know it today.

The denial of God forces this expanded concept of science to rely on "a kind of social and political process of consensus among specialists, whose data reflect decisions and choices about what is relevant and important to observe and label."[3] This is the case precisely because there is no accepted higher authority to serve as a benchmark. The only means of settling disputes between divergent or competing theories and claims is to reach a political consensus. Thus, areas of inquiry once seen as forbidden by God have become the domain of the expanded concept of science, and the final authority of God's Word to settle human disputes and questions has been dismissed and usurped by the court of human consensus.

Freud apparently wanted to develop a scientific method by which man could know, understand, and correct his psychic reality, the operations of his mind. Freud's methods were not the methods of natural science but of an expanded concept of science. Only in this expanded science could his psychoanalytic methods participate as scientific. The operations of the mind are obviously inner and subjective rather than external and objective. They obviously do not lend themselves to measuring and weighing. Freud, therefore, had to use *subjective* methods to achieve his *objective* goal. Psychoanalysis has been defined as a "self-reflective process which enables patients to retrospectively understand their own psychic reality—in other words, to reconstruct lost personal meanings."[4] For Freud then, and for insight-oriented psychotherapists today, one's psychic reality is this subjective reality that is discovered by self-reflection, remembering, repeating, interpretation, reconstruction, and the various specialized techniques originated by Freud and his successors. This reconstructed psychic reality is treated as if it were natural, measurable, weighable reality. The methods of knowing psychic reality may have no relation to empirical science, but according to psychoanalytic dogma this psychic reality is fully knowable. The methods of that knowing are considered to be "scientific" and therefore capable of generating "truth."

Freud himself became convinced that nothing we recollect from our past can or need be thought of as objective in the same way that natural, material reality is objective. For Freud and his followers, however, the obvious distinctions between fantasy and real experience became irrelevant.[5] What became important was not the objective historical *fact*, but the *meaning* that the therapist decides the assumed fact has in the subject's history.[6] Thus this psychotherapeutic "knowing" of a patient's psychic reality has more to do with what is "useful" to the concerned parties than with what is verifiable historical fact.[7]

This approach to personal historical fact and data collection represents common practice in psychotherapy: feelings, not facts—if you remember it, it happened. Whether or not it is objectively verifiable or measurable, it is as real as a rock or a brick. One can understand the concern of some, even in the psychotherapy movement itself, that patients lacking a sense of what is objectively true or "authentic" about themselves would be tempted to look to their therapists as the ultimate authority concerning their own psychic reality. Thus the dangerous possibility of suggestion by the therapist is created by the very nature and design of the psychotherapy process. Sandor Ferenczi wrote of this concern in 1933 and cautioned that patients would be subject to coercion or suggestion by the therapist in an effort to gain insight or "historical understanding."[8] Freud was more than willing to regard his patients' fantasies and recollections as "reality," and he downplayed the risk of suggestion. Ferenczi reacted against this by developing special therapeutic techniques that he theorized would help his patients accurately remember specific traumatic abuses by their parents. He blindly believed that such recollections would be more objectively real or valid than the fantasies or "re-transcriptions" so easily accepted by Freud. In a misguided effort to achieve valid historical data, however, Ferenczi actually further set the stage for the modern epidemic of "recovered memories" that has destroyed so many families in the last decade.

This is how insight-oriented psychotherapists are trained to regard historical fact vs. fantasy, evidence vs. hearsay, or proof vs. mere acceptance of a patient's "personal narrative." Therapists are not so much trained to pursue objective, verifiable facts as they are to pursue feelings. The notion of "checking out the story" is simply foreign to the psychotherapist. No wonder then that manufactured, concocted tales of long-repressed but newly remembered abuse, even satanic ritual abuse, are so blithely accepted: They are accepted because they are useful, they correspond to a prevailing theory, and they are coherent with other similar theories and with the experience of the therapist.

THE BIBLICAL STANDARD FOR TRUTH

Christians are called to be much more demanding in their approach to truth. The most important source of truth is the revealed truth of God's infallible and inerrant Word. John 17:17 says, "Your word is truth." Jesus said, "I am the Truth." That is not simply saying that the Word is accurate but that it is *truth itself.* God is truth, and His Word is therefore the ultimate standard of truth. All assertions of truth, for Christians, must be tested against God's written Word. All assertions that conform to Scripture are true, while those that violate Scripture are false. Scripture is not exhaustive on every subject of interest to the human mind, but God has given us a mind created in His own image, and even though fallen we are able to discover truth about God's created order so long as we play by His rules. For the Christian, there is the fundamental promise that God is truth and cannot be contradicted. Therefore, there are two rules for the discovery of truth:

1. the use of the authentic scientific method, and

2. the testing of all discoveries and inventions against Scripture.

God is truth and cannot be contradicted. Rigorous, honest scientific inquiry has never discovered and will never discover any fact about God's creation that will contradict His Word. The acquisition of new scientific knowledge, for a Christian, is an exciting revelation of God's creation, its wonder and majesty. It confirms the truth of Scripture and deepens our faith in God. Stephen Hawking claims to have mathematically proven that in one instant there was nothing and in the next there was the universe. As an unbeliever, Hawking looks God in the face and does not see Him. Does he practice good science? Most likely. Does his assertion fit with Scripture? Most definitely. Has he discovered truth? Yes. He simply refuses to bow before his Creator.

The first rule for the discovery of truth is the scientific method itself. This is the gold-standard rule of play for the serious scientist who seeks to discover truth about the creation around us. The scientific method begins with a question or an observation, which leads to a clearly formulated hypothesis. Out of this comes an experiment designed to be *able* to reliably prove the hypothesis correct or *able* to reliably prove the hypothesis wrong. In serious science, falsifiability is as important as verifiability. Only by proper formulation of the question, only by proper design of the experiment, only by rigorous statistical methods of data analysis . . . and then only by replication at the hands of other competent experimenters . . . can true science be conducted in a rigorous manner, so that some new recognition of facts about God's created order can be added to our prior discoveries of His truth.

The second rule is that all assertions of truth discovered by the scientific method must be benchmarked against the truth of Scripture. Our discovered truth must be tested against the ultimate written revelation of truth: Considering that our eyes and minds are flawed since the Fall, have we really proved the hypothesis true or false? The failure to test new assertions about human psychic functioning against Scripture is in part based on the reality that many things about man—such things as anatomy, neurochemistry, and genetics—are not detailed in Scripture. Man can discover truths about himself that lie outside the domain of Scripture, but these are discoveries of empirical science. Although the results from this kind of scientific inquiry lie outside of Scripture, they do not contradict Scripture.

In Jane's case, a number of the fundamental assumed truths of psychotherapy were brought into play. They were used in the assessment of her problems, the confirmation of the so-called diagnosis, the specific methods of investigation employed, and the treatment offered. Without exception, these "pillars" of psychotherapy, which we outlined in chapter 1, are products of the broadened concept of science that allowed Darwin's findings to be accepted as science. These supposed truths are popular, they sound scientific, they are accepted by other revered leaders in the field, and they are deemed efficacious. They allow therapists to ignore facts, evidence, and witnesses as less important than feelings, introspection, and the development of a personal narrative. The practice flows from the principles, and the principles have consequences.

The beliefs underlying insight-oriented psychotherapy are the products of religion, not of empirical science. Since the scientific method cannot be applied to such beliefs, the test of scriptural contradiction is of utmost importance.

Are we born innocent? Are we only a product of our upbringing? Are we all victims? Were we born with essential goodness, little bundles of potentiality?

Can we know and cure our unconscious?

How are we to look at ourselves and our lives? Whose perspective are we to seek on our own "personal narratives?"

What should a counselor do? Does a counselor speak with authority? Do his theories and methods really make sense, biblically? Is there a "right thing to do" in counseling?

Are we to avoid trial, pain, guilt, and shame? Are the goals of life the achievement of sufficient self-esteem, security, fulfilling relationships, and transcendent experiences?

As we saw in chapter 2, these questions all have clear answers from Scripture. We have a responsibility as students of the Word to apply that Word to all aspects of our lives. Human wisdom and philosophy in the psychological realm constitute a false gospel. They speak of a different anthropology, a different salvation, and a different kind of sanctification. I challenge you as students and teachers to apply the Word and the mind that God has given you to the understanding of God's truth.

In chapter 12 we will focus at length on the false-memory epidemic, a tragic outgrowth of psychotherapy's misguided definition of truth. Unfortunately, as we will see, Jane's needless suffering at the hands of the psychotherapy industry is far from unique.

TWELVE

❦

RECOVERED MEMORY THERAPY: HAVE WE RECOVERED FROM IT?

Americans frequently allow themselves to be borne away, far beyond the bounds of reason, by a sudden passion of a hasty opinion, and sometimes gravely commit strange absurdities.

—ALEXIS DE TOCQUEVILLE[1]

In a brief two-page report, published in *Science* magazine in 1983, research psychologists Jean-Roch Laurence and Campbell Perry of Concordia University in Montreal issued a warning that the "use of hypnosis may unwittingly create pseudomemories of crimes which, subsequent to hypnosis, come to be believed as true by the person hypnotized." They went on to postulate that this phenomenon grows out of the "strong demand characteristics" of the situations in which hypnosis is used, that the subjects of hypnosis are "highly motivated to help" the investigator discover required information, and that the entire process rests upon the belief in "mind as a videotape recorder and hypnosis as a means of reaching material that is stored veridically at a level not immediately available to consciousness."[2]

In addition, the researchers pointed out that "such investigative hypnosis procedures virtually require fantasy," that since "the subject ordinarily perceives the hypnotist as an expert, a process of confusing fantasy with fact may occur unwittingly and unknown to either the subject or the hypnotist," and that "there is no way to differentiate what actually happened from what a person recalls of it during hypnosis, other than obtaining verification of the hypnotically elicited recall."

Laurence and Perry concluded their report with this statement: "Such 'recall' could lead to a false but positive investigation and to all of the legal procedures and penalties that this implies. Accordingly, the utmost caution should be exercised whenever hypnosis is used as an investigative tool."

The warning of these two research psychologists proved to be prescient. "Utmost caution" was certainly not exercised, and as a result a pandemic of Recovered Memory Therapy swept across our land, devastating tens of thousands of individual and family lives. Grown children began to accuse their incredulous parents of emotional, physical, sexual, and even satanic ritual abuse after having "recovered" memories of such things through psychotherapy.

For more than a decade, this pandemic raged without any significant effort to resist or combat it. An entire industry of Recovered Memory Therapy was spawned in which a large percentage of counselors in this country willingly and enthusiastically participated. It has been conservatively estimated that, at its peak, a minimum of 62,500 professional therapists saw more than one million new cases each year in which supposedly long-repressed memories of abuse were recovered. An entire subculture of "Survivors of Incest/Abuse" grew up in response to the frenzied recovery of such memories. It is estimated that more than 2.5 million women claim to be "survivors" of such abuse, and that one out of every twenty-five families in America has been impacted by this menace.[3] Endless seminars, entire libraries of books, countless media presentations, exposés, and testimonies arose in a crescendo of power and profit. Celebrities, lawyers, politicians, and average citizens joined the bandwagon, explaining the troubles in their lives by revealing newly "discovered" memories of horrific abuse committed by their parents, pastors, teachers, and others. In the process, thousands of authority figures, claiming innocence, were accused, rejected, hauled into court, publicly shamed, and even imprisoned on charges based on evidence that already in 1972 had been identified as quite likely to produce "believed-in imaginings."[4]

After reaching its peak in the mid-1990s, the entire Recovered Memory Therapy movement and its step-child Incest/Abuse Survivor movement seem to be abating and receding quietly into the dark closet of psycho-history. This is a closet already crowded with other cast-off fads of psychotherapy. Lacking solid foundation, one movement after another has come and gone over the course of psychotherapy's one-hundred-year history. Recovered Memory Therapy is being forced unwillingly into this closet. Mounting public ridicule, increasing malpractice awards, growing professional doubt, reports of objective scientific investigation, and organizational condemnation are driving this destructive psycho-fad from the scene. This fading, however, does little to repair the broken and embittered lives of those who fell prey to the false memories and accusations.

We are now in the fortunate position of being able to look back at this movement and learn something of value from it. The movement's origins, growth, development, and decline have been voluminously reported and documented. Its adherents and practitioners are well known and are still among us. Its victims are all around us and are available to relate their experiences.

THE ORIGINS OF RECOVERED MEMORY THERAPY

The Recovered Memory Therapy movement was the understandable consequence of various ideas working their influence both independently and in concert. These ideas range in age from several centuries to just a few decades. I will try to show that these ideas include:

- Freudian psychoanalytic theory
- Freudian epistemology (his concept of truth)
- changing ideas about and attitudes toward child abuse
- the idea of victimization

- the influences of radical feminism
- the popularity of focusing on past trauma
- the "diseasification" of the human predicament

I will argue that notably absent amid the unbridled influence of these ideas was the protective bulwark of Christianity. Instead of warning and teaching, there was in fact complicity on the part of the church.

There could not have been a Recovered Memory Therapy pandemic without essentially erroneous beliefs about man, his mind, and his problems. These essential beliefs constitute the "pillars" of insight-oriented psychotherapy as formulated by Sigmund Freud a century ago. These pillars stand firm today as the fundamental beliefs underlying the practice of all insight-oriented psychotherapy.

One of these pillars was alluded to by Laurence and Perry in their prophetic 1983 paper. They stated that the representation of "mind as a video tape recorder" with "material that is stored veridically at a level not immediately available to consciousness" was fundamental to the hypnotic recovery of supposedly hidden or repressed memories. That is simply another way of stating the fundamental Freudian doctrine of psychic determinism. This "pillar" of Freudianism insists that the human mind has an active, dynamic, unconscious where all of life's experiences, sensations, perceptions, traumas, painful feelings, and memories are stored in an accurate, valid, reliable archive, hidden out of our usual awareness but actively influencing our daily thoughts, feelings, and behaviors for good or ill. The content of this hypothesized dynamic unconscious is suppressed, or kept out of our conscious awareness, by the supposed mechanisms of repression and/or dissociation, but this content expresses itself indirectly through cryptic means that allegedly cause us to have mental and emotional problems ranging from mild anxiety to florid multiple personality disorders.[5]

In addition to this pillar of psychic determinism, there are other beliefs fundamental to Freud that enabled and encouraged the Recovered Memory Therapy episode. One is the belief that reliable insight into the unconscious, the out-of-awareness mind, is both possible and necessary.[6] This pillar asserts that, with proper guidance and technique, a person can access the archives of the unconscious, obtain reliable information, and then somehow use that information to improve his or her life. The acquisition of this essential insight, however, requires the help of a therapist (another basic Freudian doctrine). Such a therapist will have been trained to understand the cryptic expressions of the unconscious, to break down repression, and to expose the causes of the problems that brought the client into therapy.

Another Freudian doctrine essential to Recovered Memory Therapy is environmental determinism, the belief that, were it not for improper environmental influences at crucial points in our development, we would all be free of any mental or emotional problems. We have seen that a confluence of ideas during the late 1800s contributed to the widespread acceptance of environmental determinism. Where there was an effect there must be a cause, and the cause of an undesirable effect must be outside of ourselves, something for which we are not personally responsible. It became popular in Freud's time to interpret the obvious human "degeneration" of the day as the result of genetics or disease or pollution or industrialization—anything but personal sin. What once would have been seen as morally reprehensible behavior came to be seen as signs and symptoms of disease. Thieves, drunkards, and arsonists became kleptomaniacs, alcoholics, and pyromaniacs.

The pillars of insight and environmental determinism, together with the pillar of psychic determinism, were essential to and set the stage for the Recovered Memory Therapy debacle. Resting on these basic ideas, psychotherapy has always sought to remember and reconstruct early life events and experiences. Those early life events are assumed to have determined the life of the client and to have caused whatever problems he or she might have. Those events must therefore be retrieved, exposed, understood, and somehow "worked through" or corrected.[7] The kinds of early life events that therapists have pursued have varied considerably over the last century, but the basic quest for awareness and understanding of such determinative past experiences has not changed.

Initially in his career, as we have seen, Freud was looking for, and attributing his clients' mental problems to, early traumatic experiences of sexual abuse.[8] During subsequent years, he and other therapists postulated and tried to discover other kinds of early adverse life experiences.[9] These included such things as parental rearing practices, age-specific fantasies and the interaction of age-specific instincts with the environment, the development and course of relationships, and the desire for autonomy or power. It is characteristic of the history of psychotherapy that new ideas constantly push old ones from the scene. These new ideas are usually the invention of a popular charismatic leader; they are typically in vogue for a time, only to be discarded when the next new idea comes along.

Underneath all this change, however, the fundamental beliefs and practices remain the same. The pillar of environmental determinism causes the therapist to search the client's past for the origin of his or her troubles. In searching for these early life experiences, the objective historical accuracy of the recall is considered of little importance. The focus instead is on the relationship between the client and therapist and how the therapist saw this past replaying itself in that relationship. In the last two decades, the search for early-life sexual trauma has been the key to the explanation for life's problems.

Another idea helping to lay the foundation for Recovered Memory Therapy—which we examined in chapter 11—was Freud's concept of truth. From the beginning of his career, Freud was troubled with the difference between what he called "historical truth" and psychic or "psychical" reality. Historical truth has been understood to refer to real events in the past that can be objectively validated and confirmed by witnesses to have actually occurred. In his earliest examinations of patients, Freud simply believed the memories of early sexual abuse that he helped his patients retrieve through free association and other techniques. He accepted the stories from these retrievals as actual historical fact. When it became clear to Freud that *all* of his patients were discovering such memories, that they were fleeing his treatment, that their accused fathers were joining in recrimination against him, and that his reputation was at stake, he jettisoned his "Seduction Theory." In its place he postulated that what was powerfully buried in the unconscious of his patients was not necessarily memories of *actual* events but rather incestuous *fantasies* that were occasioned by the vagaries of their improper rearing. It is from this base that Freud was able to assert that, "It is psychical reality which is of the decisive kind."[10] In this way Freud "replaced the reality of unconscious memories with the psychic reality of unconscious fantasies."[11] Most importantly, however, Freud established the method of arriving at truth for the entire insight-oriented psychotherapy industry. Because of Freud, truth for the therapist is not at all defined by what can be objectively established; it is defined rather by what is felt or experienced. Corroboration of or evidence for psychic reality simply does not apply. The patient's own reality is the only reality. The only test of such psychic reality is consistency, plausibility, understandability, and whether it makes sense to the patient. As a result, the goal of psychotherapy today is to develop a "personal narrative" or a rationale by which the patient is able to understand his or her life and its problems. The actual, objective truthfulness of that personal narrative is immaterial.

Over the last forty years there has been a dramatic change in our culture in its ideas about child abuse, and this also helped set the stage for the Recovered Memory Therapy movement. In 1955 it was confidently reported that incest occurred at a rate of about one or two cases per year per one million persons in America.[12] Probably such figures were the result of under-reporting. Even so, that data and its acceptance tells us much about the difference between the culture of that day and our present experience. In 1962 C. Henry Kempe, M.D., coined the term "Battered Child Syndrome."[13] He reported in the medical literature his findings on children with bruises that had been assumed to be the result of some undefined bleeding problem; his shocking discovery was that these children, in fact, were being physically abused or "battered." His report and others that quickly followed captivated public attention. Legislative bodies across the nation quickly passed laws encouraging the reporting of suspected child abuse and guaranteeing the informant protection against libel and slander actions. Within three years of Kempe's report, all fifty states had established laws penalizing health care workers for not reporting cases of suspected child abuse. Accordingly, bureaucracies were established in each state designed to respond to the ever-increasing reported cases of child abuse. By 1974 the National Center on Child Abuse and Neglect had been established to collect data, study the problem, and help prevent it.

Along the way, the definition of what constituted child abuse progressively expanded. What began as "battered" grew to include sexual abuse, emotional abuse and deprivation, environmental hardships of all kinds, the effects of economic adversity, and even parents who were present in the home but not really nurturing. As the years passed, more and more cases of this ever-expanding definition of child abuse were reported. The statistics grew more and more alarming. The effort to identify child abusers became more and more aggressive. Allegations that some were falsely accused seemed of little importance when balanced against the horror of injured and murdered children.

Few would question the value of detecting, punishing, and preventing child abuse. However, we do need to question the means. The bureaucracy formed to prevent child abuse helped pave the way toward an easy acceptance of the idea that memories in adults of abuse—long-repressed but newly retrieved through psychotherapy—could and should be used to accuse and convict other adults.

During the seventies, surveys of the background experiences of troubled and troublesome people became popular. Such surveys were based on the Freudian pillar of environmental determinism and fueled by the emerging awareness of the prevalence of child abuse. It was assumed that troubled and troublesome people had inevitably had a history of troubling experiences. Such surveys "discovered" that half of all stepdaughters were sexually abused by their stepfathers. Experiences of incestuous sexual abuse were found to be even more common in runaways, drug addicts, and prostitutes. Even worse, it was found that 20 percent of all women remembered at least one incestuous experience before the age of eighteen.[14] "In

1972, 610,000 [child abuse cases] were reported nationally, and by 1985 the number had exceeded 1.7 million."[15] By 1980 the annual incidence of child sexual abuse was "almost 43,000 cases."[16] Another report claimed that "6.8 million women nation-wide would say they had been raped once, 4.7 million more than once. . . . One in five women are incest victims."[17] The results of such surveys fostered the growth of the community mental health movement and the further elaboration of institutions and agencies designed to deal with the bad effects of improper environment. It seemed to be axiomatic that the troubles of individuals were caused by traumatic experiences earlier in their lives.

Beginning in the early 1980s and continuing into the early 90s, celebrity revelations and testimonials of past histories of child abuse became popular. LaToya Jackson, Roseanne Barr Arnold, the children of Joan Crawford, and 1958 Miss America Marilynn Van Derbur Atler came forward.[18] Long-held or long-"repressed" secrets were revealed in a most public manner. Famous parents previously held in high regard were treated with open contempt.

These were the years of the celebrated exposés of supposed systematic child abuse at day care centers. The McMartin Preschool, the Fells Acres Day Care Center, the Martensville Day Care Center, and others filled the headlines and the airwaves.[19] Ordinary people such as the Souse grandparents ended up in the headlines and in prison. Some of these cases were based on evidence that satisfied traditional legal standards of objectivity. More commonly, however, evidence of abuse accepted in court consisted of memories retrieved by hypnotists, psychotherapists, and zealous investigators who had become experts at ferreting out abuse and incest—with a special interest in satanic ritual abuse.

A convincing literature accumulated, encouraging investigators to believe the accusing child. Even when the accusation had clearly been suggested to the child, and even when the accusation was outlandish in every way and with no physical evidence, the child was to be considered the source of truth. "The more illogical and incredible the initiation scene might seem to adults, the more likely it is that the child's plaintive description is valid. . . . Children never fabricate the kinds of explicit sexual manipulations they divulge in complaints or interrogations."[20] Regardless of the lack of traditional evidence, regardless of the outrageous nature of the claimed abuse, regardless of the reputations and denials of the accused, the accusers were believed, and the overarching cause of eliminating child abuse was seen as being served.

The idea of victimization has been another factor contributing to the Recovered Memory Therapy movement. Building on the foundational idea that our troubles are caused by our environment, fueled by the relatively recent awareness of widespread child abuse, facilitated by statistics from countless surveys, and confirmed by the growing number of abuse convictions, a culture of victimization solidified. As we have demonstrated elsewhere, the culture of victimization really began taking form in Europe and America at the turn of the century. Appealing to "a rather human temptation to view all things on a balance of cause and effect," it became increasingly popular for people to view their troubled selves as victims and the cause of their troubles as being some active perpetrator.[21] "To see oneself as 'victim' can provide the illusion of a shield against the difficulties of assuming appropriate personal responsibility for one's own feelings, actions, or even inactions. Seeing oneself as 'victim' can enable one to retain an illusion of innocence and a belief that a perfect world can exist if only others were perfect in providing the sort of life we would like to have."[22]

Before the Recovered Memory Therapy movement of the mid 1980s, one version of psychotherapy after another had come and gone in faddish waves. Psychoanalysis, family therapy, encounter groups, transcendental meditation, transactional analysis, rebirthing, primal scream therapy, adult children of alcoholics, healing of the "inner child," the "dysfunctional family," codependency—all of these and more vied for the attention and investment of the troubled American. Without exception, all of these movements encouraged their clients to identify themselves as victims, to look for traumatic experiences in their past, and to attribute the causation of the troubles in their lives to those traumatic experiences.

The rise of radical feminism also had a substantial part in the origination and advancement of Recovered Memory Therapy. From the women's movement has consistently come reports of actual and imagined abuse of women by men. Unfortunately, the number of women actually battered is in fact increasing in a society with little or no fear of God. However, the temptation to attribute all of their troubles to the males in their environment is overpowering for some women. Males become perpetrators, women become victims. From the beginnings of psychotherapy, fathers have been the preferred target of attribution for the troubles of not only their daughters but also their sons. Freud ran aground on this issue in 1896, wrested himself free of it in 1897, and now, in vastly larger numbers, we are back on those shoals.

Another influence leading to Recovered Memory Therapy was the focus on past trauma. Even though the search for unacknowledged, causative, traumatic experiences in one's past has been a consistent practice since the beginning of insight-oriented psychotherapy, this focus has intensified in recent years.[23] The search for and understanding of past traumatic experiences became more important in psychotherapy after World War II but was dramatically intensified after the Vietnam War. The horrific experiences of veterans of these two wars and their mental and emotional aftereffects became fodder for this increased emphasis.

The emergence of the concept of post-traumatic stress disorder during the Vietnam War added a new dimension to the understanding and treatment of past trauma. A treatment modality termed "revivification" came into vogue among Vietnam veterans. The rationale was that the troublesome symptoms were caused by the traumatic experiences suppressed within the veteran's unconscious. Building upon previous psychological doctrine, it became a matter of course to treat such veterans by encouraging them to recall, redescribe, and relive their awful experiences. This method was considered to be especially effective if accomplished in group settings among other "survivors."

Early in the history of the treatment of post-traumatic stress disorder (PTSD), much effort was undertaken to corroborate the experiences of the returning "disordered" combat veterans. There were enough cases of sheer fabrication of combat experiences to warrant this effort, especially since monetary compensation accompanied a PTSD diagnosis. The efforts at corroboration soon waned, however, as they were increasingly viewed as unjustified, psychotherapeutically improper, non-validating of the patient, hostile to the survivors, or evidencing of distrust on the part of the therapist. The psychic reality of the disordered veteran became the accepted terrain of the PTSD therapist. Following upon this "unresolved guilt" over U.S. involvement in the Vietnam War, the psychic reality of women who had experienced their own trauma—domestic violence, incest, childhood abuse, economic oppression—was quickly allowed to become acceptable terrain for the emerging Recovered Memory Therapy movement.

The final idea abroad in American culture that contributed to the Recovered Memory Therapy movement was the notion that behavioral and emotional problems were best understood as "diseases." A disease is, of course, something one *has,* whereas behavior is something one *does.* One may legitimately be the passive victim of a disease, whereas one traditionally must own up to, or be responsible for, one's own behavior. Herein lies the advantage to the "diseasification" of behavioral and emotional troubles. One can be a victim of the "disease" of kleptomania rather than be personally responsible for stealing. One can be a victim of the disease of alcoholism rather than being responsible for habitual drunkenness. To the disease can be attributed causation as well as responsibility. "Disease definitions undermine the individual's obligation to control behavior and to answer for misconduct. . . . [Individuals] legitimatize, reinforce, and excuse all behaviors in question—convincing people, contrary to all evidence, that their behavior is not their own."[24]

In a "diseasified" culture, one is encouraged to approach personal problems from the standpoint of a victim who suffers from a disease caused by something outside of self. It becomes the norm to package one's troubles into a diagnosis such as post-traumatic stress disorder, codependency syndrome, low self-esteem, or survivor of incest or abuse. It also becomes a matter of course to then look for the cause of the disease which, by assumption, must lie outside of self.

"Diseasification" proved an easy fit for insight-oriented psychotherapy. Clients took their troubles to therapists. The therapists listened and found indicators that satisfied supposed diagnostic criteria ("Your troubles fit the category of a typical victim of child abuse, even if you don't remember it happening"). A diagnosis was made; the disease was identified ("If you think you might have been abused, it is very likely that you were"). The offending, causative agent was discovered (through the recovery of long-suppressed memories); the disease-specific treatment ensued ("You must accuse the perpetrator; if he denies the accusation, break off the relationship and join a survivor group").

The Freudian doctrine of environmental determinism, Freud's method of arriving at truth ("psychic reality"), the burgeoning awareness and concern over child abuse, the culture of victimization, the radical feminist attack on fathers, the trauma focus of therapy, and the diseasification of mental and emotional problems—all of these ideas worked together to give birth to Recovered Memory Therapy.

Because it so neatly pulled together all that had gone before in psychotherapy, because it appealed so intensely to that innate human desire to blame someone else, and because parents are such a convenient target, the Recovered Memory Therapy movement became overwhelmingly destructive like nothing before it in psychotherapy.

THE DEVELOPMENT OF RECOVERED MEMORY THERAPY

From such ideas the Recovered Memory Therapy movement took form and rapidly gained momentum. The professional literature of insight-oriented psychotherapy quickly came to regularly feature case reports in which psychotherapy clients, either through hypnosis or simply by the verbal interventions of the therapist, retrieved long-repressed memories of abuse at the hands of parents (usually fathers). These cases began to multiply dramatically, drawing positive and sympathetic media attention. They became popular fodder for television talk shows, books, and media events of all kinds.

The therapists were merely doing what they had been trained to do. Remembering, repeating, and working through is, after all, considered essential to the acquisition of insight leading to personal growth.[25] The therapeutic work is believed to rest on the retrieval of memories. Filling in gaps in those memories, and retrieving the memories even when the patient resists, is believed essential to the successful progress of therapy.[26] Complicating this basic notion is the problem of "confirmatory bias": Therapists simply ask for and look for what will confirm their suppositions.[27] They ask questions that fit their explanatory theory. It was therefore to be expected that increasing numbers of therapists began to discover exactly what they were looking for in their clients' pasts: a history of abuse.

In the late 1970s and early 80s, there were published a number of accounts of incest. This particularly loathsome form of child abuse became for many therapists and writers an important new subject of scrutiny and speculation. Case reports became more frequent, and a variety of influential books were written on the subject. Initially the case reports were of women who had remembered their abuse. As time passed, more case reports were published telling of women who, in the course of psychotherapy, suddenly retrieved "lost" memories of abuse. The fascinating nature of these case reports quickly generated further published accounts and even books on the subject. Such books were filled with lurid case descriptions as well as bold suggestions that many kinds of life troubles were often the result of early childhood abuse, with the memories of the abuse long suppressed. Such books offered checklists of "indicators" of past abuse, descriptions of "typical" abuser parents, and a variety of methods by which one might begin to retrieve such memories.[28]

To explain these experiences of retrieving supposedly lost memories, Freud's concepts of repression and/or dissociation were invoked: These awful experiences had actually taken place, had been truthfully recorded on the mind's videotape, were locked and suppressed in the unconscious, and were now causing troubles; with the help of a therapist, this could all be exposed, thus explaining the current discomfort and unhappiness of the victim. Purposeful retrieval of supposedly suppressed memories became an increasingly popular technique in therapy.

A pivotal event in the development of this movement was the publication in 1988 of *The Courage to Heal*. This book like none other legitimized and catalyzed Recovered Memory Therapy. It seems to have been singularly responsible for turning a new subject of therapy into a burgeoning movement. Combining all the fundamental ideas requisite to the very existence of memory recovery, it added the vitriol of radical feminism. "If you think you were abused, then you were" is a phrase often quoted from *The Courage to Heal*. That phrase adequately expresses the central idea of its authors: If you have problems, look first for abuse by your father; retrieve those memories; experience them; accuse him; reject him when he denies them; and finally, sever all relations with him forever.[29]

One author implicates *The Courage to Heal* in "almost all cases" of accusations stemming from recovered memories.[30] While the book is offered as a helpful guide for female survivors of child sexual abuse, it actually recruits readers to the assumption that they were abused even if the thought had never before entered their minds. It offers hints to expand the awareness of parental behaviors as abusive. It offers a lengthy roster of life troubles that are likely to be the result of past abuse.

Following upon *The Courage to Heal* came a spate of widely promulgated "check lists." Such lists were offered by therapists who, because of their vast experience, claimed to be able to detect signs or behavioral markers of long-repressed memories of abuse. These so-called high-risk markers supposedly could reliably identify victims who did not (yet) have any memory or complaint of being victimized. With these markers in mind, the therapist could focus on early experiences in order to get to the root of the problem.

The very idea that such signs could tip off a therapist depends on the notion of psychic determinism first elaborated by Freud. In that paradigm, ideas and feelings locked or repressed in the unconscious can and do exert influence on conscious thoughts, feeling, and behaviors in indirect and cryptic ways. Such is the stuff of dreams, slips of the tongue, errors, odd patterns of relating and behaving. Experienced therapists are taught that they can learn to reliably decipher such cryptic expressions of the unconscious.

Lists of the markers began to appear in women's magazines, hospital newsletters, and guidelines for childcare workers. The media became saturated with these lists. The markers or indicators included the following:

- sexual difficulties
- distrust of the opposite sex
- multiple marriages
- drug or alcohol abuse
- low self-esteem
- nightmares
- eating disorders
- homosexuality
- body shame
- depression
- a sense of overwhelming responsibilities
- anxiety
- academic difficulties
- dislike of red or black (sometimes orange, brown, purple)
- resistance to authority
- poor attention span or learning problems

If a therapist found such things in a patient, it was deemed all but certain that the patient's troubles were in fact due to long-repressed abuse.

In 1992, what has been referred to as the "lethal textbook" of the Recovered Memory Therapy movement[31] was published. *Repressed Memories: A Journey to Recovery from Sexual Abuse,* by clinical psychologist Renee Fredrickson, delineates specific methods by which anyone can retrieve supposedly repressed memories of abuse, especially early childhood incestuous abuse.[32] The methods suggested and described in vivid detail include:

- guided imagery
- dream interpretation
- journal writing
- focusing upon and interpreting bodily feelings
  (body memories)
- interpretation of artistic expressions
- hypnosis

At the same time, Judith Herman published *Trauma and Recovery*.[33] With her reputation as an academic, Herman brought to the movement an aura of scientific respectability. Her book developed the thesis that traumatic experiences can be repressed and not remembered but still influence the daily life of the victim. She postulated new forms of remembering such trauma that she believed were peculiar to victims of incestuous abuse. She conceptualized the return of "fragments" of such memories in the form of "snapshots" that need to be assembled and filled out by an expert therapist. Her work encouraged therapists to look for such memories, encourage their expression, look for more fragments, put them together in a coherent whole, add emotion and feeling to the memories, re-live and re-experience the images, rehearse the stories, and share them with other "survivors." Herman's work was accompanied in the academic and professional literature by an increasing number of articles describing case examples. It offered to inexperienced therapists the rationale and the method for the retrieval of supposedly long-repressed memories of abuse. Briere, Courtois, Olio, Summit, Terr, and Claridge are all names whose published works contributed greatly to the prestige, acceptance, and spread of the recovery of memories movement. Karen Claridge's article "Reconstructing memories of abuse: a theory based approach" is a classic "why and how-to" treatment of the subject.[34]

At this point the movement took on the characteristics of mass hysteria. One popular champion of recovered memory claimed that "millions of people have blocked out frightening episodes of abuse, years of their life, or their entire childhood."[35] Pop guru-celebrity-evangelist John Bradshaw convinced many Americans that 96 percent of all families are "dysfunctional" and 60 percent of all incest memories are repressed.[36] Increasing numbers of therapy clients were retrieving memories of past abuse, and literally thousands of families were cowering in fear and shame under the accusations of their children. Most of these cases were amazingly similar:

- More than 90 percent of the accusers are grown daughters, aged 25 to 45.
- The memories are usually retrieved through psychotherapy, although in many cases in reading a book like those mentioned above bring forth supposed memories.
- These patients are in therapy in the first place because of complaints unrelated to early abuse.
- At the outset, almost all of the daughters claim good relations with their families.
- The accused perpetrator is almost always the father, often said to be enabled or assisted by the mother.
- The families are usually middle class or above (and therefore have insurance for long-term psychotherapy!).
- The families almost always have good reputations in the community.
- There is almost never a direct witness or corroborating evidence.
- Not uncommonly, as other family members come into therapy, they too discover similar memories and thus become indirect "witnesses."
- More often than not, the abuse would have required a degree of privacy or cooperation not present in most homes.

As the movement proceeded, the stories of abuse became increasingly lurid and improbable. This culminated in the early 1990s in a true epidemic of retrieval of memories of ritualized satanic abuse. These accusations of satanic ritual abuse far exceeded the number of individuals involved in the Salem witch trials. The tales of what occurred during the rituals were, as well, far more fantastic than any recorded from the witch trials.

Thousands of families experienced what began to be called the False Memory Syndrome. Eventually, some of the hurt, embarrassed parents made contact with other such parents. They stood together accused, and together they denied the accusations. Their daughters had been advised by the therapists to sever relations with the parents until they confessed to the abuse. Many such families were eventually exposed to legal charges. Many courts chose to accept the memories retrieved by psychotherapists as legitimate and admissible evidence. Many fathers and some mothers actually went to prison solely on the basis of these memories. The daughters in these cases had taken these abuse memories as the rationale of their troubled lives, their personal narrative. They continued in therapy, joined incest survivor groups, and associated almost exclusively with other "survivors."

Almost 20,000 such families joined the False Memory Syndrome Foundation. That organization grew rapidly as parents came forward to report the accusations against them and to share their dilemma. They were uniformly shocked at the amazing similarity of their experiences. There was little solace in their sharing, however, as there seemed to be no prospect of reconciliation with their accusing children. Even today there are thousands of parents who have neither seen nor heard from their accusing adult offspring for years.

The False Memory Syndrome (FMS) Foundation has incurred the wrath of insight-oriented psychotherapists for its position on and response to the Recovered Memory Therapy pandemic. They have been accused of supporting child molesters and contributing to the increased incidence of child abuse. They have been ridiculed as being against science and being motivated by a desire to cover up the truth. Most of this acrimony has been ad hominem and vicious.

Meanwhile, the FMS Foundation has mounted an impressive public education program as well as an effort to raise awareness inside the professional psychotherapy community. Meetings of members are held regularly all across the country, and annual meetings are held with scientific and legal experts addressing large audiences. Numerous regional meetings are held for the purpose of educating physicians, lawyers, and the public. A newsletter is published monthly with a nationwide audience; this newsletter updates its readership on scientific, media, legal, and personal news related to Recovered Memory Therapy. (For the address of the FMS Foundation, see "Recommended Reading.")

As the Recovered Memory Therapy movement gathered momentum, its manifestations became increasingly bizarre. Two examples of this are the increasing frequency of the discovery of memories of satanic ritual abuse and the increasing diagnosis of multiple personalities and other so-called dissociative disorders. While the history of "dissociation" as an apparent mental phenomenon goes back to the early nineteenth century, at no time did it ever achieve such acceptance and bizarre application as during the Recovered Memory Therapy pandemic. The claimed existence of multiple personalities in individuals has an up-and-down history in psychiatry and psychology. It is a diagnosis that has gone in and out of favor. Its ascendancy in popularity has always followed upon some popularized report or case description. Following such accounts, the diagnosis would become more frequent for a time, only to fade away and depart the scene. The diagnosis of multiple personality has essentially been an American phenomenon, with little or no utilization by European psychiatrists. The dominant view worldwide is that multiple personality disorder is a product of suggestion in a troubled, susceptible patient, serving in some way to explain the patient's life.[37] Prior to the advent of the Recovered Memory Therapy movement, the most recent resurgence of the concept and diagnosis of multiple personality disorder followed upon the publication of "A Case of Multiple Personality" by Corbett Thigpen and Hervey M. Cleckley in 1954 and their subsequent publication of *The Three Faces of Eve* in 1957.[38] This was an account of a case of supposed multiple personality "discovered" through hypnosis. The paper, its derivative novel, and a subsequent movie helped reestablish multiple personality disorder as a viable concept and available diagnosis. In 1973, the book *Sybil* described a case of multiple personality.[39] This work and its subsequent movie solidified and established the concept of multiple personality disorder arising from early-life sexual abuse, through the mechanisms of repression and dissociation. Even though this work has been exposed as fiction, it served as a launching pad from which the Recovered Memory Therapy movement could attach itself to the Multiple Personality Disorder diagnosis. The fuel for the unified ascent of these two psychotherapeutic fads was without doubt their shared reliance on the supposed early experience of sexual and incestuous abuse. Because of this, the diagnosis of multiple personality became increasingly frequent and popular, and the source of the supposed discovery of multiple personalities became predominantly the attempted retrieval of long-repressed memories of sexual abuse.

No aspect of the Recovered Memory Therapy movement has been more troubling than its increasingly predominant association with the retrieval of memories of satanic ritual abuse. In retrospect, one could look over the history of the kinds of abuse memories associated with this movement and see a clear progression from simple to complex, from understandable to preposterous, from bad to horrendous, and from a single perpetrator to multiple perpetrators. What began with memories of an angry, undisciplined parent "battering" a child progressed to crowds of people conspiring together, meeting in elaborate and secret places to perpetrate upon a child unconscionable and horrific acts of sexual torture. These lurid tales became more and more the content of the movement. By the accounts of the movement, literally tens of thousands of such ceremonies took place in America every year, with tens of thousands of babies bred for ritual sacrifice and tens of thousands of girls and boys raped, tortured, and killed as part of a satanic ritual. These accounts, their vividness, their frequency, and the derivative subindustry of experts in their discovery and treatment represents the pinnacle of the Recovered Memory Therapy movement in the American culture.

THE DECLINE OF RECOVERED MEMORY THERAPY

As stated at the outset, the Recovered Memory Therapy movement is in a period of decline and seems to be quietly disappearing from the psychotherapy scene. The reasons for its disappearance have arisen from outside the world of insight-oriented psychotherapy. The industry has not cleaned its own house. Unwelcome outsiders have had to do that. The glaring light of public exposure and ridicule, warnings from other professional organizations, changes in the health insurance industry making payment for psychotherapy less likely, the increasingly successful assault in the courts, a wealth of new scientific information, increasingly common testimonials from recanters and reunited families, and even some shifts in the culture away from a victimization mentality—all of these have been instrumental in the decline of the movement.

The proprietors of the psychotherapy industry themselves have not, until very recently, been a part of this housecleaning. In fact some still not only advocate the recovery of repressed memories of past abuse, but even defiantly champion the fundamental ideas underlying the movement. Thankfully, however, a small but growing number of psychotherapists are coming forward, apparently having learned something from this destructive episode in the history of their profession.

Another part of our culture that has ignored the housecleaning is the church. The church remained silent while our culture was overtaken by the ideas that gave origin to the Recovered Memory Therapy movement; worse yet, it actually accepted those ideas. After accepting the ideas, it took on the practices that stemmed from those ideas. Church-based ministries, parachurch organizations, and independent Christian counselors across the country adopted the recovery of repressed memories of past abuse as a feasible and worthwhile therapeutic intervention. Somewhat late in getting on the bandwagon, the church now appears to be late in getting off. It appears that many of the last remaining practitioners of this black art can be easily identified as Christian counselors. As such, the church risks blame and ignominy it should have avoided and even prevented.

For no readily apparent reason, news accounts and popular reports of Recovered Memory Therapy began to shift from sympathy to doubt, moving eventually to ridicule and accusation of the therapists. The internationally reported, rapidly disproved, and rapidly withdrawn accusation of Chicago's late Joseph Cardinal Bernardin by Steven Cook may have been the turning point in the history of Recovered Memory Therapy. The accusation had all the typical features that in the past would have assured its ready acceptance: retrieval of supposedly long-repressed memory through hypnosis; lurid details of sexual abuse fascinating to the public; victimization of a young, helpless, trusting innocent; a perpetrator held in high esteem; anguished denial by the accused; and a complete lack of evidence or corroboration. In this instance, however, the story unraveled in a different manner: The accused openly and forthrightly insisted upon his innocence; the qualifications of the therapist in this case were exposed as highly questionable; and the accuser soon retracted his charges, acknowledging them to have been the product of suggestion.

The Cardinal Bernardin situation was not alone in its decisive effect on the Recovered Memory movement. A growing number of "recanters" had been coming forward over the previous few years, and many more have come forward since. From the beginning of its existence in 1992, the FMS Foundation has regularly reported in its *FMS Newsletter* the accounts of recanters. Even this aspect of the movement is amazing in its uniformity and similarity from case to case.

Typically, the recanter is a person who discovered supposedly long-repressed memories of past abuse during the course of counseling sessions. Typically, the recanter would believe the recovered memories and powerfully accuse the perpetrator, usually the father. After the accused denied the charges, the recanter would follow the prescribed course of treatment and bitterly separate from the abuser and from all other family members and friends who doubted her story. From there, the recanter would follow the typical course into extended therapy, group therapy, and immersion in the survivor movement. Thus immersed in the culture of victimization and survivorship, there she would stay—bitter, alienated, surrounded and supported by other similarly victimized persons.

The person who later becomes a recanter, however, develops a break in the therapy/survivor-support system. She runs out of money for therapy, the therapist moves away, or some outside person forces a break in the otherwise solid wall of victimization identity and support. At this point, the continuous facilitation of the survivor identity breaks down and different thoughts begin to emerge. Memories of pleasant family experiences, doubts about the veracity of the retrieved memories, a newfound openness to news accounts and published stories doubtful of Recovered Memory Therapy—all these and more come to occupy the mind of the formerly bitter and self-assured victim. As time passes these thoughts become more frequent and serious doubts emerge. This leads to seeking advice from persons outside her "survivor group," and there finally comes the awful realization that she has participated in a lie. Finally comes an admission of the truth and usually a restoration of family relationships where before there had been only hatred, blame, and desire for revenge.

The similarity between what has been recently happening with Recovered Memory and Freud's experience of exactly one hundred years ago is startling and telling. Convinced that traumatic memories of early-life physical and sexual abuse were buried in the unconscious of his patients and causing their neurotic symptoms, Freud, as we have seen, concocted his Seduction Hypothesis. Freud searched for those memories, initially through hypnosis and later by interacting verbally with his patients. Almost all of his early patients were young women. Almost all were the daughters of respected families in Vienna. They suffered from a variety of otherwise unexplainable symptoms such as fainting spells, headaches, or various other aches and pains. In every case, Freud's searching for traumatic past experiences found not only memories of abuse, but memories of incestuous abuse. Only when his patients left his care in horror, and their paying parents raised up a chorus of objection that threatened his long-hoped-for promotion at the university, did Freud conclude that he was dealing not with historically objective reality but with fantasy, with "psychic reality."

Freud was faced with a dilemma, however, as to how to explain those fantasies. He did not countenance seriously the possibility that he may have created them through suggestion and reinforcement.

Rather, he theorized that such ideas were real and inherent to the unconscious life of his patients and therefore to all mankind. He theorized that such fantasies were born of biologic instincts present in all humans, and that these instincts or "drives" were in conflict with society. Out of this conflict, he proposed, came neurotic symptoms. Thus was born his theory of the psycho-sexual stages of development, the Oedipus complex, and the other related theories upon which he built his edifice of psychoanalysis.

Over the rest of his life, Freud vacillated back and forth as to whether he had actually suggested the incestuous memories to his submissive, highly suggestible patients.[40] He ultimately decided that it really didn't matter whether the memories were real or imagined.[41] The bottom line for Freud was that, whatever the source of the unconscious material, whether real or imagined, that unconscious material *was reality* for the patient. External events, family outrage, upset patients, and public censure, *rather than a self-disciplined desire for truth and objectivity,* turned the tide for Freud, just as it is turning the tide for psychotherapists all across America today.

The crescendo of public ridicule, suspicion, and accusation has had its effect on professional organizations pertinent to the Recovered Memory Therapy movement. There has been some measure of response to the growing public outrage. In 1993 the American Medical Association issued a report from the Council on Scientific Affairs stating that "the AMA considers the technique of 'memory enhancement' in the area of childhood sexual abuse to be fraught with problems of potential misapplication." That statement and a lengthy report from the council referred to "the growing concern regarding memories of sexual abuse," the inability of establishing validity without corroborating evidence, the suggestive nature of hypnosis, concerns about lawsuits, the uncertainty and malleability of memory, and questions of medical ethics. The report concluded that "memory enhancement in the area of childhood sexual abuse produce[s] results of uncertain authenticity . . . and that all memories recovered . . . be considered seriously, although subject to external verification."[42] Later that same year the American Psychiatric Association issued a statement that said, "Human memory is a complex process, . . . expression of disbelief is likely to cause the patient further pain, . . . the issues of breaking off relationships with important attachment figures, of pursuing legal actions, and of making public disclosures may need to be addressed, . . . many individuals who recover memories of abuse have been able to find corroborating information . . . ," and stated that it was impossible to differentiate between true and false memories. The American Psychological Association and the National Association of Social Workers has yet to issue a definitive statement on the Recovered Memory Therapy issue. They have for the most part defended themselves by accusing the accusers.

A more powerful change agent has been the legal arena. Beginning in the late 1980s, more than a thousand cases of alleged childhood parental abuse have gone to trial based on the acceptance of recovered memories as admissible evidence. The first conviction came in 1989 when George Franklin was convicted of murdering a child many years before. The evidence against him was a memory of the murder recovered from his daughter during the course of her insight-oriented psychotherapy. This case was followed by many others involving individual parents, day care center operators, babysitters, and "Satan worshippers" in a frenzy of accusation, lurid testimony, and media attention. In response to all this, more than half of the state legislatures in the nation passed laws relaxing civil statutes of limitations so that the "clock would begin ticking" only when the memory of abuse was first "recovered," rather than from the time of occurrence of the alleged incident. Beginning in 1995, however, a shift began to develop in the easy acceptance of recovered memories as evidence in the courts. In April of that year, George Franklin's conviction and life sentence were overturned. Almost simultaneously two different state courts of appeal overturned a satanic ritual abuse conviction and a day care center conviction. Late in 1995, "the Alabama Supreme Court . . . allowed a patient to sue a former therapist for implanting false memories of abuse, and federal district courts in Oklahoma and Texas . . . ruled that therapists are obliged to corroborate their patients' accusations. A Baltimore judge threw out a case against a priest on the grounds that repressed memory is not scientifically valid. In Louisiana, the state supreme court ruled that expert testimony about repressed memory was inadmissible."[43] More recently, a California superior court awarded a father $500,000 for the ruination of his family by a therapist who administered truth serum (sodium amytal) to his daughter in a "successful" attempt to retrieve memories of childhood sexual abuse by the father. This case marked the first time a non-patient sued a therapist for malpractice. That decision was followed quickly by similar decisions in Dallas and Pittsburgh.[44] The issue has reached into the federal courts, where the admissibility of recovered memories as evidence in lower court trials has been called into question, and standards for admissibility are being promulgated which put the burden of proof on the plaintiff.[45]

Despite such cases, there continue to be courts where recovered memories are admitted without corroboration as evidence of past abuse. However, the tide is definitely turning as more and more courts are persuaded that uncorroborated memories may just as likely be false as true; that therapists may be held liable for suggesting to their unwitting patients that their memories are true; and that the emerging scientific understanding of human memory should be taken into account in such actions.

Spurred on by the Recovered Memory movement and surely contributing to its decline, rigorous scientific research on human memory has flourished internationally. A large scientific and popular literature has been generated. As a result, many people now understand that human memory is not infallible and is, in fact, quite malleable.

A key figure in this scientific arena has been University of Washington psychology professor and researcher Elizabeth Loftus. Her interest in memory research developed in part from her own early life experience of sexual abuse (never forgotten) and a vivid childhood experience of suggestion when she became convinced that she had witnessed an event that she actually had not witnessed.[46] Loftus came to prominence after the 1974 publication of her work on the accuracy of eyewitness accounts.[47] In that work, Loftus demonstrated that even eyewitness accounts are anything but reliable and, in fact, are subject to many influences. Her studies in that area have contributed greatly to the methods and accuracy of witness interviewing and evidence gathering for criminal trial proceedings.

While the Recovered Memory Therapy movement has spawned real disaster in human lives, it has served to awaken scientific psychology to its own history of credible research into memory. As far back as 1890 William James wrote, "False memories are by no means rare occurrences in most of us."[48] In 1908, Muensterberg documented that people do not necessarily remember specific, staged events with accuracy.[49] In 1927, Bird showed how recollection of an event in the past is influenced by subsequent experiences.[50] Bartlett in 1932 demonstrated how memories of an event or story change with retelling and sharing with other persons. He pointed out that recall is an act of "imaginative reconstruction, or construction, built out of the relation of our attitude toward a whole active mass of organized past reactions or experience." He spoke of an "effort after meaning" by which we humans attempt to make sense out of our memories using all available information past and present, as well as future aspirations.[51] In 1935, Koffka wrote extensively about misperceptions and concluded that "remembering appears to be far more decisively an affair of construction rather than one of mere reproduction."[52]

Building on that past scholarship, Loftus and others have brought the subject of memory up to date in response to the Recovered Memory Therapy movement. Ganaway reported in 1991 that people who claim that they have been victims of abuse, with all the evidence being to the contrary, are not necessarily lying; they may have been persuaded by someone or something that it actually happened.[53] Loftus and others have reported on various research efforts pointing to the fact that human recall is tenuous at best and that the recall of supposedly "repressed" memories is even more unreliable. "Every time we recall an event, we must reconstruct the memory, and with each recollection the memory may be changed—colored by succeeding events, other people's recollections or suggestions, increased understanding, or a new context. . . .

Misleading information can turn a lie into memory's truth. . . . It can make people confident about false memories and also, apparently, impair earlier recollections. Once adopted, the newly created memories can be believed as strongly as genuine memories."[54]

It is amazing the degree to which insight-oriented psychotherapy has ignored all of this impressive history of scientific psychological research into human memory—all of which attests to memory's malleability and suggestibility. In 1987, Judith Herman emphasized the extent and validity of repressed memories of childhood sexual abuse.[55] Her research found that memories of abuse were repressed in 64 percent of women attending her abuse-survivor therapy groups. Her work, fatally flawed by a built-in bias toward discovering what she believed to be there, has been widely touted as supporting the concept of repression underlying the recovery of memories. The next year the authors of *Courage to Heal* stated emphatically, "Often the knowledge that you were abused starts with a tiny feeling, an intuition. It's important to trust that inner voice and work from there. Assume your feelings are valid. . . . The progression always goes . . . from suspicion to confirmation. If you think you were abused and your life shows the symptoms, then you were."[56] These authors, one from academic counseling psychology and the other from popular self-help psychology, are but two representatives of many who believe and preach a view of human memory totally unsupported by credible research. This view that memory is a trustworthy archive, an endless videotape that can be reliably tapped for its contents and firmly believed even without external corroboration, has been essential to the entire Recovered Memory Therapy movement.

Even though the abundant information about human memory did not influence the psychotherapy industry away from Recovered Memory Therapy, it is proving to be instrumental in its decline. More and more frequently, news reports and media presentations mention the unreliability of memory and call into question the uncritical acceptance of memories of abuse retrieved in the course of therapy. More and more books are being published attesting to the unreliability of memory and eyewitness accounts. Even the very concept of repression as an explanation for failing to remember traumatic experiences is being questioned.[57] Where there was once uncritical acceptance, there is now healthy doubt. It is this doubt, rapidly spreading through the culture, that is pushing Recovered Memory Therapy from the scene. This doubt, however, is far more common among the paying clients than among the professional therapists.

As we have noted, neither the American Psychological Association nor the National Association of Social Workers has issued statements of policy or guidance to their members concerning Recovered Memory Therapy. No organization pertinent to the conduct of insight-oriented psychotherapy has accepted responsibility for the gravity of the problem, critically examined the origins of the problem, championed corrective action, or engaged in a dialogue to prevent similar problems in the future. If one can assume that the professional literature of psychotherapy in any way communicates or establishes the position of the field on a particular subject, then one can only conclude that the industry continues to defend the recovery of memories not only as valid and important, but also as a proper therapeutic modality.

Most recently, the professional journals of psychotherapy have published a number of articles that not only reassert the primacy and validity of so-called "psychic reality" over objective or "historical" reality, but that defiantly attempt to justify and even extend the concept. "Why do we need to establish whether a memory of past abuse which has surfaced during an adult's psychotherapy is true? Why should it matter?" This question opened a presentation by a clinical psychologist at the seventh annual meeting of the Association for the Advancement of Philosophy and Psychiatry. The presentation was published in the *American Journal of Psychotherapy* in 1996 and concluded that "the narrow, often fanatical focus on veridicality [truth!] supports the simplistic conceptions of psychopathology and of psychotherapy, [which] leads to impoverished ideas about the nature of the relationship to one's self and to others, and obscures less obvious but nevertheless equally destructive other kinds of family or parental pathology."[58] The author explains and ridicules the desire for objective, verifiable truth in the gathering of historical data from and about psychotherapy clients. He acknowledges the Freudian view of psychic reality in which "historically accurate perceptions and subjective fantasy are inextricably intertwined," and asserts that, "all that is possible is to create a story based on the 'here and now' of the psychotherapeutic relationship." What the author advocates, however, is a "deconstructive process," in which "veridicality [truth!] becomes a non-issue," and in which the search for objective truth is viewed as "counterproductive, covertly serving defensive needs." In fact, the author views the insistence upon truth from the perspectives of Nietzsche, Heidegger, and Marx, as "terminal estrangements of late capitalism." Historical truth should, therefore, be a "non-issue." Therapy should attend only to what occurs in the session, and should focus on "removing obstacles to intrapsychic freedom." It should accept whatever story the patient brings to the session and "not tell our patients that they have misjudged a life situation . . . [not] correct a misapprehension. . . . Instead we attempt to correct those distortions of self-observation which become evident in the analytic situation."

For this respected author, there is no such thing as a true story. Every patient's story is to be "deconstructed" in a search for a highly personalized meaning, which is not related to objectivity but is accepted as decisive and important for personal growth. In a similar vein a recently published special issue of *Psychoanalytic Dialogues* contains a symposium on the false memory controversy in which three of the several papers from respected insight-oriented psychotherapists not only aggressively challenge critics of the Recovered Memory Therapy movement but go beyond that to underscore the validity and importance of recovered memories. According to one of the writers, J. Davies,

> The only truth we can prove is that there is no singular truth, nor is there only one way to access personal truth. . . . But, through the give and take of the therapeutic process, [we] come to believe in the essential integrity and reality of their own internal experiences. . . . We are free at last from the unto-

ward burden of deriving a singular meaning from our patient's communications. . . . It is our task . . . to stand ready to engage actively with the patient's internal self and object world and to recognize and confirm meaning when that meaning is offered to us within a shared context.[59]

Davies defiantly stands against the awakening of public distrust in recovered memory. As Frederick Crews wrote in response, "Rather than face this predicament, [Davies] chooses to make a virtue of irrationalism, not only couching her explanatory discourse in mystifying poststructuralist bafflegab but also actually recommending that a therapist's critical intelligence be overruled by passion."[60]

Insistence upon truth is not only defied, it is labeled as symptomatic of pathologic and oppressive cultural influences. In Davies's view, patriarchalism or more simply male oppression, by its insistence on provable facts, distorts the discovery by victimized women of their fathers' past abuses. Somehow truth is characterized as a "male thing." Whether it is a symptom of late capitalism or male oppression, the search for objective, verifiable, historical truth in the assessment of a psychotherapy patient's problems is viewed as a problem.

So while the culture is waking up to the horrific abuses and basic underlying irrationalities of the Recovered Memory Therapy debacle, significant spokespersons within insight-oriented psychotherapy are championing "business as usual." In their defense of business as usual, it should not be surprising that any available rationale—be it late capitalism, postmodernism, patriarchalism, male oppression, or child abuse prevention—would be drawn upon to validate their profession.

In the same fashion, key representatives of psychotherapy try to undermine even the scientific psychologists and other hard scientists from within their own professional ranks who have contributed so much to the understanding of human memory. From that scientific psychological community, the central question is "whether a supposed multitude of horrific events spanning years of childhood can be serially banished from memory, be kept in a safe place for as long as two or three decades, and then be retrieved with a precision that defies both our present knowledge of the brain and our awareness of the fragmentariness and corruptibility of [even] *unrepressed* memories."[61]

Those who would demean scientific criticism of Recovered Memory Therapy generally do so by appealing to the primacy of clinical experience over the results of research. They try to dismiss those results of rigorous, objective, scientific scrutiny that do not fit with the subjective experience of therapists and patients. Those stories and personal narratives depend on the traditional ideology concerning environmental determinism, the dynamic unconscious, powerful repression, dissociation, the feasibility and value of insight into the unconscious, the reliability of recovered memory, and the reliance upon telltale signs and cryptic indicators of past abuse. The stalwart defenders of Recovered Memory Therapy also tend to offer as proof any and every bit of experimental evidence "whose results look even remotely compatible with the theory behind Recovered Memory Therapy."[62]

No critic has been more attacked by the defenders of Recovered Memory Therapy than Elizabeth Loftus. Many other researchers have accomplished work replicating hers; other researchers have added to the body of knowledge clearly incompatible with the theories upon which the Recovered Memory Therapy movement depends. However, Loftus continues to be the principal target of the movement's defenders.[63] Her work was the recent subject of a lengthy article in *American Psychologist,* the most respected professional journal in American psychology. In that journal Kenneth Pope, claiming concern for ethics within clinical psychology, outlines the issues surrounding the False Memory Syndrome epidemic.[64] He stipulates that scientific psychology has a long and impressive history of research into the functioning of human memory, but he does not explain why clinical psychology and psychotherapy have chosen to ignore it. He extensively criticizes research demonstrating that memory is malleable and unreliable, without offering credible research findings to the contrary. He questions whether there is in fact an epidemic of false memories, pointing to supposed problems of definition of words such as *false* and *epidemic*. He insists that claims critical of Recovered Memory Therapy must be "grounded most firmly in the scientific tradition . . . from hypotheses that are falsifiable," ignoring the long chorus of protest from clinical psychology that its hallowed psychic reality should not be expected to live by the scientific doctrine of falsifiability. He disagrees that the recovery of memory should be thought of as "risky" and denies that research has confirmed that fact. He stringently avoids dealing with the accusation of malpractice or the need for validation of historical data.

Pope makes constant accusations against any and all critics of the Recovered Memory Therapy movement. All such criticism, says Pope, fosters and actually increases the incidence and prevalence of child abuse. He singles out the False Memory Syndrome Foundation for the most vitriolic accusation. He characterizes it as an organization of child molesters who have banded together to cover their crimes and protect their reputations. He demeans and ridicules its board of scientific advisors, which includes a roster of highly respected researchers, academicians, and clinicians of mental health, as if they were blinkered ideologues, turncoats, or worse. He accuses the Foundation of foisting upon the American public the baseless notion that there is an epidemic of something foolishly called a False Memory Syndrome, by the use of dishonest and hysterical manipulation of public attention.

Pope's accusations of child abuse are a powerful defensive tactic, available and useful to the defenders of Recovered Memory Therapy. Few issues resonate more strongly through our culture than that of child abuse. No caring person would stand directly or indirectly in denial of that awful reality of fallen mankind. No caring person would do any less than his all to protect a child from abuse. One must ask, however, to what degree "social attention to the here-and-now plight of neglected and abused children is actually hampered by 'near mass hysteria regarding childhood experiences told by adults.'"[65]

THE CHURCH'S FAILURE TO CHALLENGE
RECOVERED MEMORY THERAPY

It should come as no surprise that the therapy industry has not been instrumental in the decline of Recovered Memory Therapy. Self-correction has never characterized the industry, and the current defensive responses of its leadership offer little hope that such will happen in the future. What ought to be surprising, however, is the utter failure of the American Christian church to act as a bulwark against the movement.

Though biblically the repository of God's truth, the church has remained silent while lies have moved throughout society. For the past century, the American church has raised little opposition to the doctrine of environmental determinism. The church raised no opposition to the belief that man can reliably access his out-of-awareness mind. Thus, it raised no question about the claimed truthfulness of supposedly retrieved memories or the acceptance of such "psychic reality" as truth. No caution was offered as to the value of focusing on one's past. Instead of theological confrontation of these destructive ideas, Christian radio, many seminaries, Christian publishers, and individual counseling practitioners latched onto the Recovered Memory movement, making it a profitable industry within the church. The church appeared to forget that we are sinners responsible for our own trespasses. It offered no counsel about the meaning and purpose of our past and our suffering from the perspective of a holy and merciful Creator, before whom each of us will one day stand without a professional therapist as mediator.

Scripture has specific answers to all of the beliefs that gave rise to Recovered Memory Therapy. It has a complete psychology that answers sufficiently and with authority all questions about mankind, his nature, his problems, and their solution. Yet as the movement gained momentum, the church, rather than sounding an alarm, quietly joined the bandwagon. Scientific psychology had sufficient studies and warning to have held back the Recovered Memory movement. Far more did the church have sufficient truth in the Word of God to have confronted the movement. Now the church must share with the psychotherapy industry the ignominy of involvement in this debacle.

It is not difficult to find evidence of the church's participation in the Recovered Memory movement. The tremendous popularity of church-sponsored "Survivors of . . ." or "Adult children of . . ." groups easily speaks to this fact. Recovered Memory had swept across the culture and was in its popular and unquestioned phase for some time before the church attached itself to the cause; the popularity of the movement placed before the church a powerful temptation to involve itself in the culture and be a part of "the action." To be sure, a Christian spin was often placed on these "recovery ministries," but the underlying belief system was Freudian, not biblical.

This modern-day example of syncretism was successful, if measured by numbers of individuals and dollars. Drawing in the "seekers" by offering self-help psychology was so much less "off-putting" than the message of sin and salvation. Offering the world's psychotherapeutic products to the troubled and needy, inside a house of Christian worship, quickly proved a sure-fire method of expansion—so much so that the American Christian church is now openly seen by many as dispensing a "therapeutic gospel."

Nor did it take long for the steady flow of recovery-related Christian books and other media to gain momentum. At present, the shelves of most Christian bookstores are filled with offerings that pander to the survivor, the victim, the recoverer of memories of past abuse. Even more ominous is the preponderance of such books in the bookstores of Christian colleges and seminaries. The reader should peruse such bookstores to see the extent of the courses and the textbooks required for students of Christian psychology and pastoral counseling. Compare the number of those courses and textbooks with the number of theological courses and textbooks. Look at the sources of such textbooks and you will see that secular authors predominate. There is little there for Christian students interested in counseling material truly biblical in its base

or authored by someone who considers Scripture to be authoritative and sufficient for matters of counseling.

Many Christian counselors followed suit and took on the ways
of the Recovered Memory movement. It became common to hear
from such counselors case reports replete with the recovered memories of lurid sexual abuse. Respected church members and leaders
were pilloried by the accusations of their grown children "recovering" with the help of Christian counselors. Support groups for the
"survivors" became common fixtures not only in the offices of
Christian counselors but also within growing and respected
churches. Accounts of satanic ritual abuse within church families
became more and more common, as did accounts of multiple personality disorder. Often these more incredible case reports were
presented by Christian counselors with almost an aura of, "Eureka!
Guess what I heard about this week!" Church elders, including pastors, were accused and relieved of their positions solely on the basis
of memories recovered in therapy.

Along the way the Christian counselor, the support group,
Christian recovery literature, the therapeutic radio and television
programs have, for all too many Christians, become a replacement
for the church itself. "Some go to a support group and find a level
of honesty and integrity about life that is in contrast to what they
experience in church. They wonder why one seems real and one
seems pretend. It can be very confusing."[66] Rather than caring for
souls in the biblical sense, the church's leadership too often has
given over its authority and its prerogative to the "professionals."
"Overpromotion of professional [psychological] services has
undermined the confidence of clergy and laypersons in their capacity to minister effectively in the name of Christ."[67] Even as long ago
as 1991, a *Christianity Today* survey found that only one in four
Christians who sought counseling sought it from a pastor.[68] Such
has been the extent of the abrogation of the church's responsibilities to the world, all in the name of modernity, seeker sensitivity,
and "science."

The destruction of families, the embitterment of grown children, the enslavement of clients to their therapists and support

groups, the slander and defamation of formerly respected parents—all that was so common in the secular Recovered Memory Therapy movement soon was present in Christian congregations all across America. It happened rapidly and without significant opposition. As noted, the presence of "adult children of" or various other survivor ministries became a badge of modernity for the church. This was especially true of the megachurches, but it became true of any church aggressively out to enroll "seekers" by offering popular programs. Church brochures and new visitor packets offered rosters of support groups of various kinds. Recovery became a byword and survivorship a by-product of the therapeutic church.

There were a few who spoke out, early, often, vigorously, and truthfully, such as Martin and Deidre Bobgan, Dave Hunt, and John MacArthur, Jr. (see "Recommended Reading"). They were uniformly criticized, marginalized, and dismissed by those for whom the increasing numbers appeared to confirm the success of recovery ministries.

"Christian counselors tend to be the worst kind of suggestive therapists, encouraging memories of satanic ritual abuse," says Mark Pendergrast in *Victims of Memory*.[69] This book, published in 1995, is the most thoroughly documented, easily read, and popular work to expose and debunk the Recovered Memory Therapy movement. His statement, sadly, reflects the perception of the church in the declining days of the movement.

One has only to turn the clock of history back a century and a half to see recorded a very similar response on the part of the church to a very similar challenge to its doctrines. At that time the challenge came from Charles Darwin and his followers. The challenge presented was a view of human origins that contradicted Scripture and left God entirely out of creation and nature. It was a view that set in motion the naturalistic metaphysic of science that holds sway to this day: There is no God; there is nothing supernatural; there is no intelligent design; there is only matter, energy, and the laws of physics; everything about humanity and the cosmos can and will be explained by objective, natural, atheistic science. These are the fundamental beliefs of science today. The church had the answers to all the questions about man's origin, his nature, his purpose, his problems. It had the answers to questions about the material and the immaterial, the past, the present, and the future. It had the answers about life and death. It had all these answers revealed by God Himself; it had Scripture and the Holy Spirit, through which and through whom God addresses mankind directly. The church had all of this with absolute authority and sufficiency; yet too often it chose to accommodate itself with popular, plausible, modern ideas rather than speak out its truth against those ideas. Instead of clear, absolute answers, it offered comparative religious studies and higher critical approaches to the interpretation of Scripture. Instead of absolute revealed truth, it embraced relativism and granted validity to subjective experience. Instead of standing as a bulwark against evolution by natural selection, it espoused theistic evolution and retreated from a meaningful dialogue with science in general.

Similarly the church has accommodated itself to the Recovered Memory movement. Instead of speaking the truth of Scripture, it offered to "integrate" its theology with modern psychology. Instead of using Scripture as a benchmark, it allowed Scripture to be interpreted through the lens of psychology. Instead of absolute revealed truth, the church embraced psychic reality. Even therapists should have known better than to embrace the Recovered Memory Therapy bandwagon. They should have remembered what happened to Freud in 1897. They should have remembered what their own colleagues already understood about the inherent unreliability and malleability of human memory. How much more should Christians have known better! They should have seen the popular emphasis on self-esteem as unscriptural. They should have known from Scripture that man is not determined by his environment. They should have known better than to look to one's past for the answers to one's present. They should have known that only God has access to the unconscious, the "heart."

Christians bear responsibility because they have access to absolute, revealed, authoritative, and sufficient truth through the Scriptures with the guidance of the Holy Spirit. Christians bear responsibility because they know a supreme, perfect, holy, sovereign God who addresses them through His Word. Christians bear responsibility because they chose to "integrate" this treasure with the "godless chatter and the opposing ideas of what is falsely called knowledge [or science]." In so doing they "wandered from the faith" and into disaster (1 Tim. 6:20).

THE RESULTS OF RECOVERED MEMORY THERAPY

Can we learn from the Recovered Memory Therapy episode?

Because of the Recovered Memory Therapy debacle, there is in some quarters a much clearer understanding of the workings of human memory. Many now understand that human remembering is not at all akin to replaying a videotape, and that human memory is malleable and can range in accuracy from totally wrong to totally right. Many now understand that humans are suggestible and, depending on the circumstances of their efforts at recall, can be induced to fully believe something that never took place at all. Most courts now understand that therapists can unwittingly create in their clients false but vivid and fully believed memories even of horrific experiences of abuse. Most authorities would now agree that there is a "lack of evidence that any special type of psychological procedure or practice is capable, even in trained hands, of leading people to recover memories that can be accepted as valid without corroboration."[70] Finally, the media has now publicized widely the fact that accusations based on false memories can be astonishingly destructive.

Out of this has come an increased distrust in the fundamental psychological notions of repression and dissociation. These concepts, which have for a century served as pillars of insight-oriented psychotherapy, are now increasingly understood to rest, not on the evidence of hard science, but rather on anecdotal case reports and tradition. Especially questioned, more so now than ever before, are the notions that repeated, sustained, horrific abuse over years of time could be repressed or dissociated completely out of awareness or recall, yet still evidence its effects through multiple personality disorder, body memories, or other cryptic psychic symptoms. Thus most would now agree that there are "no compelling findings to support the practice of a therapy aimed specifically at the recovery of memories that have been totally unsuspected and absent since early childhood."[71]

The very fact that "the place of truth and the validity of long-delayed memories of abuse in childhood have become the focus of a debate that has polarized the behavioral science community" is a positive outcome of the Recovered Memory Therapy debacle.[72] The exposure of the dangers of the application to real life of the concept of psychic reality is a positive outcome. Treating the recollections of a therapy client and building a personal "story" or "narrative"—as if truth were being assembled—is now viewed by many therapists as dangerous; this is a significant ethical and practical advancement.

Because of the widespread media coverage of the Recovered Memory Therapy debacle, more people now distrust the ability of hypnotists or therapists to reliably discover truth in the out-of-awareness mind. The public has been made aware of the harm that can be done, and some believe that therapists *have* done harm in attempting to recover memories without corroboration. As a result, there is now caution where there was once naive acceptance.

One benefit of all this may be the growing popularity of a here-and-now approach to counseling. One has only to listen to popular radio or watch daytime television to witness the growing popularity of a kind of "in your face" counseling in which real day-to-day problems of *what* people are doing (rather than *why* they are doing it) are being forthrightly addressed. Rather than searching for some influence in their past as causative, these talk show therapists are confronting real behaviors as right or wrong. The popularity of these programs hopefully indicates some shift in our culture away from the victim/survivor mentality that was so much a part of Recovered Memory Therapy. The Menendez brothers basically claimed that their parents deserved to die because they abused them, and the Unabomber's actions were attributed by *Newsweek* magazine to his not being held by his mother enough during a crucial period in infancy.[73] When talk show hosts ridicule such self-pity and blaming of others, this may be a sign of a culture shifting away from irresponsibility.

Possibly the experiences of the Recovered Memory Therapy movement will have some lasting positive effects on the legal system in this country regarding the importance of physical evidence, as well as upon the efforts of our social institutions to combat real child abuse and neglect. Already, as we have seen, there is a trend in the courts toward reversing earlier decisions made on the basis of uncorroborated retrieved memories. This will likely continue. As malpractice decisions are handed down against the therapists and clinics who pandered this debacle upon us, this should further hasten the disappearance of the movement from the scene. As efforts are turned away from mining the unconscious for supposed experiences of abuse, perhaps more effort can be devoted to the real plight of real children living in real time.

The acquiescence and complicity of the church in the Recovered Memory Therapy movement should be an opportunity for evaluation by church leadership of its proper responsibilities in the face of cultural trends. When the church allowed the pillars of insight-oriented psychotherapy to be "integrated" into the fabric of its caring for souls, it laid the foundation for the outcome before us. What formerly had been pastoral care became in the seventies something called Christian counseling. What was Christian counseling in the seventies became little different from secular counseling shortly thereafter. What was once a church-based caring for souls, with pastors and elders ministering to the troubled in their flocks, became a professional cadre of Christian psychologists and counselors. Soon came franchised Christian counseling corporations and national organizations of Christian counselors. Seminaries and Christian colleges opened departments of psychology and counseling, which soon became overwhelmingly popular. Along the way, Christian counselors incorporated not only the doctrines of insight-oriented psychotherapy but its business practices as well.

From where did the Recovered Memory Therapy movement come? It came as a logical and thoroughly expected outcome of the fundamental beliefs of insight-oriented psychotherapy. It was eagerly accepted by a culture of people eagerly looking for causes outside of themselves for problems that ultimately reside within themselves. It created both oppressors to hate and victimized selves to love. It offered the tantalizing excuse of blame to a people in love with resentment.

Where is the church in all of this? Its involvement is reflected in the faces of the embittered daughters and sons and their broken-hearted parents, whose lives have been torn apart by accusations based on memories concocted by a therapy process born in evil and conducted in brazen rebellion against God. The church is paying a price for its syncretistic attraction to modernity, relativism, psychology, and pragmatism.

ALTERNATIVES TO PSYCHOTHERAPY

Introduction to Section Four

In section 1 we discussed the fundamental "pillars" that guide the insight-oriented psychotherapy industry. We examined them in light of Scripture and found them to be offering a false gospel with disastrous consequences. We further discussed these consequences in section 3, in which we contrasted the Puritan caring for souls with modern-day Christian counseling, looked at the concept of "psychic reality," and finally examined one of the most recent and most awful consequences of the industry, the Recovered Memory Therapy debacle. Important in all this is the realization that the fundamental beliefs of insight-oriented psychotherapy do indeed have their consequences and are indeed harmful.

In section 2 we looked back to critical moments in history for the sources of the ideas that ultimately found their expression in psychotherapy. We found the ancient denial of man's inherent sinfulness (Pelagianism), man's endless search for his own secret wisdom (gnosticism), and his hope in the saving power of human reason (Platonism). We saw in the Enlightenment the beginnings of what would become today's overarching metaphysic of all science: atheistic materialism. No wonder, then, that the mind scientists of today deny any existence of the immaterial or the supernatural. No wonder, also, that in spite of Descartes' example and advice, they deny that Christianity has any truth by which to understand the immaterial, and they accept no limits to the domain of science.

In this section we will briefly examine some alternatives to insight-oriented psychotherapy. In chapter 13, "Psychiatry's Twin Failure: No Cause, No Cure," we will take another look at the history of psychotherapy, noting the ongoing futility of its quest for an understanding of and adequate cure for psychological complaints. This will underscore the great need for a viable alternative to Freud's failed system. In chapter 14, "One Person, Two

Paradigms," we will consider two approaches, one based on traditional psychotherapeutic practice and the other based on biblical principles. We will see that, when the true cause of human mental suffering is addressed, substantial healing becomes a real possibility. In chapter 15, "A Biblical Approach to Depression," we will discover how Scripture applies to the most common "mental illness" in our society today.

THIRTEEN

PSYCHIATRY'S TWIN FAILURE: NO CAUSE, NO CURE

Ever since Eve believed the serpent's lie, mankind has sought a kind of understanding of the human mind that can only be possessed by the Creator of that mind. This search to know and control the mind largely explains the history of the medical specialty called psychiatry.

In earlier times, what is now called mental illness was explained in many ways, including: magical influences of malevolent deities; improper mixtures of earth, air, fire, and water; atoms in motion; imbalance of humoral spirits; imbalance of vital substances or tendencies; excesses of phlegm; excesses of yellow or black bile; passions uncontrolled by the soul; and adverse external circumstances playing upon predispositions or unsatisfied desires. These ancient views held sway in one form or another until the late 1400s. During the time of the Inquisition, witchcraft and demon possession became the most common explanation for aberrant behavior. Subsequent to that period, ancient views again became popular, including Galen's (A.D. 130–200) view attributing mental illness to imbalances of humoral spirits.

By 1600, "animism" supplanted Galenism. Animism postulated that the anima (soul, psyche) held sway over the body (soma). This notion fueled speculation as to the "psychological" causation of mental illness, in addition to the already assumed bodily (natural, somatic) causation. Thus began an ongoing debate: Is mental illness psychic or somatic? Is it of the soul-mind-reason (immaterial), or is it of the body-tissue-chemistry (material)? Does the explanation lie in the psyche (mind) or in the soma (body)?

The hyper-rational Enlightenment brought speculation concerning specific brain diseases that had specific signs and symptoms. Mental illnesses were grouped into diseases claiming objective anatomic causation, even though there was no evidence for this fundamental pathogenesis (cause). Neuroses were said to be caused by spasm or flaccidity of muscles and blood vessels when influenced by a brain in unequal states of excitement or collapse. The phrenologic mapping of the skull was evidence of the theories attempting to connect disease with malshaped brain structures, unequal distributions of bodily fluid, and what was called "animal magnetism."

Historians of psychiatry, especially those of the twentieth century,[1] are inclined to weave a rich and colorful tapestry making psychiatry appear to be as old as recorded history itself. They include the most ancient concepts of mental illness under the rubric of psychiatry, and thereby establish a robust and authoritative history for the field. The term *psychiatry,* however, was not used until the dawn of the nineteenth century. Not until 1805 was the first professional journal of psychiatry founded, in Germany.

Wilhelm Greisinger (1817–1868) published his textbook in 1845, when the "Somatic School" of psychiatry had reached its fullest flower.[2] Greisinger and his followers asserted that all mental illness was of objective physical causation, and that there was no need at all for psychological explanations. With this textbook, psychiatry was acknowledged as a medical specialty even though it was combined with neurology. Greisinger was named in Berlin the first professor of neurology and psychiatry.

Much work was done in proposing specific sites of disease within the brain. Many refined definitions of mental diseases were codified. Schizophrenia, manic-depressive psychosis, paraphrenia, Alzheimer's disease, and general paresis were names of mental illnesses established in an attempt to comply with the disease concept.

Each diagnostic category was proposed as having a recognized and typical onset, presentation, course, and outcome. In spite of great effort, however, all of these essential elements of a true disease continued to elude investigators for each of the above diagnoses.

A true disease has a specific, observable etiology (cause) resulting in a pathophysiologic (abnormal) bodily process. This results in physically measurable signs and usually in felt symptoms. For a true disease, the cause, course of illness, and outcome can be predicted. For any specific disease, there will be a specific recommended treatment that can be expected to lead to the disappearance of abnormal signs, the lessening of symptoms and, ideally, a cure.

Because of the continued lack of known causes or effective treatments, Greisinger's somatic school of psychiatry lost influence by the end of the nineteenth century, to be replaced by the psychic school. By this time, psychiatry was so well established as a medical specialty that it continued under the guise of scientific medicine even though its diagnoses and treatments became increasingly subjective.

The ideas as to psychic causes of mental illness traced their roots to animism (the belief that the psyche held sway over the body) and were strengthened by claims of success with psychic treatment. The philosophical movement called Romanticism, with its emphasis on subjective experience, introspection, and self-awareness, swept across Europe and America in the nineteenth century and thoroughly facilitated the rise of the psychic (subjective) over the somatic (objective) view.[3]

The 1800s brought improvement in the treatment of patients termed mentally ill who had been placed in asylums. Dungeons, chains, and beatings were replaced by exercise, activity, entertainment, good food, pleasant environs, conversation, and education. These new "moral" treatments fostered psychological explanations of mental illnesses as improvement was seen in the patients under these improved conditions. The psychic school of psychiatry grew and argued for new diagnoses, such as *neuroses* and *neurasthenia,* which were postulated as having no somatic (organic) basis. But the psychic school had a deficiency similar to the somatic school: no real evidence for psychic causation.

Into this milieu came Sigmund Freud. Freud was trained by the chief theoreticians of the somatic school and was a neurologist. Unable, however, to discover any organic explanation for mental illness using the scientific methodology of his day, Freud adopted psychic views from varied sources. He proposed an entirely new concept of the workings of the human mind by taking paradigms from the field of hydraulics and hydrostatics. His concept of the unconscious and its effect on daily life was new and bold, and his theories as to the means of exploring the unconscious, with the possibility of correcting its content, sounded plausible to many. His Grand Theory was easily accepted by the Romanticized culture of his day.[4] Freud and his followers solidly established the psychic school of psychiatry, such that it has remained predominant to this day.

During the twentieth century, so heavily influenced by Freud, psychiatrists seemed to forget that they were trained as medical doctors. They lost sight of the disease concept in favor of the concept of "syndromes" or what they called "disorders." Although infections, endocrine disease, diabetes, poisonings, nutritional problems, tumors, lack of sleep, heart and lung disease, medication side effects, as well as many other known organic diseases can produce changes in personality and behavior, the typical psychiatrist today takes only a cursory medical history, does no physical exam at all, and does little or no rigorous diagnostic testing. Various studies show that psychiatrists overlook anywhere from 41 to 75 percent of significant, detectable medical illnesses in their patients.[5] Since the time of Freud, psychiatry has distanced itself from the rest of the medical profession by ignoring the medical model and the disease concept.

Psychiatry has failed to progress beyond a syndromal concept of diagnosis, and it shows no inclination to do so. The psychiatrist collects subjectively experienced *symptoms,* usually unaccompanied by objectively measurable *signs.* These symptoms are grouped into packages in order to fit the diagnostic manual, even though these groupings have no scientific foundation or validity. The syndromes and disorders have no known cause, no predictable course of illness, no specific and reliable treatment, and no reliable response to treatment.

This method of diagnosis leads to a continual revision of the criteria for differentiating one supposed disorder from the next. Lacking objective data, the "diagnostic criteria" change with individual experience. The *Diagnostic and Statistical Manual of Mental Disorders*[6] is now entering its fourth revision since its initial publication in 1952. Psychiatry is riddled with defective communication, sloppy definition, inadequate criteria for labeling symptoms and signs, sub-rational treatment, and an inability to predictably cure or even lessen symptoms.

Effective medical research in psychiatry is essentially impossible, since a treatment cannot be tested when researchers cannot be sure they are reliably separating one disorder from another. The known physically based (organic) mental diseases represent the only diagnoses in psychiatry that have "advanced from mere syndromal diagnosis to disease diagnosis and a comprehensive understanding of pathophysiology."[7] Examples of these would be neurosyphilis, certain vitamin or enzyme deficiencies, and alcoholic encephalopathy where objective measurements of brain structure and function as well as blood chemistries have shown definite abnormality. Such conditions fit the definition of disease; however, these true diseases, when discovered, become the domain of neurologists or other medical specialists. The diagnoses left to psychiatry, such as depression, schizophrenia, passive-aggressive personality, and narcissism, fail to fit the definition of true diseases.

Because psychiatric diagnoses are based largely on subjectively described symptoms rather than on objectively measurable signs, the likelihood of two psychiatrists labeling the same patient with the same diagnosis is quite low.[8] This "inter-rater reliability" is high only when the psychiatrist is dealing with true diseases such as Korsakoff's psychosis, vitamin B_{12} deficiency dementia, mental retardation, and the other established organic diseases. When the psychiatrist tries to diagnose "functional" disorders (those having no known physical base), the inter-rater reliability is very low.[9] This is the case for diagnoses such as bipolar disorder, anxiety disorder, schizophrenia, dysthymic disorder, and especially the personality disorders.

Only in the last twenty years has the long-dormant somatic school of psychiatry been reawakened, with its interest in an organic basis to mental illness. The availability of scientific methods for new kinds of measurement and observation, the apparent successes of "somatic" therapy (drugs, electroshock), and the increasing refusal of insurance payment for talking therapy have all combined to bring the resurgence of the somatic school. However, no specific pathogenesis has yet been found for the so-called functional illnesses (schizophrenia, manic depressive illness, depression, neuroses); however exciting this somatic line of inquiry may be to its adherents, they have not yet provided any closure of the loop of the disease concept. Lacking any cure, modern psychiatry remains stuck in a cycle of observing subjective symptoms, categorizing those symptoms according to the latest theory-based diagnostic manual, then following the patient indefinitely through talking therapy or support groups. The logic of psychoanalytic theory is circular, as would be expected in a theory based on entirely subjective data. A psychiatrist who believes in the theory of repression, for instance, observes what he believes to be repressed content in a patient's report of his dreams—he observes what he believes he ought to observe and thus is confirmed in his belief in the existence of repressed content.

Aware of this failure, some psychiatrists continue to try to bring a measure of objectivity to the specialty. They have tried to find certain signs that can be observed in the patient aside from any theory that might predict or explain them. They attempt to define the form of a psychiatric symptom rather than rest on vague, personalized descriptions of the symptom. They seek to avoid interpretive words such as *repressed, narcissistic, oedipal conflict,* and *neurotic,* which are inherently speculative and thus used in different ways by different examiners. Terms such as these "have no demonstrated reliability, often substitute for objective observation, and should not be used in clinical diagnosis."[10]

The "biological" (somatic) psychiatrist, on the other hand, will search among similar individual patients for bits of data that lend themselves to easy recognition and measurability and that would be recognized by multiple observers with a high inter-rater reliability. One example of this would be hallucinatory voices that occur in a clear state of consciousness, are distinct, clear, and loud to the hearer, and are believed to come from "outside" the hearer. This sign, when observed with several other such signs in individuals free of demonstrable organic brain disease, is claimed to select out the worst cases of so-called schizophrenia with the very highest degree of inter-rater reliability.[11]

This is termed the "phenomenological" method of diagnosis, because certain signs (phenomena) are sought in the patient in an attempt to be rigorously scientific.[12] However, this method, like many methods before it, has not brought the elucidation of true diseases in the proper understanding of that term. In a continuing effort to move toward this end, numerous lists of "research diagnostic criteria" for schizophrenia, depression, and a panoply of other mental "diseases" have been proposed.[13] To date, none of these efforts have brought success. Instead of discovering true disease, modern psychiatry continues to invent ever more elaborate lists. The lists are useful in giving names to the customers of psychiatry, but in terms of actual diagnosis and treatment, confusion reigns.

The modern psychiatrist usually approaches his patient in a pseudoscientific but authoritative manner and claims to be prescribing a specific cure for a specific disease. Psychiatric medications are usually truly powerful substances that have major effects on the function of the brain and the rest of the body. These effects are so desirable to both the psychiatrist and the patient that it seems to matter little that the drugs' mechanisms of action and long-term side effects are entirely unknown.

With few exceptions, the practice of psychiatry continues to be subjective and irrational. Contrary to what the public is allowed to believe, no disease called depression, manic-depression, or schizophrenia has ever been discovered, and no rational treatment for these "disorders" has been devised or proved to be effective. Science understands little about the function of the brain and even less about how the various psychiatric medications affect the brain. Neuroscience can regularly claim to be on the verge of complete understanding of human consciousness and can regularly display colorful scans of human brains in the process of various types of thought. However, any humility combined with honesty in these scientists should cause them to admit that they have barely scratched the surface of an organ more complex than we can begin to comprehend.

𝒶

ONE PERSON,
TWO PARADIGMS

What does it look like in real life when souls are truly cared for in a biblical way? How does the biblical method of soul care differ from the traditional approach of insight-oriented psychotherapy? Most importantly, can truly biblical counseling lead to the substantial cures that continue to elude practitioners of psychotherapy? Paradigm One, below, will present the traditional psychotherapeutic approach, with the psychiatrist firmly in charge of diagnosis and treatment. Paradigm Two will suggest a biblical way in which a concerned Christian friend of a troubled individual, in partnership with a psychiatrist, can help bring that person back to emotional and spiritual health.

PARADIGM ONE

A married forty-three-year-old woman, mother of teenage sons, arrives thirty minutes early for her appointment with a psychiatrist. Alone in the waiting room, she nervously pages through popular magazines. She wonders whether she should have agreed to this "consultation" but is sure that her Christian counselor knows best. When, some months before, she had told her pastor of her mounting difficulties with insomnia, anxiety attacks, and fears of leaving her home, she could not have anticipated the possibility of actually being mentally ill, of having a mental disease.

During the ten minutes the psychiatrist allows himself between patients, he reviews the consultation/referral letter for his next patient: "Forty-three-year-old hysterical and narcissistic female, apparent panic attacks . . . agoraphobia . . . three years duration . . . worsening . . . insomnia . . . marital disharmony . . . dysfunctional family . . . low self-esteem . . . massive repression with neurotic defenses, not too productive in therapy . . . request consultation for medication management to facilitate therapy process."

To this first session come a physician/psychiatrist, a patient, knowledge, experience, fact, and opinion, in response to symptoms, signs, disorder, and perhaps a disease.

Because of his medical training, the psychiatrist will seek from his new patient a full description of her subjective symptoms. He may ask about attendant physical changes or objective signs of illness. He will compile a case history of her problems. In so doing, he will also explore alternative explanations (the differential diagnosis) before arriving at a diagnosis (an educated guess). Along the way he may request some additional information (personality testing, tests for diabetes, thyroid disorder, etc.). However, his medical goal as a physician is to determine the "disease" and then apply a treatment that either eliminates the underlying causative disease process itself or at least blunts or blocks its effect on the sufferer's health.

What the patient thought would be a single session becomes three more visits with the psychiatrist, one more visit to a psychologist for personality testing, and a visit to her internist for "lab work."

One month later she sits in the now-familiar book-lined office awaiting her "final diagnosis." She has developed respect and a kind of affection for this fatherly, caring psychiatrist, and she speaks highly of him to her Christian counselor. After the usual pleasantries, the psychiatrist begins his explanation of her illness, her disease.

"You have a classic case of panic disorder with agoraphobic features." Her hearing dulls as he reassuringly imparts to her the nature, frequency, projected treatment, and likely outcome of the disease he has astutely diagnosed. She is considerably more attentive to his explanations of "the course . . . deep-seated . . . stress . . . repression . . . neurotic defense mechanisms . . . breaking through." Convinced that she is, in fact, diseased, she is only mildly shaken by his instructions of her need for long-term, insight-oriented psychotherapy and, of course, medication.

As his patient leaves, the psychiatrist basks in the glow of a job well done. Using his professional powers, he once again has asked the correct questions, satisfied the accepted diagnostic criteria, and fitted his new patient into the appropriately labeled slot. He has deduced the "disease" causing the patient's discomfort. He understands the workings of the disease, he believes he knows its cause (even though psychological and vague), and he is sure the treatment will relieve her of her suffering. Isn't that the bottom line?

Some time later, the patient speaks with her pastor during the Sunday morning fellowship hour. "My psychiatrist has cured me," she says breathlessly. "No anxiety, no insomnia; I even went to the mall this week; I am back on top of the world!" Her pastor listens attentively as she recounts her experiences with "my psychiatrist," her diagnoses, her medication, and its positive effect. She is delighted to say, "I am a panic disorder sufferer. There are lots like me out there; I think I may join a Panic Disordered Anonymous survivor group at the community center. I am considering in-depth psychoanalysis to really get to the bottom of my problems and turn my life around!"

Concern shapes the pastor's countenance as he asks, "Are you still seeing the Christian counselor I referred you to?"

Somewhat startled and not a little uncomfortable, the woman quickly replies, "Oh, there's no need for that now!" She then turns her attention to another acquaintance in the crowded room.

The pastor briefly reflects before his thoughts are drawn away by the next parishioner: *That psychiatrist—does he have any real understanding of human suffering. Does he have any real understanding of the human mind?* And, having pastoral knowledge of the patient, her life, her family, and her faith, he wonders, *Has that doctor really helped her?*

This pastor has a deep and thorough understanding of theology and of what the revealed Word of God says. He knows that the Bible is not and does not pretend to be an exhaustive textbook of medicine. He does know, however, that the Bible is a sufficient and authoritative guide even for physicians, as to how to view the human personality and the meaning and experience of illness and suffering. The pastor understands that illness and suffering exist as a result of the Fall, but that God is sovereign, holy, and always perfectly just, working all things to His glory and for the believer's good.

The pastor regularly hears medical scientists reporting on ever more minute and complex discoveries about the healthy and unhealthy human organism. Regular features in the media document the relentless progress of medicine in its efforts to help people flee from all suffering to what they call "quality of life." The amelioration of suffering is the obvious and seemingly sufficient goal of medicine and medical research.

The pastor wonders whether the psychiatrist he has just heard so highly praised has any real understanding of the purposes of a sovereign, holy God, the God who has revealed Himself in Scripture. Might this patient's illness have a purpose? Could it be a means to lessen pride, the chastisement of a beloved child? (2 Cor. 12:7). Could it be used to further spiritual growth? (Heb. 12:7-11). Might her discomfort, her illness, be the wages of sin? (Acts 13:11). Could her body be responding to a spiritual problem that needs desperately to be exposed, confronted, and taken to her Lord and Savior? Is not her illness and her response to it an opportunity to glorify God and serve Him more fully? (John 9:1-4). The pastor is concerned that the answers to all these questions, and the related opportunities for growth and maturation in the faith, have been bypassed by the quick, easy diagnosis of mental illness and the accompanying successful elimination of her symptomatic discomfort.

The pastor sees that an opportunity has been lost. The psychiatrist, however, believes he has helped his patient in accordance with the guidelines and ethics of his profession.

Our patient will now embark on the psychotherapeutic lifestyle. She will invest much time and money attempting to examine and reveal her innermost thoughts, feelings, and recollections. She will be encouraged to "remember, repeat and work through" in order to gain "insight." From this personal understanding, she will expect to somehow derive the strength and ability to change herself. She will visit her therapist often and will consume various medications. Sometimes she will feel better; sometimes she will feel worse and conclude that she needs more therapy. She will attend groups where similarly afflicted people "support" each other. Her relationships will more and more center on group, therapist, and self. She will discard relationships that seem "destructive, codependent, or non-affirming." She will seek to develop "adaptive" skills such as self-esteem. Self-actualized and empowered through therapy, she will become a "modern woman," ready for life on her own terms. She will see no need for guilt, shame, or the conviction of personal sin. Following the gospel of felt needs, she will have no room for the Jesus of Scripture with His off-putting demands.

How could this awful outcome have been avoided? Had the psychiatrist had a biblical concept of man, his problems, and the human mind, and had he had a biblically tested concept of his role as a physician, what might he have done? Is there a biblical paradigm for psychiatry?

PARADIGM TWO

A married forty-three-year-old woman, mother of teenage sons, arrives thirty minutes early for her appointment with a psychiatrist. She is accompanied by her husband as well as by one of the church elders and his wife. The elder and his wife have been praying for the patient and her husband, discipling them, and ministering to them from the Word over the last few weeks. The elder's wife has come alongside this troubled mother as part of their church's ministry of caring for souls within the church body. In the same way, the elder has come alongside the husband after he brought the history of his wife's difficulties to the pastor of the church. In the waiting room, the woman nervously pages through popular magazines. She and her husband have been assured by their pastor that this visit, this evaluation, is a part of his plan to understand their problems from both the spiritual and the physical aspects, so that he and the church elders might assist them in their Christian life. They want this couple to more fully serve and glorify God through times of trial as well as times of ease.

During the ten minutes the psychiatrist allows himself between patients, he reviews the consultation/referral letter for his next patient: "Forty-three-year-old female, apparent panic attacks . . . agoraphobic . . . three-years duration . . . worsening. Obvious spiritual problems manifest in marital disharmony and problems raising teenage sons. Believes she is a failure and unable to do what she knows is right. Is preoccupied with anxiety, fears, insomnia, and is unable to really concentrate on spiritual things, counseling homework, or follow-through. Requests evaluation and recommendations."

He is pleased that the letter is from a pastor he knows and with whom he has worked many times in the past. He considers this pastor not just a source of professional referrals but a partner with him in achieving his goals as a physician, a psychiatrist, and a Christian. They share a biblical understanding of illness and of the spiritual challenges and opportunities that illness represents. To the pastor, he provides his expertise in the physical aspects of the human body—how as a fallen entity, it has defects and can be diseased, injured, and misused; he shares with the pastor his knowledge as to how the body can produce signs and symptoms as it physically responds to spiritual problems.

To *this* first session come a Christian/physician/psychiatrist, a patient, wisdom, and established science, in response to symptoms, signs, disorder, and perhaps a disease. This physician, with prayer, will approach his next patient from not only a medical but also a spiritual model. He will seek from his patient the fullest possible range of physical data and objective historical information that he believes might have some bearing on her current state. In addition to assessing the likelihood of any medical illnesses that could have caused or contributed to her symptoms, he will look for any ways that her body's response to her underlying spiritual difficulties might be worsening her situation.

Along the way, he will pay special attention to the functioning of his patient's brain. Knowing of the supernatural unity of the physical brain and the immaterial spirit, he will assess the functioning of the physical aspect of the whole. He will test specific mental functions that measure organic brain function, such as consciousness, the ability to pay attention, and the power of concentration. He will test language abilities, memory, and the ability to do some simple calculations and answer thought-provoking questions. He will perform a physical and neurological examination. Were there any indications of physical brain dysfunction, he would order additional objective examinations. These might include brain imaging, computerized EEG, and neuropsychological testing such as a Halstead-Reitan Battery or a Boston Aphasia Screening Exam.

Having gone through such procedures and finding nothing abnormal, the psychiatrist can assure himself and his patient that she does not suffer any organic brain disease.

He will then examine specific phenomena of mental functioning by asking questions and observing his patient, focusing on the objective process of those answers. Rather than asking only what a hallucinated voice might say, he will ask, "How loud is the voice? Where does it come from? Is it clear? Is it you or something outside of you?" He is interested in the history of his client's present complaints, but he is even more interested in what they are and how they have developed. He is more interested in how they are manifested rather than in what they mean in an interpretative psychological sense.

One week later, our patient and her husband sit in the now familiar office awaiting the results of her evaluation. They both have been pleasantly surprised by the thorough and meticulous questioning of this fatherly, caring, psychiatrist; they have spoken highly of him to their pastor. The woman is convinced that the psychiatrist knows as much as another person can as to what her discomfort is like. She is surprised at his offer to pray with her that she might come to understand not only the physical but also the spiritual aspect of her discomfort, and through that might be better able to glorify God in her life. She is surprised at the lack of "Freudian" questions about her self-concept, early memories, or sexual fantasies. After prayer, the psychiatrist speaks with her concerning her difficulties.

"You do not have any medical, physical, or brain disease that could explain your felt discomfort. You clearly have some important issues, spiritual issues, with which you need sound biblical help."

The woman becomes more alert as she listens. The psychiatrist goes on to explain that the symptoms of anxiety are to be expected, and that she should not see them as "the problem," the disease, but more as a physiological indicator of her spiritual problem and her need to participate in the counseling and discipling ministry of her church. He advises her that such symptoms work in conjunction with her conscience as an indicator of spiritual conflict. He goes on to say that, as such, they are a gift from God to draw us to Him. He assures her that her symptoms will abate as she works with her counselor. He expresses his confidence that, with the help of the Holy Spirit, she will be more and more able to put off the wrong and put on the right in her goal of serving and glorifying God.

The psychiatrist points out that some patients do benefit from medication, but only those whose physical responses to their own spiritual problems are so extreme as to become an impairment to progress in biblical counseling. Even in those cases, he adds, once the counseling is stabilized, the medications would be tapered off and discontinued as quickly as possible. He goes on to assure her that he has spoken with her pastor; together, they have agreed on this plan and will remain in contact to monitor the progress they expect she will enjoy.

As the couple leaves the office, the woman is able to express gratitude. She is grateful for the doctor's help and advice and for his plan to maintain contact with her counselor. Only later, on the way home, does it come to her mind that she is *not* suffering a mental illness, that there is no disease controlling her, that she is not a victim, and that the kind of hope and understanding she was given is the best there can be from the medical profession today.

A few weeks later, the pastor listens attentively after he asks the couple how they are doing in the discipling and counseling he has arranged: "With the Lord's help, I'm doing better," the woman says excitedly. "I still get anxious; sometimes I can't sleep, but the truth will set me free. I am able to get out, take some responsibility, and I'm actually able to do my counseling homework."

The husband and wife are both delighted to relate how much they have grown during their "time of trial," and how much their perseverance and growth is proving to be a witness for Christ to those around them.

FIFTEEN

A BIBLICAL APPROACH TO DEPRESSION

Nothing fills the calendar of the modern counselor more than clients complaining of "depression." This is true whether the counselor styles himself as Christian or secular. "Office visits for depression increased from 10.99 million in 1988 to 20.43 million in 1993. Visits for depression doubled for both primary care physicians and psychiatrists."[1]

Those who suffer depression typically characterize it as a state in which feelings of guilt, shame, and fear predominate. Depressed people typically describe their thought-life as focused on ideas of sadness, worthlessness, and hopelessness. Out of these feelings and thoughts come the usual behaviors of the depressed person: sleeplessness, eating problems, withdrawal, crying, listlessness. Almost universally, people who complain of depression are very introspective and crave an inordinate amount of attention to their thoughts and feelings. Sufferers of depression strive to "understand" the causes of the depression, as do most of those who seek to help them. These efforts to understand the cause of depression have produced over the last century a multitude of theories, books, and schools of counseling.

More recently, as the following quotes illustrate, it has become popular to assume that depression is always a biologically mediated disease, meaning that, like any other well-understood disease, it has a specific and identifiable environmental or biologic cause, a particular slate of measurable signs and symptoms, a rational cause-directed treatment, and a predictable response to that treatment:

> Ultimately, depression is mediated by the brain, where chemicals such as an amine called serotonin evidently have much to do with maintaining an individual's self-esteem in the face of life's tribulations. In persons . . . who think they are failing, or in those who actually are failing, serotonin levels may drop, and depression becomes likely.[2]

> "If you have vulnerabilities associated with low serotonin functioning—guilt, submissiveness, low self-esteem—you can learn to compensate for them." And if you're lucky, you'll be rewarded with a rise in serotonin.[3]

> Anger kept inside and unleashed against oneself causes depression. Loss of psychic energy causes the person to approach a zero balance; finally depression appears when there is no longer sufficient psychic energy to perform. Don't use the Bible or prayer without first listening to the helpee . . . the helpee was not ready to accept these passages.[4]

Such comments reflect the prevalent view that depression is by definition a noxious state to be avoided at all cost; that it is caused by something bad outside of us or by chemical aberrations inside us; that by understanding these causes we can conquer them; that a professional therapist is essential; and that by a variety of methods we can be victorious over depression and achieve a state of pleasure.

What should we as Christians do with someone seeking help with depression? Where should we begin if we are to answer the call to minister to such a person? We can begin by reviewing a few examples of what the Bible says about the thoughts, feelings, and behaviors popularly defined today as depression:

> Then the LORD said to Cain, "Why are you angry? Why is your face downcast? . . . Sin is crouching at your door; it desires to have you, but you must master it." (Gen. 4:6-7)

When Rachel saw that she was not bearing Jacob any children, she became jealous of her sister. So she said to Jacob, "Give me children, or I'll die!" (Gen. 30:1)

Naomi said, . . . "I am too old to have another husband. . . . It is more bitter for me than for you, because the Lord's hand has gone out against me!" (Ruth 1:11-13)

Saul was very angry. . . . "They have credited David with tens of thousands," he thought, "but me with only thousands." . . . And from that time on Saul kept a jealous eye on David. (1 Sam. 18:8-9)

Elijah . . . went a day's journey into the desert. He came to a broom tree, sat down under it and prayed that he might die. "I have had enough, LORD," he said. "Take my life; I am no better than my ancestors." (1 Kings 19:3-4)

Ahab said to Naboth, "Let me have your vineyard." . . . But Naboth replied, "The LORD forbid that I should give you the inheritance of my fathers." So Ahab went home, sullen and angry. . . . He lay on his bed sulking and refused to eat. (1 Kings 21:2-4)

When I heard these things, I sat down and wept. For some days I mourned and fasted and prayed before the God of heaven. . . . The king asked me, "Why does your face look so sad when you are not ill? This can be nothing but sadness of heart." (Neh. 1:4; 2:1)

When I kept silent, my bones wasted away through my groaning all day long. For day and night your hand was heavy upon me; my strength was sapped as in the heat of summer. (Ps. 32:3-4)

Some became fools through their rebellious ways and suffered affliction because of their iniquities. They loathed all food and drew near the gates of death. Then they cried to the

LORD in their trouble, and he saved them from their distress. (Ps. 107:17-19)

My soul is weary with sorrow; strengthen me according to your word (Ps. 119:28). Before I was afflicted I went astray, but now I keep Your word (Ps. 119:67, NKJV). My soul faints for Your salvation, but I hope in Your word. My eyes fail from searching Your word, saying, "When will You comfort me?" (Ps. 119:81-82, NKJV). I rise before the dawning of the morning, and cry for help; I hope in Your word. My eyes are awake through the night watches. (Ps. 119:147-148, NJKV)

"The word of the LORD has brought me insult and reproach all day long. . . . All my friends are waiting for me to slip. . . . Cursed be the day I was born! May the day my mother bore me not be blessed! . . . Why did I ever come out of the womb?" (Jer. 20:8, 10, 14, 18)

Lest we conclude that such countless expressions and descriptions of depression are limited to the Old Testament, let us turn to the New:

When Judas, who had betrayed him, saw that Jesus was condemned, he was seized with remorse and returned the thirty silver coins to the chief priests and elders. "I have sinned," he said. . . . They replied, "That's your responsibility." So Judas threw the money into the temple and left. Then he went away and hanged himself. (Matt. 27:3-5)

Praise be to the God and Father of our Lord Jesus Christ, the Father of compassion and the God of all comfort, who comforts us in all our troubles, so that we can comfort those in any trouble with the comfort we ourselves have received from God. . . . We were under great pressure, far beyond our ability to endure, so that we despaired even of life. Indeed, in our hearts we felt the sentence of death. But this happened that we might not rely on ourselves but on God, who raises the dead. . . . On him we have set our hope. (2 Cor. 1:3-4, 8-10)

During the days of Jesus' life on earth, he offered up prayers and petitions with loud cries and tears to the one who could save him from death, and he was heard because of His reverent submission. Although he was a son, he learned obedience from what he suffered. (Heb. 5:7-8)

Hopefully, these Scriptures are enough to rid us of the common view that depression is an abnormal event in the Christian life. The Bible does not present what we now call depression as a noxious, environmentally-caused, or biologically-caused disease that will therefore require and respond to a specific technique or chemical treatment. Scripture does not present depression as repressed anger, loss of psychic energy, low serotonin, low self-esteem, or even as the result of an abusive childhood. This being so, we should not respond to depression in ourselves or in others with scream therapy, yoga, visualization, selective serotonin reuptake inhibitors, St. John's Wort, assertiveness training, hypnosis, or "flood therapy."

Since the world and Scripture present incompatible views of depression, we must take a rather radical departure from the ways of the world when confronted by a "depressed" person. A Christian must always begin with Scripture.

What we describe as depression is truly a kind of suffering. Few would argue this. From the world's viewpoint, all suffering is inappropriate, unjustified, unacceptable, and to be avoided. From the viewpoint of Scripture, suffering has both meaning and purpose:

Now if we are children, then we are heirs . . . if we indeed share in his sufferings in order that we may also share in his glory. I consider that our present sufferings are not worth comparing with the glory that will be revealed in us. (Rom. 8:17-18)

This sharply distinguishes the perspective of the Christian from the perspective of the nonbeliever as it pertains not only to depression, but to suffering in general. We must remember this fundamental scriptural truth when we are called to minister to an individual labeled as depressed. From Scripture, we make the following conclusions:

1. Each of us will stand alone before the judgment seat of God to answer for the sin in our life. There will be standing beside us no oppressor, no bad parent, no bad environment, no abuser, no molester whom we can blame for our sin. There will be no other person or environmental condition to cover or mitigate our sin before a holy God who cannot look on sin. If other people or the environment were the problem, then Christ's death was unnecessary and even a bit ridiculous.

> The dead were judged according to what they had done. . . . If anyone's name was not found written in the book of life, he was thrown into the lake of fire. (Rev. 20:12, 15)

> The soul who sins is the one who will die. The son will not share the guilt of the father, nor will the father share the guilt of the son. (Ezek. 18:20)

Blaming others for our depressed thoughts and behaviors is common today, but it is unbiblical and helps no one. No matter what the past, no matter what the oppression, no matter what the abuse, the child of God is not in bondage to the past. Remind the depressed person of this wonderful news:

> Brothers, I do not consider myself yet to have taken hold of it. But one thing I do: Forgetting what is behind and straining toward what is ahead, I press on toward the goal to win the prize for which God has called me heavenward in Christ Jesus. (Phil. 3:13-14)

If we try to respond to a depressed person's suffering by blaming his or her past or by employing techniques supposedly able to make up for the deficiencies of that past, we will be at cross-purposes with God. Such efforts will not be blessed.

2. We cannot know the heart and mind of another individual. The pursuit of "insight," "deep understanding," or the supposed unconscious determinants of the depressed state of mind is, by biblical definition, not only fruitless but rebellious (Jer. 17:9-10). It is the natural desire of our fallen hearts to know as only God can know. We can never reliably discover the why of a person's depression by searching for it in the subconscious mind. This kind of knowledge remains with the Creator alone. We must avoid the use of techniques and booklets that lead us to believe otherwise. As regards the use of Scripture, we cannot reliably know when a person is "ready to accept" what the Bible says, but that should by no means keep us from calling that person to God's Word. We are called to walk by faith and not by sight. We are armed solely with the Word of God and with the Holy Spirit pointing always to that Word. God will be as angry with us as He was with Job's counselors (Job 42:7-9) if we claim deep knowledge related to the heart and mind of another individual.

3. It is not within our power to restructure another person's life. We should not presume that we are able to prevent suicide, make someone happy, restore a marriage, or give joy in relationships. Life, contentment, and fellowship are gifts of God.

> We proclaim to you what we have seen and heard, so that you also may have fellowship with us. And our fellowship is with the Father and with His Son, Jesus Christ. We write this to make our joy complete. (1 John 1:3-4)

Don't assume that, armed with the latest psychological techniques, you are able to offer more than does the apostle John in this passage. Your task is to communicate to the depressed person with clarity the love of God. Your concern should be related to your obedience to God and your willingness to sacrifice for the depressed person. The priority must be to fix your eyes on Jesus and to persevere in what is set before you with this depressed individual. Do not allow your priority to become suicide prevention, the attainment of good feelings, divorce prevention, or even preservation of relationships. These are by no means unimportant, but they are ultimately in God's control; you are clay in the hands of the potter. Don't forget this truth. If suicide, divorce, or other tragedy occurs, it does not mean that you failed in your duty. Many labor under the fantasy that they can attach attractive fruit to a dead tree and see it flourish. Fruit is a gift from God, and it comes through suffering. This is in stark contrast to the thinking of the world:

> We also rejoice in our sufferings, because we know that suffering produces perseverance; perseverance, character; and character, hope. And hope does not disappoint us, because God has poured out his love into our hearts by the Holy Spirit. (Rom. 5:3-5)

4. Remind the depressed person from Scripture that thoughts of suicide, focusing on self, wallowing in ideas of hopelessness or worthlessness, blaming others, and sloth (laziness) are sinful decisions. Remind him that his focus needs to be on serving God that day rather than on how he feels inside. Take it one day at a time. Tell him that God expects him to get out of bed and get dressed regardless of how he may feel. Arrange activities for the day so that he will be busy and accountable to others for productive labor. Urge him to get his mind on others and on the tasks at hand. Constantly draw the person outward, to service and to others; remind him that thinking of self is not honoring to his Creator:

> Religion that God our Father accepts as pure and faultless is this: to look after orphans and widows in their distress. . . . the royal law found in Scripture, "Love your neighbor as yourself" . . . (James 1:27; 2:8)

Do not allow the depressed person to dwell on his early morning wakefulness, loss of appetite, feeling better later in the day, lack of sexual feelings, and so on; he has likely read in the latest magazine or hospital newsletter these symptoms of the disease called depression which, "if not treated rapidly will become worse and worse, lasting a lifetime." With these warnings so widely disseminated today, the depressed person is usually living in despair and fear of such an outcome. Explain that these lists of symptoms with their calls to "early treatment" come from a huge industry ill-based in science and with no base in Scripture. This knowledge alone will often lift a heavy load from the depressed individual. Explain to him that everyone who is in touch with reality has experienced depression at some time in life.

Read John Bunyan's *Pilgrim's Progress* to him, and show him how quickly Christian and Pliable fell into the Slough of Despond. Spend time studying the difference in the way Christian and Pliable responded to the Slough. Your depressed comrade will not be the only one to grow as you review the time Christian and Hopeful spent in "Doubting Castle which is kept by Giant Despair who despiseth the King of the Celestial Country." *The Pilgrim's Progress* is a precious and timeless portrayal of the Christian walk, written by Bunyan amid his own suffering, and as such it can be used to clear the thinking of a depressed person. It will help him understand that he is "surrounded by such a great cloud of witnesses" (Heb. 12:1) who have walked this same way and felt this same hopelessness. The depressed person needs to understand that the thoughts, feelings, and behaviors associated with depression are a part of life on this fallen planet, and are expected to be a part of our sanctification. It is beyond human understanding, but it is a biblical truth that God makes His children holy through suffering, both physical and mental.

THE DEPRESSED WOMAN

What American society terms depression remains largely a problem for females. Women account for the vast majority of counselor visits and hospitalizations for depression. Various reasons are offered for this, all of which are mere speculation, reflecting more the bias of the observer than anything resembling science. Suffice it to say, however, that a secular therapy clinic or a Christian counseling ministry will be busy with women who complain about their depression. Because of this predominance, we should give special attention to depression among women. From experience as well as from Scripture, I advise the following:

1. It is always wise to talk with the spouse of the depressed individual if at all possible, and to do so with both spouses present. Listening individually and exclusively to complaints of one marital partner about the other often leads to divorce. However, a caring woman should talk privately with the depressed woman, to give her the opportunity to confess sin that she may have confessed to no one else. It is very common to find the depressed woman living with sin on the part of her husband about which she has feared to speak to anyone. She may rightfully fear that public knowledge of the sin would hurt the children. She may rightfully fear that her husband would physically harm her if she told anyone. Listen for this type of fear, and pray for wisdom in asking the depressed woman about this. She may have gone to church leaders for help related to the husband's adultery, theft, sexual perversion, physical violence, or refusal to hold a job, and found those leaders unwilling to confront the husband. Often, in these situations, the focus will have been turned to the wife's refusal to submit, to her repressed anger or bitterness, to her failure to love her husband. Anyone ministering to a depressed woman needs to listen for signs of this kind of situation in the home. It is a frequent cause of depression in women in the modern church, where psychotherapy is so popular and church discipline is so unpopular. Reassure this woman that you will protect her confidence, taking it only to elders in the church who will deal with the husband biblically. Assure yourself that you have such elders before you make such a promise to the frightened woman.

2. If depression in a woman is related neither to her own unconfessed sin nor to that of an undisciplined husband, look for lack of godly purpose in her life. Some women have mistakenly concluded that to stay at home, out of the work force, is the sum total of God's will for them. Gently and with respect, learn what this woman does

with her time. Is she watching Oprah Winfrey and soap operas? Does she spend her day in idleness? Does she spend her day gossiping with other idle women? If so, speak to her of laziness and the need to transform her mind toward the things of God.

3. Does the depressed woman spend her day indiscriminately watching Christian television or listening to Christian radio? If so, she may have become burdened by false teachers, "who tie up heavy loads and put them on [women's] shoulders," and who "love the place of honor at banquets" and love to "have men call them ['Doctor']" (Matt. 23:4, 6-7). Seek to discover whether this woman has gone to seminars where she has been given notebooks and tapes by which she can learn to keep demons out of the home and out of the children. She may be laboring under the task of remembering "where Satan got a foothold," making lists, and writing endless letters to people asking for forgiveness. She may have reached a point of refusing to hire a baby-sitter for fear of evil influences. This sort of thing is especially common with young mothers who are devoted to perfection in the home. Show such a woman from Scripture that the devil is a created being, that he is not "the dark side of God," and that Jesus has defeated him. Show her that her focus is to be on Jesus rather than on Satan; tell her to leave Satan to Jesus, and reassure her that her Redeemer is far more powerful than Satan. Show her from Scripture that she doesn't have to go through rituals and repetition, claiming her position in Christ aloud daily. "Even the archangel Michael, when disputing with the devil about the body of Moses, did not dare to bring an accusation against him, but said, 'The Lord rebuke you'" (Jude 9).

Baby-sit for this young mother; visit her and work with her in the home; take her and/or the children out to breakfast. If a woman has turned to antidepressants or psychotherapy, help her see that it is often easier and less humiliating to turn to a pill or write a check to a therapist than to accept the help and counsel of a fellow believer—but that the easier thing is not always the right thing.

As you relate to this woman, remind her that God expects us to help one another, to exhort one another. Let her know that your relationship with her is a blessing to you also. Show her that refusing the help and advice of other believers may be pride on her part. Scripture calls us to care for one another; it never calls us to seek "good feelings" as a goal in life. Draw her steadily away from self, and help her recognize ways in which she may be using Christ as a "means to an end" rather than seeing Him for what He is, the beginning and end of our faith. Draw her toward the Word, and show her from Scripture that good works are the evidence rather than the cause or means of her salvation:

> For it is by grace you have been saved, through faith, . . . not by works, so that no one can boast. For we are God's workmanship, created in Christ Jesus to do good works, which God prepared in advance for us to do. (Eph. 2:8-10)

4. As you get to know the depressed woman, listen for indications that she may perhaps view her husband as the mediator between God and herself. This is not an uncommon situation in Bible-believing churches. At times it is due simply to poor teaching, while at other times it may be due to irresponsibility on the woman's part. Watch for such an attitude and help her to see from Scripture that it is her own sins that placed her under God's wrath and in need of a Redeemer; she is responsible before God, and Jesus is her only mediator.

Help her see that a miserable marriage, though it may feel to her like a prison, is no excuse for her failure to serve and glorify the One who bought her with His blood. Remind her that Paul wrote many of his letters while locked in a Roman dungeon. Gently help her face the reality that God did not promise anyone a happy marriage and that many women make this an idol without realizing it. She may have goals for the home as well as demands of her husband and children that are based far more on romance novels and women's magazines than on Scripture. Help her see that she must constantly compare Christian radio and her daily devotional booklets with Scripture. Help her trust more in the Word and less in the latest seminar.

Point to the fact that Scripture actually says very little about marriage and the home. What it does say is easy to understand but impossible to obey without the strength of the Holy Spirit. Show her from Scripture that it is normal for Christians to struggle in their obedience to God:

> If we claim to be without sin, we deceive ourselves and the truth is not in us. (1 John 1:8)

> For in my inner being I delight in God's law; but I see another law at work in the members of my body, waging war against the law of my mind and making me a prisoner of the law of sin at work within my members. What a wretched man I am! Who will rescue me from this body of death? Thanks be to God—through Jesus Christ our Lord! (Rom. 7:22-25)

Show her from Scripture that the victory has been secured by Christ's perfect obedience, and that the struggle will continue as regards her own obedience until the day she dies. Show this depressed woman that all of Scripture is for her, not just the few verses on marriage, and that God expects her to study it seriously. God does not honor ignorance in males or in females. "Do your best to present yourself to God as one approved, a [workwoman] who does not need to be ashamed and who correctly handles the word of truth" (2 Tim. 2:15).

The Bible shows clearly that the darkness that modern society terms "depression" is to be expected as a part of this life. Depression provides the ripest of times for the evangelist to clearly proclaim the truly hopeless state of the unbeliever and his or her need for a Savior. Depression provides the ripest of times for the ministering believer to enjoy fellowship in the Word with another believer, calling out for insight, crying aloud for understanding, looking for wisdom as for silver and searching for it as for hidden treasure, and together finding the knowledge of God and understanding the fear of the Lord (see Prov. 2:3-6). We are called to exhort one another, to encourage one another, and to bear one another's burdens. Armed with the full armor of God (Eph. 6:10-20), we should humbly enter the battle with our depressed brother or sister. In doing so, we will come to say with Paul:

> Oh, the depth of the riches of the wisdom and knowledge of God! How unsearchable his judgments, and his paths beyond tracing out! "Who has known the mind of the Lord? Or who has been his counselor?" "Who has ever given to God, that God should repay him?" For from him and through him and to him are all things. To him be the glory forever! Amen. (Rom. 11:33-36)

Epilogue

One autumn day several years ago my wife, Carol, received a phone call from one of her college classmates who now lives and works in another state. This friend was alarmed by the plight of a colleague whose wife was in the depths of depression and had been admitted to a psychiatric hospital because of the risk of suicide. These people were serious Christians who feared the worst in a secular psychiatric setting where she was not even allowed to read her Bible. The patient was described as constantly tearful, wringing her hands, sleeping very little, losing weight, unable to function, hopeless, and describing herself as worthless. She was five months postpartum, and the depression was getting worse.

The next day I spoke with the patient's husband, a meticulous professor, who was distraught over his wife's awful and worsening condition. He believed she had a "chemical imbalance" that would respond to medication, but he desperately wanted her out of the hospital. He stated that he was unable to keep her at home because she was truly suicidal. They had five small children and no family willing or able to stay with her at home.

He recounted, in well-prepared, textbook-like fashion, his wife's past and their married life together. Her mother had been hospitalized for depression, and a brother had committed suicide. He believed that his wife's depression was "genetic." He knew that it would be recurrent and that it would always plague them. He feared that their children would likely suffer the same outcome. They had married after high school. The first of their children had accidentally died at age two. Through that trauma, they both came to faith in Christ and have been serious Christians ever since.

They had a Catholic background and early in their Christian

walk were involved in a charismatic church. In recent years they had become involved in a well-known national Christian renewal movement, about which they were extremely zealous. The wife homeschooled, ground wheat for making their own bread, and avoided all associations that were not in harmony with the movement. They had dropped out of Bible study groups and most social activity. She spent much of her days studying "wisdom journals" with their children while her husband left for the university at 6 A.M. to return at 7 or 8 P.M.

After attending a seminar sponsored by another organization, they decided to no longer hire baby-sitters, for fear of "demonic influence entering their home." She gradually became tired and morose. As the delivery date approached and especially when she became more seriously depressed after the delivery, they sought to cast out the demons of despair and depression. Numerous art objects the husband had received as gifts when lecturing in the Orient were burned because of their supposed demonic content; multiple "warfare" prayer sessions were held, but they never felt certain that all the demons were gone. The husband became frustrated with his wife; tension erupted; her state of mind and his tolerance nosedived.

"What should I do with my wife?" he asked. "The doctor started her on an antidepressant just today and promises all will be normal in three or four weeks. I can't have her at home until she is ready to function like before!"

Carol and I discussed this situation with much prayer. I told him, with more than a little hesitation, to put her on a plane and send her to our home.

Never having met these people in person, and having spoken only once by phone with the husband, we held up a sign with their name on it in the arrival area at the airport. Off the plane that day came what seemed to be an endless stream of jubilant children with their happy but exhausted parents fresh from Disneyland. The last people off the plane were the most pitiful-looking souls we had seen in a long time. The tall, athletic husband looked exhausted, but he managed a thin smile. He seemed somewhat embarrassed at the bent, weeping, hand-wringing wife who followed him off the plane.

All the way home from the airport and for the next several days, she continued just as she had been. The husband was clearly exasperated with her. He could not see how all this could be simply due to her being chemically imbalanced. He was totally resistant to considering that some of the aspects of their life might have been too hard for his wife. He saw that as impossible, because all they were doing was simply putting the "Bible into action" in their home.

The husband soon returned home, and Carol went into action. Conversation was diverted from the disease recovery model and replaced with conversation based on a scriptural understanding of whatever topic was at hand. Instead of, "Will I get well?" (which was her constant question) she was directed toward asking, "How can I serve God today? What is His will for me today?"

A few days of sleep medication normalized her sleep pattern and lessened the likelihood that she would wake up in the middle of the night terrorized by overwhelming fears. Chores were assigned, a schedule was maintained, and tasks were accomplished. Our closets were never more orderly! She mowed the grass, gathered sticks off the lawn, and made wild grape jelly with our kids. She attended a Bible study held in our home, and we were relieved of our constant observation of her for two evenings by some of the dear ladies in Carol's Bible study group. Carol helped her see from Scripture the sinful pride back of what had been her increasingly self-centered isolation disguised as a pursuit of "family values."

We encouraged her toward the study of Scripture to investigate some of the practices that seemed especially oppressive and spiritually exhausting in her life. When she raised some of these issues with her husband over the telephone and suggested the possibility that not all of the legalistic practices were really based in truth, he replied that she might expect him to commit suicide if she upset their life with talk like that! She did, however, persist in sorting out truth and was slowly encouraged by that truth.

She did her homework and continued daily to lovingly speak by phone with her husband about their life, their beliefs, and what the

Bible actually taught. She kept busy and went to the office with Carol, working there with the Christian office girls. She also spent a few hours with a pastor, who discipled her from the Word. He helped her search Scripture even more thoroughly in relation to the exhausting legalistic and demon deliverance techniques she and her husband had practiced. He showed her that the fears that had developed from those false teachings had no biblical base.

A missionary from Papua New Guinea visited our home while she was there. He showed a video of his work with the animistic tribes. She watched in amazement as she saw how the teaching of God's Word was breaking the strongholds of fear and superstition in the tribes of New Guinea. She could clearly see that what she and her husband considered true Christianity had been building fear and superstition in her of the same sort that had held those tribes in bondage for so long.

After about ten days, the husband flew in for a visit to check on his wife's progress. He thankfully came with an attitude all too rare among Christians—that whatever discussion he and his wife would have about changes in their life should be biblically based. We confronted him about some of the ministry techniques and writings related to the seminars he and his wife had attended. We confronted him about the separation of his family from Christian fellowship and group Bible study. We lovingly confronted him about his own absence from the home as well as his exaggerated headship in the home, where he seemingly assumed the role of mediator between his wife and God. These thoughts were all new to this husband; he had thought he was obeying the Lord. He wanted time alone to search the Scripture.

The Holy Spirit was at work in this man. He compared his beliefs with Scripture, and he changed his mind. He came to see his wife's plight as largely a state of physical and spiritual exhaustion brought on by wrong doctrine, and together they planned changes.

The husband left for home. Two days later, after thirteen days with us and ahead of the earliest time that any antidepressant medication could have been credited with any positive effect, the woman purchased her own airline ticket, stood in line at the airport, and said to my wife, "Carol, I stand amazed in the presence of Jesus the Nazarene!" She changed planes alone in a large airport, was met by her family, and took up her responsibilities as wife and mother the next day.

She calls occasionally. Gone is the legalism, and gone are the techniques for bondage-breaking. She realizes now that the bonds were broken for her 2,000 years ago on a hill called Calvary when the Messiah said, "It is finished." She no longer tries to add to that finished work and thus has found that truth really does set you free.

The family is now in a Bible-believing church, participating with grateful vigor. They are in a group Bible study going line by line through the Word. She is in a home-school mothers' program. She helps out with Cubbies in AWANA. She sleeps well and has gained back her weight. They have a growing circle of Christian friends and are doing things socially as well as in Christian service. Carol's classmate is still amazed at the positive changes in the husband as he functions at the university.

What were the fundamental principles guiding Carol's and my work with this troubled woman?

Did we view her as a helpless victim of her past, her circumstances, or her genes? No, we viewed her as a sinner saved by grace, in need of help along the course of her new life in Christ.

Did we view her as being controlled by her unconscious? No, we saw her as having a heart that can be changed by the Spirit and obedience to God's Word.

Did we call her to dwell on her past? No, we did not even discuss her parents and upbringing. Instead, we asked her to examine herself and test herself to see how her beliefs and actions "squared with Scripture."

Did we claim secret knowledge and affirm her every utterance? No, the absolutes of Scripture were our guide in teaching, rebuking, correcting, and training her in righteousness.

Did we urge her to seek self-esteem, empowerment, and revenge? No, we directed her toward submission, humility, servanthood, and the glorification of God in her life.

Did we aim her toward pleasure and comfort as a goal—toward a spa, a cruise, or more make-up? No, we aimed her toward glorifying God in the tasks before her; we pointed her toward Scripture, showing that God would bring her joy in those tasks in His own good time.

What were the fundamentals of this woman's care? Was she treated as a patient? Were fees charged? Did Carol have any degrees or certificates in psychotherapy or counseling? Were highly technical skills brought to play in caring for her soul? Were complex psychological insights brought to bear on her situation? The answer is no to all the above. Christians merely came alongside this woman and her husband with the authority and sufficiency of the Word, the power of the Holy Spirit, and the priesthood of believers. The outcome is always in God's hands, not ours; and because that is true, obedience to Him (1 Sam. 15:22) is far better than any of our independent human efforts, abilities, or credentials.

Recommended Reading

Adams, Jay E. *The Biblical View of Self-Esteem, Self-Love, and Self-Image*. Eugene, Ore.: Harvest House, 1986.

_____. *From Forgiven to Forgiving: Discover the Path to Biblical Forgiveness*. Amityville, N.Y.: Calvary Press, 1994.

Bobgan, Martin and Deidre. *The Four Temperaments, Astrology and Personality Testing*. Santa Barbara, Calif.: EastGate, 1992.

_____. *Larry Crabb's Gospel*. Santa Barbara, Calif.: EastGate, 1998.

_____. *The End of Christian Psychology*. Santa Barbara, Calif.: EastGate, 1997.

_____. *Competent to Minister: The Biblical Care of Souls*. Santa Barbara, Calif.: EastGate, 1996.

Brownback, Paul. *The Danger of Self-Love*. Chicago: Moody, 1982.

Bulkely, Ed. *Why Christians Can't Trust Psychology*. Eugene, Ore.: Harvest House, 1993.

_____. *Only God Can Heal the Wounded Heart*. Eugene, Ore.: Harvest House, 1997.

Conyers, A. J. *The Eclipse of Heaven, Rediscovering the Hope of a World Beyond*. Downers Grove, Ill.: InterVarsity, 1992.

Dineen, Tana. *Manufacturing Victims*. Montreal: Robert Davies Publishing, 1996.

Ganz, Richard. *Psychobabble: The Failure of Modern Psychology and the Biblical Alternative*. Wheaton, Ill.: Crossway, 1993.

Horton, Michael, ed. *Power Religion: The Selling Out of the Evangelical Church*. Chicago: Moody, 1992.

_____. *In the Face of God*. Dallas, Tex.: Word, 1996.

Hunt, Dave. *Beyond Seduction*. Eugene, Ore.: Harvest House, 1987.

Hunt, Dave and T. A. McMahon. *The New Spirituality*. Eugene, Ore.: Harvest House, 1988.

Ice, Thomas and Robert Dean. *Overrun by Demons*. Eugene, Ore.: Harvest House, 1990.

Kilpatrick, William K. *Psychological Seduction*. Nashville, Tenn.: Thomas Nelson, 1983.

Lewis, C. S. *The Abolition of Man*. New York: Macmillan, 1947.

MacArthur, John. *Our Sufficiency in Christ*. Dallas, Tex.: Word, 1991.

Matzat, Don. *Christ-Esteem*. Eugene, Ore.: Harvest House, 1973.

Owen, Jim. *Christian Psychology's War on God's Word: The Victimization of the Believer*. Santa Barbara Calif.: EastGate, 1993.

Pendergrast, Mark. *Victims of Memory*. Hinesburg, Vt.: Upper Access, 1995.

Playfair, William, with George Bryson. *The Useful Lie*. Wheaton, Ill.: Crossway, 1991.

Vitz, Paul C. *Psychology as Religion: The Cult of Self-Worship*. Grand Rapids, Mich.: Eerdmans, 1977.

Wells, David. *No Place for Truth or Whatever Happened to Evangelical Theology?* Grand Rapids, Mich.: Eerdmans, 1993.

_____. *God in the Wasteland*. Grand Rapids, Mich.: Eerdmans, 1994.

Valuable Newsletters

The Berean Call, P. O. Box 7019, Bend, OR 97708-7019.

Psychoheresy Awareness Letter, 4137 Primavera Road, Santa Barbara, CA 93110.

Resource Groups

Christian Counseling and Education Foundation West
3495 College Avenue
San Diego, CA 92115

False Memory Syndrome Foundation
3401 Market Street, Suite 130
Philadelphia, PA 19104-3315
(215) 387-1865

International Association of Biblical Counselors
11500 Sheridan Blvd.
Westminster, CO 80020

L.I.F.E. Fellowship
11500 Sheridan Blvd.
Westminister, CO 80020
(303) 451-LIFE

Notes

Introduction: From Psychoanalysis to Caring for Souls

1. It is impossible to estimate the total number of Christian professional counselors (or of pastors involved primarily in a counseling ministry). In an article titled "Hurting Helpers: Will the Christian Counseling Movement Live Up to Its Promise?" (*Christianity Today*, September 16, 1996, 78), Steve Rabey reported that the American Association of Christian Counselors had a membership of 17,500; the Minirth-Meier/New Life Clinics had more than 600 employees; and the Rapha counseling ministry had 3,500 churches in its RaphaCare network.

2. John Bynyan, *The Pilgrim's Progress* (Westwood, N.J.: Barbour, 1985), 75.

3. Jay Adams, *Competent to Counsel* (Grand Rapids, Mich.: Zondervan, 1986).

Chapter 1: The Freudian Foundation

1. Paul C. Vitz, "A Christian Theory of Personality," in Robert Roberts and Mark Talbot, eds., *Limning the Psyche: Explorations in Christian Psychology* (Grand Rapids, Mich.: Eerdmans, 1997). Vitz is also the author of *Psychology as Religion: The Cult of Self-Worship* (Grand Rapids, Mich.: Eerdmans, 1994).

2. O'Brien, C. P., "Evaluation of Psychotherapy," in Harold Kaplan and Benjamin Saddock, *Comprehensive Textbook of Psychiatry*, 5th edn. (Baltimore: Williams and Wilkins, 1989).

3. Kaplan and Saddock, *Comprehensive Textbook of Psychiatry*, 1568.

4. Paul Gray, "The Assault on Freud," *Time* (November 29, 1993), 46.

5. Richard Webster, *Why Freud Was Wrong: Sin, Science and Psychoanalysis* (New York: Basic Books, 1995); Frederick Crews, *The Memory Wars: Freud's Legacy in Dispute* (New York: New York Review of Books, 1995).

6. J. Horgan, "The Intellectual Warrior" in *Scientific American* (November 1992), 38-44.

7. Crews, *Memory Wars*.

8. "For God knows that when you eat of it your eyes will be opened, you will be like God, knowing good and evil" (Gen. 3:5).

9. Richard Noll, *The Jung Cult: Origins of a Charismatic Movement* (Princeton, N.J.: Princeton University Press, 1994), 44-47.

10. R. P. Corsini, ed., *Encyclopedia of Psychology*, 2nd edn. (New York: John Wiley and Sons, 1994).

11. Gray, "Assault on Freud," italics mine.

12. Alan A. Stone, M. D., "Where Will Psychoanalysis Survive?" *Harvard Magazine* 99, no. 3 (January–February 1997): 34-39.

13. Ernst Haeckel, *The History of Creation*, vol. 1, 3rd edn., trans. Lankester (London: Kegan Paul, Trench & Co., 1883).

14. Sigmund Freud, *The Standard Edition of the Complete Psychological Works of Sigmund Freud,* ed. James Strachey (London: Hogarth Press and the Institute for Psycho-Analysis, 1953–1974), 21:5-6.

15. Freud, ibid., 4:250.

16. Ibid., 15:210.

17. Webster, *Why Freud Was Wrong,* 332.

18. Freud, *Standard Edition,* 4:250.

19. Ibid.

20. Ibid.

21. Ibid., 23:260.

22. Ibid., 7:174-176.

23. Ibid., 5:578.

24. Rabey, "Hurting Helpers," 78.

25. Tana Dineen, *Manufacturing Victims* (Montreal: Robert Davies Publishing, 1996), 19.

26. *Encyclopedia of Psychology,* 255.

27. Ibid.

28. Ibid.

29. Ibid., 256.

30. Ibid.

31. Carl Rogers, *Client Centered Therapy* (Boston: Houghton Mifflin, 1951), 62.

32. *Encyclopedia of Psychology,* 153.

Chapter 2: The Biblical Foundation

1. J. C. Ryle, *Holiness: Its Nature, Hindrances, Difficulties and Roots* (London: Evangelical Press, 1991), 1.

2. Sigmund Freud, *The Standard Edition of the Complete Psychological Works of Sigmund Freud,* ed. James Strachey (London: Hogarth Press and the Institute for Psycho-Analysis, 1953–1974), 12:145-155.

3. Wayne Grudem, *Systematic Theology: An Introduction to Biblical Doctrine* (Grand Rapids, Mich.: Zondervan, 1994), 482.

4. Alan A. Stone, M.D. "Where Will Psychoanalysis Survive?" *Harvard Magazine* 99, no. 3 (January–February 1997): 34-39.

5. Grudem, *Systematic Theology,* 73-135.

6. Nicholas Wolterstorff, *Divine Discourse: Philosophical Reflections on the Claim That God Speaks* (Cambridge, England: Cambridge University Press, 1996), quoted by Mark Talbot, "Divine Discourse," in *First Things* (December 1996), 42-44.

7. John Calvin, *Institutes of the Christian Religion*, ed. John T. McNeill, trans. Lewis Battles Ford, The Library of Christian Classics (Philadelphia: Westminster, 1960), vol. 9, iv.

8. Mark Talbot, "Divine Discourse" in *First Things* (December 1996), 42-44.

9. Grudem, *Systematic Theology,* 746.

10. Ryle, *Holiness,* 17.

11. Ibid.

12. Ibid.

13. Ibid., 20.

14. Ibid., 30.

15. Ibid., 31.

16. Ibid., 88ff.

17. Ibid.

18. Harold O. J. Brown, *The Sensate Culture* (Nashville: Word, 1996).

19. Quoted in David Hackett Fischer, *Albion's Seed: Four British Folkways in America* (Oxford, England: Oxford University Press, 1989), 69.

20. *The Westminster Shorter Catechism* (Phillipsburg, N.J.: Presbyterian and Reformed, 1986).

Chapter 3: Ideas Have Consequences

1. Richard Weaver, *Ideas Have Consequences* (Chicago: University of Chicago Press, 1948).

2. Evan Thomas, "Blood Brothers," *Newsweek* (April 22, 1996), 28-34.

3. Elizabeth Moberly, "Homosexuality and Truth," *First Things* (March 1997): 31.

4. Linda Cochrane, "Women in Ramah: A Post Abortion Bible Study" (Sterling, Va.: Christian Action Council's Care Net, 1991).

5. Ellen Willis, "Down with Compassion," *The New Yorker* (August 23, 1996), 4-5.

6. Alan A. Stone, "Where Will Psychoanalysis Survive?" *Harvard Magazine* 99, no. 3 (January–February 1997): 34-39.

7. Ernest Gellner, *The Psychoanalytic Movement: The Cunning of Unreason* (Evanston, Ill.: Northwestern University Press, 1996), 100. The late Dr. Gellner, professor of social anthropology at Cambridge, wrote this book to "offer an account of how, within the span of less than half a century, this system of ideas could conquer so much of the world, at any rate to the extent of becoming the dominant idiom for the discussion of the human personality and human relations." He does this by "relating its central ideas and practices to the major social and intellectual changes of the time." This is only one of a burgeoning number of scholarly (and secular) works looking dispassionately at the corrupt history of the entire modern psychotherapy movement. One can only lament the lack of response in the church during this period.

8. Ibid., 69.

9. Quoted in Barry A. Shain, *The Myth of American Individualism: The Protestant Origins of American Political Thought* (Princeton, N.J.: Princeton University Press, 1994), 106-107.

10. Harold O. J. Brown, *The Sensate Culture* (Nashville: Word, 1996), 142-143. The Franklin Forman Chair of Ethics in Theology at Trinity Evangelical Divinity School, Dr. Brown picks up on the work of Russian expatriate Pitirim Sorokin and speaks to the decline of Western culture compellingly, relating it to a loss of our spiritual roots. Although we are in a "late stage of degenerate, sensate culture," Brown offers a combination of warning and scriptural encouragement to guide us through the coming chaos.

11. Ibid., 102.

12. John Calvin, *Institutes of the Christian Religion*, ed. John T. McNeill, trans. Lewis Battles Ford, The Library of Christian Classics (Philadelphia: Westminster, 1960), vol. 2, chap. 7.

13. Quoted in Shain, *Individualism*, 203.

14. Ibid.

15. Quoted in Hugh J. Hughes, *Life of Howell Harris* (Hanley, Stoke-on-Trent, England: Tentmaker, 1996), 117.

16. Quoted in David B. Calhoun, *History of Princeton Seminary: Volume 2: The Majestic Testimony* (Edinburgh: Banner of Truth Trust, 1996), 317.

Chapter 4: Darwin, Haeckel, Fliess, and Freud

1. J. Robertson McQuilkin, "The Behavioral Sciences Under the Authority of Scripture," paper presented December 30, 1975, at the Evangelical Theological Society, Jackson, Mississippi.

2. See, e.g., Max Nordau, *Degeneration* (New York: D. Appleton, 1895); M. Teich and R. Porter, eds., *Fin de Siecle and Its Legacy* (Cambridge, England: Cambridge University Press, 1990); George Mosse, *The Culture of Western Europe: The Nineteenth and Twentieth Centuries,* 3rd edn. (Boulder, Colo.: Westview, 1988).

3. Richard Noll, *The Jung Cult: Origins of a Charismatic Movement* (Princeton, N.J.: Princeton University Press, 1994), 27.

4. Nordau, *Degeneration.*

5. See Ian Dowbiggin, *Inheriting Madness: Professionalization and Psychiatric Knowledge in Nineteenth Century France* (Berkeley, Calif.: University of California Press, 1991); Daniel Pick, *Faces of Degeneration: A European Disorder c. 1848–1918* (Cambridge, England: Cambridge University Press, 1989).

6. Dowbiggin, *Inheriting Madness*; Pick, *Faces of Degeneration.*

7. Mosse, *Culture of Western Europe,* 228.

8. Friedrich Nietzsche, *Thus Spake Zarathustra* (New York: Viking Penguin, 1982), 187; see also Karl Beckson, ed., *Aesthetes and Decadents of the 1890s* (Chicago: University of Chicago Press, 1981).

9. Owen Chadwick, *The Secularization of the European Mind in the 19th Century* (Cambridge, England: Cambridge University Press, 1975).

10. L. P. Thiele, *Friedrich Nietzsche and the Politics of the Soul: A Study of Heroic Individualism* (Princeton, N.J.: Princeton University Press, 1990).

11. Walter Kaufmann, *Nietzsche: Philosopher, Psychologist, Antichrist* (New York: Free Press, 1991), 262.

12. David Luft, "Schopenhauer, Austria and the Generation of 1905," *Central European History* 26 (1983): 53-75.

13. Frank R. Freemon, reviewing *Charcot: Constructing Neurology,* by Goetz, Bonduelle, Gelfarb (New York: Oxford University Press, 1995), in *Journal of the American Medical Association* 278, no. 24, 2196; J. Goldstein, *Console and Classify: The French Psychiatric Profession in the Nineteenth Century* (Cambridge, England: Cambridge University Press, 1987).

14. W. Kontstaal, "Skirting the Abyss: A History of Experimental Explorations of Automatic Writing in Psychology," *Journal of the History of Behavioral Sciences* 28 (1992): 55-27.

15. William James, "Frederick Myers' Service to Psychology," in Burkhardt and Bowers, eds., *The Works of William James: Essays in Psychical Research* (Cambridge, Mass.: Harvard University Press, 1986).

16. Carl Jung, *The Psychology of the Unconscious: Collected Works of C. G. Jung,* vol. xx (Princeton, N.J.: Princeton University Press, 1970).

17. J. Barzun, *Darwin, Marx, Wagner: Critique of a Heritage* (New York: Basic Books, 1958).

18. L. von Schroder, *Fulfillment of the Aryan Mystery at Bayreuth* (Munich, 1911).

19. D. F. Strauss, *The Life of Jesus Critically Examined,* trans., ed. Eliot (Philadelphia: Hodgson Fortress, 1972); H. David Harris, *Friedrich Strauss and His Theology* (Cambridge, England: Cambridge University Press, 1973).

20. A. Desmond and J. Moore, *Darwin* (New York: Michael Joseph, 1991), 477.

21. B. A. Morel, *Traite des Degenerescences,* cited in Nordau, *Degeneration,* 16.

22. E. Mayr, *The Growth of Biological Thought: Diversity, Evolution and Inheritance* (Cambridge, Mass.: Harvard University Press, 1982), 505-510.

23. Ibid., 693-694.

24. Frank Medawar, *The Limits of Science* (Oxford, England: Oxford University Press, 1985).

25. Roger Penrose, *Shadows of the Mind: A Search for the Missing Science of Consciousness* (Oxford, England: Oxford University Press, 1994); Antonio R. Damasio, *Descartes' Error: Emotion, Reason and the Human Brain* (New York: G. P. Putnam's Sons, 1994).

26. W. Montgomery, "Germany," in Glick, ed., *The Comparative Reception of Darwinism* (Austin, Tex.: University of Texas Press, 1974).

27. R. Grigg, "Ernst Haeckel: Evangelist for Evolution and Apostle of Deceit," *Creation* 18, no. 2 (March–May 1996), 1-2.

28. Ernst Haeckel, *The History of Creation,* vol. 1., 3rd edn., trans. Lankester (London: Kegan Paul, Trench & Co., 1883).

29. Ernst Haeckel, *The Riddle of the Universe* (Berlin: Watts, 1929).

30. Damasio, *Descartes' Error.*

31. Haeckel, *Riddle of the Universe.*

32. Koppen, E., "Wagnerism as Concept and Phenomenon," in Muller and Wapnewski, eds., *Wagner Handbook,* trans. Deathridge (Cambridge, Mass.: Harvard University Press, 1992).

33. Gilbert Romanes, *Mental Evolution in Man: Origin of Human Faculty* (London: Hewich, 1888).

34. Sigmund Freud, *The Standard Edition of the Complete Psychological Works of Sigmund Freud,* ed. James Strachey (London: Hogarth Press and the Institute for Psycho-Analysis, 1953-1974), 7:98.

35. Ibid.

36. Mayr, *Growth of Biological Thought,* 70.

37. Ibid.

38. Holt, N. "Ernst Haeckel's Monistic Religion," *Journal of the History of Ideas* 32 (1971): 270.

39. Grigg, "Ernst Haeckel," 2.

40. Quoted in Freud, *Standard Edition,* 14:13.

41. J. Mousaieff, ed., *The Complete Letters of Sigmund Freud to Wilhelm Fliess 1887–1904* (Cambridge, Mass.: Harvard University Press, 1985).

42. Wilhelm Fliess, "The Relations Between the Nose and the Female Sex Organ from the Biological Aspect," in ibid.

43. Michael Gardner, quoted in Frank Sulloway, *Freud, Biologist of the Mind: Beyond the Psychoanalytic Legend* (New York: Basic Books, 1979), 140; Benjamin Ry, quoted by Masson in *Complete Letters of Freud to Fliess,* 310.

44. Marie Bonaparte, Anna Freud, and Ernst Kris, eds., *The Origins of Psycho-Analysis: Letters to Wilhelm Fliess, Drafts and Notes 1887–1902* (New York: Basic Books, 1950).

45. Richard Webster, *Why Freud Was Wrong: Sin, Science and Psychoanalysis* (New York: Basic Books, 1995); Frederick Crews, *The Memory Wars: Freud's Legacy in Dispute* (New York: The New York Review of Books, 1995); Sulloway, *Freud, Biologist of the Mind.*

46. Webster, *Why Freud Was Wrong.*

47. Gardner, quoted by Sulloway, *Freud, Biologist,* 144.

48. Crews, *Memory Wars,* 298.

49. See Noll, *Jung Cult;* Webster, *Why Freud Was Wrong;* Crews, *Memory Wars.*

50. J. M. Charcot, *Clinical Lectures on Diseases of the Nervous System,* vol. 3, trans. Savil (London: New Sydenham Society, 1889); M. Macmillan, *Freud Evaluated: The Completed Arc* (New Holland, Conn.: Hogarth, 1991).

51. Webster, *Why Freud Was Wrong,* 98.

52. Ibid., chapter 7, "Mysterious Mechanisms."

53. H. Ellenberger, *The Discovery of the Unconscious: The History and Evolution of Dynamic Psychiatry* (New York: Basic Books, 1970), 13.

54. Ibid.

55. *Complete Letters of Freud to Fliess,* 152.

56. Ibid., 261.

57. See Webster, *Why Freud Was Wrong;* Crews, *Memory Wars.*

58. *Complete Letters of Freud to Fliess,* 266.

59. Ibid.

60. Sulloway, *Freud, Biologist,* 275.

61. Freud, *Standard Edition,* vol. 5.

62. Ibid., vol. 7.

63. Ibid., 7:231-243.

64. P. B. Medawar, review of Irving S. Cooper, *The Victim Is Always the Same,* in *New York Review of Books* (January 23, 1975).

65. Crews, *Memory Wars,* 61-62.

Chapter 5: Descartes' Dualism vs. Materialistic Monism

1. Adrien Baillet, quoted in Sigmund Freud, *The Standard Edition of the Complete Psychological Works of Sigmund Freud,* ed. James Strachey (London: Hogarth Press and the Institute for Psycho-Analysis, 1953–1974), 21:199-204.

2. Antonio R. Damasio, *Descartes' Error: Emotion, Reason, and the Human Brain* (New York: Grosset/Putnam, 1994), 248.

3. Daniel C. Dennett, *Kinds of Minds: Toward an Understanding of Consciousness* (New York: Basic Books, 1995), 15-16.

4. Damasio, *Descartes' Error* (see note 2, above).

5. Ibid., xvi.

6. Ibid., 254.

7. Francis Crick, *The Astonishing Hypothesis: The Scientific Search for the Soul* (New York: Charles Scribner's Sons, 1994).

8. Ibid., 127.

9. Ibid., 141.

10. John R. Searle, "The Problem of Consciousness," in *Thinking and Literacy: The Mind at Work in the Classroom,* eds. Carolyn Hedley and W. Eugene Hedley (Hillsdale, N.J.: Antonacci, Rabinowitz, Erlbaum Associates, 1995), 21-30.

11. Ibid., 3-7.

12. W. Teed Rockwell, "On What the Mind Is Identical With," in *Philosophical Psychology* 7, no. 3 (1994): 307.

13. Jean Delacour, "An Introduction to the Biology of Consciousness," *Neuropsychologia* 33, no. 9 (1995): 1066.

14. Rockwell, "On What the Mind Is Identical With," 308.

15. Ibid., 321.

16. Oliver Sacks, "A New Vision of the Mind," in *International Review of Neurobiology* 37 (1996): 348.

17. Richard Lewontin, "Re-creating Creation," *National Review* (December 31, 1997), 63.

18. Stephen Hawking, *A Brief History of Time: From the Big Bang to Black Holes* (New York: Bantam, 1988), 13, 175.

19. Roger Penrose, *Shadows of the Mind: A Search for the Missing Science of Consciousness* (Oxford, England: Oxford University Press, 1994).

20. Ibid., 411.

21. Ibid., 201.

22. Ibid., 208.

23. Dennett, *Kinds of Minds* (see note 3, above).

24. Daniel C. Dennett, *Darwin's Dangerous Idea* (New York: Simon and Schuster, 1995).

25. Daniel C. Dennett, *Consciousness Explained* (Boston: Little, Brown, 1991).

26. Bo Dahlbom, ed., *Dennett and His Critics: Demystifying Mind* (Cambridge, Mass: Blackwell, 1993), 47.

27. Ibid., 83.

28. Dennett, *Kinds of Minds,* 74.

29. Ibid., 92.

30. Rockwell, "On What the Mind Is Identical With," 307.

31. Valerie G. Hardcastle, *Locating Consciousness,* vol. 4 of *Advances in Consciousness Research* (Philadelphia: Benjamins, 1996), 2.

32. Ibid., 4.

33. Edwin A. Locke, "Beyond Determinism and Materialism, Or Isn't It Time We Took Consciousness Seriously?" *Journal of Behavior Therapy and Experimental Psychiatry* 26, no. 3 (1995): 265-273.

34. Hardcastle, *Locating Consciousness,* 194.

35. Hedley and Hedley, *Thinking and Literacy.*

36. Searle, "Problem of Consciousness."

37. Delacour, "Introduction," 1072.

38. Brand Blanshard, "Behaviorism and Thought," in Brand Blanshard, ed., *The Nature of Thought* (New York: Humanities Press, 1964), 2:313-340.

39. Locke, "Beyond Determinism," 266.

40. Ibid.

41. Ibid., 265.

42. Leonard Peikoff, *Objectivism: The Philosophy of Ayn Rand* (New York, Dutton, 1991).

43. Ingrid Wickelgren, "Getting a Grasp on Working Memory," *Science* 275 (March 14, 1997): 1580-1582.

44. M. Barinaga, "Visual System Provides Clues to How the Brain Perceives," *Science* 275 (March 14, 1997): 1583–1585; M. S. Seidenberg, "Language Acquisition and Use: Learning and Applying Probabilistic Constraints," ibid., 1599–1603; A. Prince and P. Smolensky, "Optimality: From Neural Networks to Universal Grammar," ibid., 1604–1610; W. Schultz, P. Dayan, P. Montague, "A Neural Substrate of Prediction and Reward," ibid., 1593-1598.

45. Nancy Andreasen, "Linking Mind and Brain in the Study of Mental Illnesses: A Project for a Scientific Psychopathology," *Science* 275 (March 14, 1997): 1586-1592.

46. Sigmund Freud, "Project for a Scientific Psychology," *Standard Edition,* 1:295-341.

47. S. Hameroff, A. Kaszniak, and A. Scott, eds., *Toward a Science of Consciousness: The First Tucson Discussions and Debates* (Cambridge Mass.: MIT Press, 1966).

48. Hawking, *Brief History,* x.

49. Quoted in ibid.

50. Stephen Jay Gould, "Nonoverlapping Magisteria," *Natural History* 106, no. 2 (March 1997): 62.

51. Ernest Hemingway, *A Farewell to Arms* (New York: Charles Scribner's Sons, 1929), 313.

Chapter 6: Augustine's "Anti-Psychoanalytic Influence"

1. Augustine, *Confessions,* VIII, 5.

2. Hanna Arendt, "Understanding and Politics," in *The Partisan Review,* July/August, 1953, 390.

Chapter 7: Pelagian Roots; Augustine's Answer

1. Harold O. Brown, *Heresies* (Garden City, N.Y.: Doubleday, 1984), 22.

2. Paul Lehman, "The Anti-Pelagian Writings," in R. W. Battenhouse, ed., *A Companion to the Study of Saint Augustine* (Grand Rapids, Mich.: Baker, 1955), 204.

3. Augustine, *On the grace of Christ and on Original Sin,* I, 17 and II, 14.

4. Philip Schaff, *History of the Christian Church* (Peabody, Mass.: Hendrickson, 1996), 3:791.

5. Pelagius, quoted in ibid.

6. Schaff, *History,* 3:799.

7. Lehman, "Anti-Pelagian Writings," 206.

8. Schaff, *History,* 3:813.

9. Ibid., 814.

10. Ibid., 815.

11. Brown, *Heresies,* 205.

12. Silvano Arieti, "Anti-Psychoanalytic Cultural Forces in the Development of Western Civilization," *American Journal of Psychotherapy,* VI, no. 1 (1952): 68-78, 466.

13. Ibid., 470.

14. Ibid., 471.

15. Paul Enns, *The Moody Handbook of Theology* (Chicago: Moody, 1989), 437.

16. Wayne Grudem, *Systematic Theology* (Grand Rapids, Mich.: Zondervan, 1994), 496.

17. Augustus H. Strong, *Systematic Theology* (Valley Forge, Pa.: Judson, 1907), 601.

18. Grudem, *Systematic Theology,* 663.

19. Ibid., 338.

20. Brown, *Heresies,* 200.

21. See Ed Bulkley, *Why Christians Can't Trust Psychology* (Eugene, Ore.: Harvest House, 1993).

22. Robert Schuller, *If It's Going to Be, It's Up to Me* (New York: HarperCollins, 1998).

Chapter 8: Gnostic Roots; Augustine's Answer

1. Harold O. Brown, *Heresies* (Garden City, N.Y.: Doubleday, 1984), 39.

2. Ibid.

3. Kurt Rudolph, *Gnosis: The Nature and History of Gnosticism* (New York: HarperSan Francisco, HarperCollins, 1987), 276.

4. Ibid., 277.

5. Ibid., 285.

6. Ibid., 287.

7. Brown, *Heresies,* 39.

8. Ibid., 47.

9. Ibid., 42.

10. Ibid., 49.

11. Rudolph, *Gnosis,* 61-62.

12. Nag Hammadi Codex I, 3, 22, 1ff, quoted in Rudolph, *Gnosis,* 56. The discovery by grave-robbers of the thirteen Nag Hammadi Codices in 1945 in Egypt brought to the light of day for the first time actual gnostic writings from the second and third centuries. Prior to that discovery our only knowledge of ancient gnosticism was indirect, as it was described, quoted, or criticized by others, especially the early Church Fathers.

13. Nag Hammadi Codex II, 3, 77 (125)14f.; 84 (132), 10, quoted in ibid., 56.

14. Nag Hammadi Codex I, 3, 22, 1ff., quoted in ibid., 56.

15. Clement of Alexandria, *Stromata,* II, 114, 3-5, quoted in ibid., 88. Clement, along with Origen, were significant early church theologians in Alexandria. Clement lived from the mid-second into the early third centuries. He was highly educated in the wisdom and philosophy of the Greeks. He advocated reconciliation of Christianity with the challenge of gnosticism by equating the truth of the Gospel with what he believed was true in gnosticism. He accommodated gnosticism to Christianity, and his works (*Stromata* is a collection of essays comparing Christian and pagan wisdom) provide much of the record of what the gnostics of the early church period believed.

    Origen was a contemporary of Clement but lived into the mid-third century. He wrote "against" the gnostics in the same manner as Clement, but in a similar fashion he adopted and advocated for the early church some of the views and practices advocated by gnosticism. The most important of these was a gnostic method of interpreting Scripture by which Origen, like the gnostics, claimed that there is a deeper, more esoteric meaning in Scripture, behind the text, that is available through allegorical or symbolic methods of exegesis. These methods of exegesis remain with the church today and continue to be a method by which the truth of the Gospel is contaminated by the "truth" of human opinion, desire, prejudice, and pride.

16. Rudolph, ibid., 92.

17. Nag Hammadi Codex II, 7, 138, 8-18, quoted in: Rudolph, *Gnosis,* 113.

18. Hippolytus, *Refutatio Omnium Haeresium,* V, 17, 6, quoted in ibid., 115. Hippolytus of Rome was an early Church Father who died in 235. His "Refutation of All Heresies" is an encylopedic exposure of the heresies of his day.

19. Rudolph, *Gnosis,* 117.

20. Ibid., 119.

21. Nag Hammadi Codex VI, 4, 39, 33-40, 7, quoted in ibid., 120.

22. Nag Hammadi Codex I, 3, 22, 2-19, quoted in ibid., 120.

23. Ibid., 119.

24. Ibid.

25. Ibid.

26. Corpus Hermeticum, 132, quoted in ibid., 120. The Corpus Hermeticum is a collection of Greek writings from the second and third centuries. Rudolph states that they "present an occult revelation-wisdom intended to promote the effort after the vision of God, rebirth and the liberation or redemption of the soul. Here alongside mysticism, ecstasy, and meditation, magic and astrology also had a part to play" (Rudolph, *Gnosis,* 26). The New Age is not so new after all!

27. *Acts of John,* 95, 1, quoted in Rudolph, *Gnosis,* 122. The *Acts of John* is an apocryphal and highly gnostic work. Here it quotes a song supposedly sung by Christ. Such works, obviously uninspired and spurious in their origin, were extensive in number and highly popular in early church times. These works, like many other apocryphal works, included romance, fantasy, and fable. In style they were not significantly different from the popular literature of the day. They often served to spread gnostic and other pagan ideas to Christians.

28. Rudolph, *Gnosis,* 257-258.

29. Brown, *Heresies,* 49.

30. Rudolph, *Gnosis,* 26.

31. Augustine, *Confessions,* V, X, 18, quoted in Ronald W. Dworkin, *The Rise of the Imperial Self* (Lanham, Md.: Rowman and Littlefield, 1996), 7.

32. Quoted by al-Biruni from the *Shapuragan,* cited in James Hastings, ed., *Encyclopedia of Religion and Ethics* (London: T. & T. Clark, 1926), VIII, 397a.

33. Irenaeus, Adv. Haer. II, V, 2, cited in Rudolph, *Gnosis,* 62.

34. Pierre Bayle, quoted in R. W. Battenhouse, *A Companion to the Study of Saint Augustine* (Grand Rapids, Mich.: Baker, 1955), 166.

35. Augustine, *De Duabus Animabus, contra Manichaeos,* 10, 14.

36. Augustine, *Disputatio contra Fortunatum Manichaeum,* II, 20.

37. Augustine, *Confessions,* VIII, 10, 22.

Chapter 9: Plato's Faith in Reason; Augustine's Faith in God

1. H. Kaplan and B. Saddock, eds., *Comprehensive Textbook of Psychiatry,* 5th edn. (Baltimore: Williams and Wilkins, 1989), 1777.

2. Ibid.

3. Paul Dewald, *The Psychoanalytic Process* (New York: Basic Books, 1972), 622.

4. Lewis R. Wolberg, *The Technique of Psychotherapy* (New York: Grune and Stratton, 1967).

5. Kaplan and Saddock, ibid.

6. Sigmund Freud, *The Standard Edition of the Complete Psychological Works of Sigmund Freud,* ed. James Strachey (London: Hogarth Press and the Institute for Psycho-Analysis, 1953–1974), 21:48.

7. Silvano Arieti, "Anti-Psychoanalytic Cultural Forces in the Development of Western Civilization," *American Journal of Psychotherapy,* VI, no. 1 (1952).

8. Arieti, "Anti-Psychoanalytic Cultural Forces," 466.

9. Ibid., 460.

10. Augustine, *The City of God* (New York: Modern Library, 1993), VIII, 3.

11. Ibid.

12. Ibid., 4.

13. T. Honderich, ed., *The Oxford Companion to Philosophy* (Oxford, England: Oxford University Press, 1995), 284.

14. E. Hamilton and H. Cairns, eds., *Plato: The Collected Dialogues* (Princeton, N.J.: Princeton University Press, 1985), xvii.

15. Ibid., xiv.

16. Honderich, *Oxford Companion,* 837.

17. Hamilton and Cairns, *Plato: The Collected Dialogues,* 420 b, c.

18. Augustine, *City of God,* VIII, 4.

19. Ibid., 3.

20. Plato, *Phaedo,* 107sq, 113a sq.

21. Ibid., 107c, d.

22. Plato, *Theaetetus,* 176b.

23. Plato, *Phaedo* 69b, c, d.

24. Plato, *Laws,* X 906b.

25. Ibid., X 904c sq.

26. Augustine, *City of God,* VIII, 8.

27. Plato, *Protagoras,* 358c.

28. Plato, *Laws,* X 906b.

29. Freud, *Standard Edition,* 21:48.

30. Augustine, *City of God,* VIII, 5.

31. Augustine, *Christian Doctrine,* II, 40, 60.

32. Augustine, *City of God,* VIII, 5.

33. Augustine, *The Enchiridion,* V.

34. Augustine, *On the Gospel of St. John,* XV, 19.

35. Augustine, *City of God,* VIII, 7.

36. Ibid, X, 28.

37. Augustine, *Christian Doctrine,* II, 7, 11; *On the Gospel of St. John,* I, 8; I, 19; III, 18; XIX, 16; XX, 11; CXI, 3.

38. Augustine, *Exposition on the Psalms,* XL, 20, quoted in R. Cushman, "Faith and Reason," in R. Battenhouse, ed., *A Companion to the Study of Saint Augustine* (Oxford, England: Oxford University Press, 1969), 299.

39. Augustine, *On the Holy Trinity,* IX, 1, 1; *City of God,* X, 28.

40. Augustine, *On the Holy Trinity,* I, 2, 4.

41. Augustine, *Confessions,* VI, 4, 6.

42. Battenhouse, *Companion,* 300.

43. Augustine, *City of God,* X, 29.

44. Ibid., 28, 29.

45. Ibid., 29.

Chapter 10: Caring for Souls: Then and Now

1. Andy Crouch, "A Generation of Debtors," *Christianity Today* (November 11, 1996), 31-33.

2. John Bunyan, *The Pilgrim's Progress* (Westwood, N.J.: Barbour, 1985), 141.

3. Joseph Hartunian, *Piety vs. Moralism: The Passing of New England Theology* (New York: Harper, 1932), 145, quoted by Michael S. Horton in "Christianity and Popular Culture," White Horse Inn tape series (Philadelphia: Alliance of Confessing Evangelicals), audio-cassette.

4. David Hackett Fischer, *Albion's Seed: Four British Folkways in America* (New York: Oxford University Press, 1989), 20.

5. Ibid., 25.

6. Barry A. Shain, *The Myth of American Individualism: The Protestant Origins of American Political Thought,* (Princeton, N.J.: Princeton University Press, 1994), xvii-xviii. Shain, a professor of political science at Colgate University, demonstrates that our nation did not begin with the pursuit of "American individualism" but rather with pursuing the "freedom to order one's life in accord with the demanding ethical standards found in Scripture and confirmed by reason." He tries to show that the individualism and autonomy championed and cherished by so many today is actually the result of the loss of trust in and obedience to Scripture. Shain says it well when he notes that, outside the walls of the kind of community that the Puritans sought to establish, "humans could only live like beasts, slaves, or tyrants, but never as free beings."

7. Fischer, *Albion's Seed,* 24.

8. Shain, *Individualism*, 13.

9. Fischer, *Albion's Seed,* 69.

10. Ibid., 72.

11. Ibid., 73.

12. Ibid., 74.

13. Ibid., 89.

14. Ibid., 99.

15. Shain, *Individualism*, 216.

16. Martin and Deidre Bogban, *Against Biblical Counseling: For the Bible,* (Santa Barbara, Calif.: EastGate, 1994), 29.

17. Shain, *Individualism*, 197.

18. John Calvin, quoted in Bobgan, *Against Biblical Counseling,* 31.

19. Jonathan Mitchell, quoted in Fischer, *Albion's Seed,* 69.

20. Shain, *Individualism*, 22.

21. Ibid., 233.

22. Samuel Davies, quoted in ibid., 39, note 88.

23. Samuel Sherwood, quoted in ibid., 39, note 90.

24. Richard Baxter, *A Christian Directory* (Ligonier, Pa.: Soli Deo Gloria, 1990), 43.

25. Shain, *Individualism,* 40.

26. Ibid., 40, note 100.

27. Bobgan, *Against Biblical Counseling,* 55.

28. Baxter, *A Christian Directory* (see note 24, above).

29. Ibid., 8, 36.

30. Jay E. Adams, *Competent to Counsel* (Phillipsburg, N.J.: Presbyterian and Reformed, 1970).

31. Gary and Carol Almy, and Jerry Jenkins, *Addicted to Recovery* (Eugene Ore.: Harvest House, 1994); Ed Bulkley, *Why Christians Can't Trust Psychology* (Eugene, Ore.: Harvest House, 1993).

32. Jay E. Adams, *How to Help People Change* (Grand Rapids, Mich.: Zondervan, 1986); Martin and Deidre Bobgan, *Psycho Heresy* (Santa Barbara, Calif.: EastGate, 1987); Martin and Deidre Bobgan, *Prophets of Psychoheresy I* (Santa Barbara, Calif.: EastGate, 1989); Martin and Deidre Bobgan, *Prophets of Psychoheresy II* (Santa Barbara, Calif.: EastGate, 1990).

33. Martin and Deidre Bobgan, *Competent to Minister: The Biblical Care of Souls* (Santa Barbara, Calif.: EastGate, 1996).

34. Ibid., 123.

Chapter 11: Jane's Story: Modern Psychotherapy vs. Truth

1. Ellen Bass and Laura Davis, *The Courage to Heal: A Guide for Women Survivors of Child Sexual Abuse* (New York: HarperCollins, 1988), 22.

2. Sigmund Freud, *The Standard Edition of the Complete Psychological Works of Sigmund Freud,* ed. James Strachey (London: Hogarth Press and the Institute for Psycho-Analysis, 1953–1974), 20:8.

3. Suzanne R. Kirshner, *The Religious and Romantic Origins of Psychoanalysis: Individuation and Integration in Post-Freudian Theory* (Cambridge, England: Cambridge University Press, 1996), 220.

4. J. Victor Haberman, "A Criticism of Psychoanalysis," *Journal of Abnormal Psychology* 9 (1914): 265-280.

5. Freud, *Standard Edition*, 17:3-122.

6. P. Ricoeur, *Freud and Philosophy* (New Haven, Conn.: Yale University Press, 1970).

7. Richard Rorty, *Philosophy and the Mirror of Nature* (Princeton, N.J.: Princeton University Press, 1979).

8. Jurgen Habermas, "Hermeneutic and the Social Sciences," in K. Meuller-Vollmer, ed., *The Hermeneutic Reader* (New York: Continuum, 1989); J. Habermas, *Knowledge and Human Interests* (Boston: Beacon Press, 1971).

Chapter 12: Recovered Memory Therapy: Have We Recovered from It?

1. Alexis de Tocqueville, *Democracy in America*, trans. Henry Reeve (New York: Vintage, 1958), 2:142.

2. Jean-Roch Laurence and Campbell Perry, "Hypnotically Created Memory Among Highly Hypnotizable Subjects," *Science* 222 (November 4, 1983): 523-524.

3. Mark Pendergrast, *Victims of Memory: Incest Accusations and Shattered Lives* (Hinesburg, Vt.: Upper Access, 1995), 491.

4. T. Sarbin and W. Coe, *Hypnosis: A Social-Psychological Analysis of Influence Communication* (New York: Holt, Rinehart and Winston, 1972).

5. Sigmund Freud, "The Aetiology of Hysteria," *The Standard Edition of the Complete Psychological Works of Sigmund Freud,* ed. James Strachey (London: Hogarth Press and the Institute for Psycho-Analysis, 1953–1974), 3:191-221; P. Janet, *Psychological Healing: A Historical and Clinical Study,* trans. E. Paul and C. Paul (New York: Macmillan, 1925), 1:589-698; M. H. Erdelyi, *Psychoanalysis: Freud's Cognitive Healing* (New York: W. H. Freeman, 1985), 218-221.

6. See F. H. Frankel, "Discovering New Memories in Psychotherapy," *New England Journal of Medicine,* 333, no. 9, 591.

7. Freud, *Standard Edition,* 3:191-221.

8. Ibid.

9. Ibid., 17:3-123; S. Wetzler, "The Historical Truth of Psychoanalytic Reconstructions," *International Review of Psychoanalysis,* 12:187-197.

10. Freud, *Standard Edition,* 16:368.

11. A. Ornstein, "Fantasy or Reality? The Unsettled Question in Pathogenesis and Reconstruction in Psychoanalysis," in A. Goldberg, ed., *The Future of Psychoanalysis* (New York: University Press, 1983), 381-396.

12. K. Weinberg, *Incest Behavior* (New York: Citadel, 1955).

13. C. H. Kempe, et al., "The Battered Child Syndrome," *Journal of the American Medical Association* 181 (1962): 105-112.

14. G. Milne, "Repressed Memories Sometimes a Minefield," in *Australian Journal of Clinical and Experimental Hypnosis* 23, no. 2 (1995): 158-165; D. Finkelhor, *Sexually Victimized Children* (New York: Free Press, 1979); D. Finkelhor, *A Sourcebook on Child Sexual Abuse* (Beverly Hills, Calif.: Sage, 1986); D. Russell, *The Secret Trauma: Incest in the Lives of Girls and Women* (New York: Basic Books, 1986).

15. R. A. Baker, *Hidden Memories* (Buffalo, N.Y.: Prometheus, 1992), 37.

16. D. Nathan, *Women and Other Aliens* (El Paso, Tex.: Cinco Puntos Press, 1991), 154.

17. D. Johnston, "Survey Shows Number of Rapes Far Higher than Official Figures," *New York Times,* April, 24, 1992, A9.

18. Roseanne Barr Arnold, *A Star Cries Incest* (Venice, Fla.: Darnton, 1991); Marilyn Van Derbur, *The Darkest Secret* (Venice, Fla.: Darnton, 1991).

19. Elizabeth F. Loftus, "The Reality of Repressed Memories," *American Psychologist* 48, no. 5, 519.

20. R. Summit, "The Child Sexual Abuse Accommodation Syndrome," in *Child Abuse and Neglect* 7, no. 2 (1983).

21. M. A. Austin, "Recovered Memories of Childhood Sexual Abuse: Problems and Concerns," in J. Edward and J. Sanville, eds., *Fostering Healing and Growth: A Psychoanalytic Social Work Approach* (Northvale, N.J.: Jason Aronson, 1996), 179-194.

22. C. Young, "Victimhood Is Powerful," in *Reason* (October 1992), 18-23.

23. Judith Herman, *Trauma and Recovery* (New York: Basic Books, 1992), 180.

24. Stanton Peele, *Diseasing of America: Addiction Treatment Out of Control* (Lexington, Mass.: D.C. Heath, 1989), 27-28.

25. Freud, *Standard Edition,* 12:145-155.

26. H. Muslin, "The Role of the Transference in the Wolf Man Case," *Journal of the American Academy of Psychoanalysis* 19, no. 2 (1991): 294-306; Freud, *Standard Edition,* 12:147.

27. J. Baron, J. Beattie, and J. Hershey, "Heuristics and Biases in Diagnostic Reasoning: Congruence, Information and Certainty," in *Organizational Behavior and Human Decision Processes* 42 (1988): 88-110.

28. E. Sue Blume, *Secret Survivors: Uncovering Incest and Its After-Effects in Women* (New York: Ballantine, 1990); Steven Farmer, *Adult Children of Abusive Parents* (New York: Ballantine, 1989); Carol Poston and Karen C. Lison, *Reclaiming Our Lives: Hope for Adult Survivors of Incest* (New York: Bantam, 1990).

29. Ellen Bass and Laura Davis, *The Courage to Heal: A Guide for Women Survivors of Child Sexual Abuse* (New York: HarperCollins, 1988).

30. H. Wakefield and R. Underwager, "Recovered Memories of Alleged Sexual Abuse: Lawsuits Against Parents," in *Behavioral Sciences and the Law* 10 (1992): 486.

31. Pendergrast, *Victims of Memory,* 69.

32. Renee Fredrickson, *Repressed Memories: A Journey to Recovery from Sexual Abuse* (New York: Simon and Schuster, 1992).

33. Herman, *Trauma and Recovery* (see note 23, above).

34. J. Briere and J. Conte, "Self-Reported Amnesia for Abuse in Adults Molested as Children," in *Journal of Traumatic Stress* 6, no. 1 (1993): 21-31; C. A. Courtois, *Healing the Incest Wound* (New York: Norton, 1988); K. Olio, "Memory Retrieval in the Treatment of Adult Survivors of Sexual Abuse," *Transactional Analysis Journal* 19 (1989): 93-94; L. Terr, "What Happens to Early Memories of Trauma," *Journal of the American Academy of Child and Adolescent Psychiatry* 27 (1988): 96-104; Karen Claridge, "Reconstructing Memories of Abuse: a Theory Based Approach," *Psychotherapy* 29, no. 2 (1992): 243-251; Blume, ibid.; Farmer, ibid.

35. Fredrickson, *Repressed Memories,* 15.

36. John Bradshaw, *Bradshaw On: The Family* (Deerfield Beach, Fla.: Health Communications, 1988); John Bradshaw, "Incest: When You Wonder If It Happened to You," *Lears,* August, 1992, 43-44.

37. H. Merskey, "The Manufacture of Personalities," *The British Journal of Psychiatry* 160 (1992): 327-340.

38. Corbett Thigpen and Hervey M. Cleckley, "A Case of Multiple Personality," *Journal of Abnormal and Social Psychology* 49 (1954): 135-151; Thigpen and Cleckley, *The Three Faces of Eve* (New York: McGraw-Hill, 1957).

39. Flora R. Schreiber, *Sybil* (New York: Warner, 1973).

40. Pendergrast, *Victims of Memory,* 417.

41. Freud, *Standard Edition,* 16:370.

42. Report of the Council on Scientific Affairs, CSA Report 5-A-94, Yank D. Coble, Jr., M.D., Chair.

43. C. Sileo, "Unearthed Memories Lose Ground in Court," *New York Times* (June 3, 1995).

44. R. Clifford, "Families Target Therapists in Memory Cases," *Chicago Lawyer* (March 1996).

45. See "Testimony of Recalled Memories Not Per Se Inadmissible, Court Rules," *BNA Health Law Reporter* 4 (November 2, 1995): 1663-1664.

46. Pendergrast, *Victims of Memory,* 109.

47. Elizabeth Loftus, "Reconstructing Memory: The Incredible Eyewitness," *Psychology Today* (June 1974), 26-34.

48. William James, *The Principles of Psychology,* vol. 1 (New York: Dover, 1890).

49. H. Muensterberg, *On the Witness Stand: Essays of Psychology and Crime* (New York: McClure, 1908).

50. C. Bird, "The Influence of the Press upon the Accuracy of the Report," *Journal of Abnormal and Social Psychology* 22 (1927): 123-129.

51. F. Bartlett, *Remembering: A Study in Experimental and Social Psychology* (New York: Macmillan, 1932).

52. K. Koffka, *Principles of Gestalt Psychology* (New York: International Library of Psychology, 1935).

53. I. Wielawski, "Unlocking the Secrets of Memory," *Los Angeles Times* (October 3, 1991), 14B.

54. Elizabeth Loftus and Katherine Ketchum, *Witness for the Defense* (New York: St. Martin's, 1991); Elizabeth Loftus, "The Reality of Repressed Memories," *American Psychologist* 48, no. 5 (May 1993): 518-537.

55. Judith Herman and E. Schatzow, "Recovery and Verification of Memories of Childhood Sexual Trauma," *Psychoanalytic Psychology* 4, no. 1 (1987): 1-14.

56. Bass and Davis, *Courage to Heal,* 22.

57. Elizabeth Loftus, *The Myth of Repressed Memory* (New York: St. Martin's, 1996); M. Austin, "Recovered Memories of Childhood Sexual Abuse: Problems and Concerns," in J. Edward and J. Sanville, eds., *Fostering Healing and Growth* (Northvale, N.J.: Jason Aronson, 1996), 179-194.

58. L. Berger, "Cultural Psychopathology and the 'False Memory Syndrome' Debates: A View from Psychoanalysis," in *American Journal of Psychotherapy* 50, no. 2 (Spring 1996): 167-177.

59. J. Davies, "Dissociation, Repression and Reality Testing in the Countertransference: The Controversy Over Memory and False Memory in the Psychoanalytic Treatment of Adult Survivors of Childhood Sexual Abuse," in *Psychoanalytic Dialogues* 6, no. 2 (1996): 189-218.

60. Frederick Crews, "Forward to 1896?" in *Psychoanalytic Dialogues* 6, no. 2 (1996): 235.

61. Crews, ibid., 236.

62. Ibid.

63. D. Payne, M. Toglia and J. Anastasi, "Recognition, Performance Level and the Magnitude of the Misinformation Effect in Eyewitness Memory," *Psychonomic Bulletin and Review* 1 (1994): 376-382; I. Hyman, T. Husband, and F. Billings, "False memories of childhood experiences," in *Applied Cognitive Psychology* 9 (1995): 1-7; K. Pope, "Memory, Abuse, and Science: Questioning Claims About the False Memory Syndrome Epidemic," in *American Psychologist* 51, no. 9 (September 1996): 957-974; J. Herman, "The Abuses of Memory," in *Mother Jones* (March–April 1993), 3-4; F. Crews, "Forward to 1896?" 233; B. J. Cohler, "Memory Recovery and the Use of the Past," *Applied Cognitive Psychology* 8 (1994): 365-378.

64. Kenneth Pope, "Memory, Abuse, and Science: Questioning Claims About the False Memory Syndrome Epidemic," *American Psychologist* 51, no. 9 (September 1996): 957-974.

65. Frankel, "Discovering New Memories," 593.

66. Michael Maudlin, "Addicts in the Pew," *Christianity Today* (July 22, 1991), 21.

67. S. Jones, "Demonizing the Head Doctors," *Christianity Today,* September 16, 1991, 21.

68. Ibid.

69. Pendergrast, *Victims of Memory,* 477.

70. Frankel, "Discovering New Memories," 591-594.

71. Ibid.

72. Ibid.

73. Evan Thomas, "Blood Brothers," *Newsweek* (April 22, 1996), 28-34.

Chapter 13: Psychiatry's Twin Failure: No Cause, No Cure

1. G. Zilboorg and G. W. A. Selesnick, *History of Medical Psychology* (New York: Norton, 1941); Franz Alexander and S. T. Selesnick, *The History of Psychiatry* (New York: Harper & Row, 1961).

2. Wilhelm Greisinger, *Mental Pathology and Therapeutics* (New York: Hafner, 1965).

3. Edward Welch, "12-Steps and Co-Dependency" Workshop at the annual meeting of the National Association of Nouthetic Counselors, October 4–6, 1993, Greenville, South Carolina.

4. Ibid.

5. Sidney Walker, M.D., *A Dose of Sanity: Mind, Medicine, and Misdiagnosis* (New York: John Wiley and Sons, 1996).

6. *Diagnostic and Statistical Manual of Mental Disorders,* 3rd edn., rev. (Washington, D.C.: American Psychiatric Association, 1987).

7. Harold I. Kaplan and Benjamin J. Saddock, *Comprehensive Textbook of Psychiatry,* 5th edn. (Baltimore: Williams and Wilkins, 1989), 639.

8. J. Leff, "International Variations in the Diagnosis of Psychiatric Illness," *British Journal of Psychiatry* 131 (1977): 329-338.

9. N. Kreitman, "The Reliability of Psychiatric Diagnosis," *Journal of Mental Science* 107 (1961): 876-86.

10. Michael A. Taylor, Frederick Sierles, and Richard Abrams, *General Hospital Psychiatry* (New York: Free Press, 1985).

11. J. B. Kurionsky, et al., "Trends in the Frequency of Schizophrenia by Different Diagnostic Criteria," *American Journal of Psychiatry,* 134 (1977): 631-636.

12. A reading list on the phenomenological approach would include: Taylor, Sierles, and Abrams, *General Hospital Psychiatry* (see note 10, above); M. A. Taylor and J. P. Heiser, "Phenomenology: An Alternative Approach to the Diagnosis of Mental Illness," *Comprehensive Psychiatry* 12 (1971): 480-486; Karl Jaspers, *General Psychopathology* (Manchester, England: Manchester University Press, 1963); Kurt Schneider, *Clinical Psychopathology* (New York: Grune and Stratton, 1959).

13. J. P. Feighner, E. Robins, S. B. Guze, et al., "Diagnostic Criteria for Use in Psychiatric Research," *Archives of General Psychiatry* 26 (1972): 57-63. This classic paper was the beginning of twentieth-century efforts in psychiatry to achieve precision in diagnostic terminology.

Chapter 15: A Biblical Approach to Depression

1. Harold A. Pincus, et al., "Prescribing Trends in Psychotropic Medications," *Journal of the American Medical Association* 279, no. 7 (February 18, 1998): 526-531.

2. Paul C. Nagel, *John Quincy Adams* (New York: Alfred A. Knopf, 1997), 60.

3. G. Cowley and A. Underwood, "A Little Help from Serotonin—Could a Single Brain Chemical Hold the Key to Happiness?" *Newsweek* (January 5, 1998), 81.

4. Training Manual: 1986 Stephen Ministries (St. Louis), 5, 7, 33-34.

GENERAL INDEX

SCRIPTURE INDEX